THE

SOKAL

HoaX

The Sham That Shook the Academy

Edited by the editors of Lingua Franca

University of Nebraska Press   Lincoln and London

Acknowledgments for the use of
copyrighted material appear on pages 267–69,
which constitute an extension of the copyright page.

Library of Congress Cataloging-in-Publication Data
The Sokal hoax : the sham that shook the academy /
edited by the editors of *Lingua Franca*. p. cm.
"A *Lingua Franca* book."
Includes bibliographical references.
ISBN 0-8032-7995-7 (pa: alk. paper)
1. Fraud in science.   2. Science—Philosophy.   3. Science—
Social aspects.   4. Humanities.   5. Sokal, Alan D., 1955–
I. Sokal, Alan D., 1955–   II. *Lingua Franca.*
Q175.37 .S65 2000   501—dc21   00-026113
𝒩

CONTENTS

5 LONGER ESSAYS

THE SOKAL HOAX

THE EDITORS OF *LINGUA FRANCA*
Introduction

May 18, 1996, was not a slow news day. The front page of the *New York Times* featured the suicide of the highest-ranking officer in the navy, claims that Bob Dole resigned from the Senate under political siege, and a photograph of President Clinton signing a law against child molesters. And yet the editors of the *Times* also found room that day for a front-page item about an obscure NYU physics professor who had published an article in an academic journal. What made this a top story? Exactly this: the physicist's article had been revealed as a hoax. It was a hodgepodge of unsupported arguments, outright mistakes, and impenetrable jargon designed to "test" its host journal's intellectual integrity. Apparently the journal had failed.

By his own account, physicist Alan Sokal was inspired to submit such a piece of writing out of a growing concern over the state of the political left. He felt that a number of leftists (mostly academics in the humanities) were betraying their cause by challenging standards of logic, truth, and intellectual inquiry, in general, and the role of these concepts in the natural sciences in particular. His concerns echoed those of several writers who believed that the academic left had become increasingly irrelevant or antithetical to the political left—because of its detachment from political life or, worse, its engagement with ideas that actually belong to the right.

Sokal's views crystallized when he read a book coauthored by a biologist and a mathematician who shared his disdain for critiques of science done in the name of postmodernism, cultural studies, and science studies: *Higher Superstition* (1994) by Paul Gross and Norman Levitt argued that such work ranged from the misguided to the absurd. The book has been hailed by its supporters (among them many scientists) as the brave dissenting voice that revealed the Emperor's nakedness—and assailed by its critics as a vicious attack that misrepresents the work it describes. In the midst of the controversy, Gross and Levitt have gone through several printings and sold thousands of copies, one of them to Alan Sokal. Upon reading *Higher Superstition*, Sokal moved beyond being, as he put it, "troubled by an apparent decline in the standards of rigor in certain precincts of the academic humanities," and decided to act.

Early in 1994, Sokal set himself to writing an article full of what he saw as the worst sins of cultural studies and science studies: appeals to authority rather than logic to support arguments, unreadable prose, mistaken claims about scientific theories, and a general failure to give the scientific method its due. But he had to do his work carefully. The article had to be "bad" enough to make his point—but "good" enough to find a perch from which to make it. He needed to create a piece full of nonsense and errors—but one that could, nonetheless, make it past the editorial board of whichever unfortunate journal Sokal would finally choose as his target.

Like any conscientious scholar, Sokal spent hours researching his topic, performing electronic searches for certain combinations of terms. (The combination "Derrida and quantum physics" initially led him astray because the nephew of the philosopher is, in fact, a quantum physicist.) Unlike most scholars, however, Sokal was searching for references that struck him as nonsensical. He gathered a collection of the best (or worst) he could find and built an impenetrable essay around them. The result: a mix of plausible claims that go too far, implausible claims that go nowhere at all (concealed in syntax so dense as to be almost unreadable), and fringe philosophical theories set forth as widely accepted scientific advances. He topped these off with a vast number of endnotes and the occasional truth, and christened the piece "Transgressing the Boundaries: Toward a Transformative Hermeneutics of Quantum Gravity."

When Sokal first told friends of his plan to send his piece to *Social Text*, they warned him that, there, he might well be caught and advised him to try a less well-known publication. But in many ways, his was an obvious choice. Founded in 1979 by Stanley Aronowitz (now a professor of sociology at the City University of New York [CUNY], and still a member of the *Social Text* editorial board), John Brenkman (now a professor of English at CUNY and editor of the literary journal *Venue*), and Fredric Jameson (now chair of the graduate program in literature at Duke), *Social Text* has published many of the academic left's leading lights. Edward Said's article on Zionism in the first issue was followed by Michel de Certeau's "The Oppositional Practices of Everyday Life," Gayatri Chakravorty Spivak's "Finding Feminist Readings," Cornel West's "The Paradox of Afro-American Rebellion," and Eve Kosofsky Sedgwick's "How to Bring Your Kids Up Gay." By the early 1990s, *Social Text* had become one of the more sought-after publication options for scholars in the expanding field of cultural studies. These same characteristics, however, made the journal difficult to breach; after all, it was certainly not in need of submissions. In the end, though, *Social Text* was Sokal's choice, and exactly how much this choice shaped the course of events depends on who is telling the story.

In the weeks after the revelation of the hoax, *Social Text* would be characterized as "a respected social science journal" by the Associated Press, "an influential academic magazine" by the Gannett News Service, "a journal that helped invent the trendy, sometimes baffling field of cultural studies" by the *New York Times*, "a left-wing 'critical studies' publication" by the *Boston Globe*, a "hapless postmodern social science journal" by the *Washington Post*, and, finally, in the phrase of its own editors: "in the 'little magazine' tradition of the independent left." So, depending on where you get your news, Sokal's target was either trendy, respected, and influential, or independent, hapless, and little. And Sokal, by implication, was either David, the solitary man of the left struggling against the widespread trends of obscurity, or Goliath, the man backed by the power and money of science, attacking the already-besieged humanities.

In many ways, the uncertainty over the identity of *Social Text* reflects the uncertainty surrounding the field of cultural studies itself. In general, cultural studies has come to stand for the interdisciplinary study of how popular culture interacts with its audiences. The discipline's first institutional incarnation was the Centre for Contemporary Cultural Studies, a postgraduate research institute established in 1964 at the University of Birmingham in England.[1] Today, anthologies of cultural studies come out regularly, and with the exception of one or two early Birmingham Centre pieces, they contain none of the same essays. American cultural studies is often said to be characterized by a movement away from the Birmingham school's emphasis on social class toward other aspects of identity, such as race and gender; it has also come to be associated with the ideas of the French poststructuralists targeted by Sokal; and it is just as often said to be characterized by a myopic enthusiasm for celebrities. In fact, none of these characterizations account for the bewildering diversity of the work done under its name. Such ambiguity lent the Sokal debate an added resonance, since arguments about whether or not his article was a successful send-up of cultural studies could not help but presume what the real thing looked like.

To add to this complexity, discussions of the Sokal hoax have often conflated cultural studies with its cousin, "science studies." Like cultural studies, science studies encompasses an unwieldy collection of interests, methodologies, scholarly backgrounds, and institutional affiliations.[2] The arguments of science studies range from claims that the practice of science is more contaminated by social values than scientists admit to the idea that the pursuit of truth and objectivity is itself a value system and should be analyzed as such, in terms of what it accomplishes and for whom.

In contrast with earlier, more heroic narratives of scientific progress, these analyses of the culture and practice of science are often skeptical in spirit, and they have met with vehement resistance from scientists. In books like *Higher Superstition,* opponents of science studies have rejected the attempt to explain scientific progress in sociological terms, claiming that the uniqueness of science lies precisely in its refusal to place any value system above truth, objectivity, logic, and the scientific method. Others claim that non-scientists are unlikely to know enough to analyze a scientific field. There seems to be little room, however, for science studies within scientific departments and institutions—indeed, though several science studies scholars have come from science departments, they have usually ended up elsewhere. Take, for example, the special double issue that *Social Text* published on science studies, called "The Science Wars." It included work by professors in anthropology, English, history, law, political science, public health, science and technology studies, social studies, and sociology. But it contained only one article by a bona fide scientist: Alan Sokal. Though Sokal didn't know it would turn out this way, it was *Social Text*'s special issue on science studies that would end up containing his article.

For the editors at *Social Text*, the "Sokal affair" began in November of 1994. Sokal's "Transgressing the Boundaries" made its slow way through the ordinary editorial channels at *Social Text*, and Sokal received a polite e-mail from coeditor Andrew Ross thanking him for the submission of his "interesting article." "The editorial committee is reviewing it," Ross writes, "and we hope to get word to you soon." In the meantime, Ross had begun work on the special double issue of *Social Text* that would focus on *Higher Superstition* and the controversy surrounding science studies. In early March 1995 Ross wrote to invite Sokal to revise his piece for the "Science Wars" issue and requested that Sokal remove some of the philosophical references and endnotes (remember, there were several pages of them). Sokal expressed his enthusiasm for having his article appear in the "polemical context" of the special issue, but refused to cut his many references, claiming that "the endnotes are an integral part of the reasoning . . . and that evidence is crucial to my argument and can't be omitted or even much shortened." The difficulty, Sokal's e-mail continued, is that he has "had to write the article for two audiences simultaneously: the usual readership of *Social Text*, but also the scientists who will subsequently become aware of it, whether I like it or not." He expressed concern that removing references might leave his argument "wide open to attack by uncharitably disposed scientists."[3] Despite the editors' later claim that Sokal's article seemed "a little hokey," *Social Text* accepted it in essentially its original form—and as they prepared their special issue, Sokal began to prepare the revelation of his hoax.

The tendency in the media accounts has been to identify the *Social Text* editorial board with its coeditor Andrew Ross, a tendency that is not completely due to the fact that Ross had handled the initial correspondence with Sokal. There was always the added twist that Ross, like Sokal, was a NYU professor: they both had offices on the same campus. But their proximity in space may be less important for this story than the considerable professional distance between them. For one thing, NYU's physics department is not especially well known. Ross, on the other hand, is something of an academic celebrity. Born in Scotland, he made his name working on American popular culture (though his early work was on modern poetry), and heads a high-profile American Studies program. As the *enfant terrible* of cultural studies, he warranted a full-page photograph in the *New York Times Magazine* (wearing a now infamous Comme des Garçons mango-colored jacket). Far from the bespectacled tweedy myth, Ross signaled a new (to some compelling and to some horrifying, but always startling) possibility—the professor as popstar.

In other words, Ross represented, in more ways than one, much of what Sokal was attacking—not just a certain field of study, but the considerable success enjoyed by that field in recent years. In the end, Ross's visibility helped to ensure that Sokal's hoax reached a wide audience.

Sokal's original plan was to wait two or three months after the publication of his article and then reveal that it was a hoax. But well over a year had passed since the submission of the article, and there was an ever-growing circle of people who had heard that something was rotten in the upcoming issue of *Social Text*. Sokal had told a few friends, and they had told more than a few others—though, for a while, none of them went public with the information or felt compelled to share the rumor with *Social Text*. One breach came in the winter of 1996, when someone leaked the story to Roger Kimball, managing editor of *The New Criterion*, a neo-conservative cultural journal. Before Kimball could reveal the hoax, though, rumors of his intentions made it back to Sokal, who asked him to hold off. As Kimball later explained, he was "reluctantly prevailed upon by Mr. Sokal . . . to let him have the first word." Thus, the Kimball leak was contained.[4]

But the secret didn't keep for much longer. The events leading to Sokal's own revelation began when a New York City freelance reporter heard that something was amiss with an article in the upcoming "Science Wars" issue of *Social Text* and took the news to *Lingua Franca*. After examining an advance reviewer's galley of the issue, the writer and the *Lingua Franca* staff identified the suspect article and then contacted Sokal, who had already begun work on a piece that would reveal his trick. Sokal made the piece available to *Lingua Franca*. And in its May–June 1996 issue, shortly after the *Social Text* special issue had come out, *Lingua Franca* published Sokal's "A Physicist Experiments with Cultural Studies" (pt. 2, "Revelation").

In the headlines alone, Sokal's article has been called a hoax, a joke, a sting, an affair, a *paródia*, a prank, *uno sfregio*, a spoof, a con, *un canular*, a fraud (delicious and malicious), a ruckus, *la farce parfaite*, a Pomolotov Cocktail, a *brincadeira*, a *mystification pédagogique*, double-speak, *un'atroce beffa*, nonsense, gibberish, rubbish, and hokum. From the front page of the *New York Times* to the front page of *Le Monde* to the online *People* magazine "quote of the day," the story seemed to have something for everyone. Scholars in departments throughout the university rallied to Sokal's side, considering this to be their own battle against obscurity and pretension or political cant. Readers across America saw their fears about the waste of their tuition dollars confirmed. Intellectual sophisticates around the world threw up their hands and sighed, "Only in America." Others believed that a right-wing campaign was underway to discredit the social critique of science, or that know-nothing scientists were misrepresenting the work of the humanities.

The outpouring of reactions to the Sokal affair is often not very pretty. Many are strident; almost none are conciliatory. Several make insightful and articulate arguments about what is at stake, but few of these are in accord. Partly because it began with a hoax, this event has been an occasion for taking sides, for finding holes in arguments, rather than building on them. At the same time, the discussion has inspired scholars to write with unusual passion and vividness on both sides of the issue; and it has put crucial questions about the baneful influence of academic jargon squarely on the academic agenda. It has also provided a remarkable occasion to witness the spread of an academic debate into the public arena, for good or ill. For all of these reasons, the editors of *Lingua Franca* decided to put together a collection of how the Sokal hoax was presented by the media and discussed in the academy.[5]

Though news of the hoax spread like wildfire, it is unlikely that more than a handful of people have actually read Sokal's original article. Indeed, Andrew Ross has claimed that the "Science Wars" issue of *Social Text* sold eight hundred copies in the six months it was on the newsstands. Therefore, part 1 of this book presents the article itself, as it was published in *Social Text*.[6] The rest of the volume explores the responses to the event. Part 2 includes the full text of Sokal's original confession, a response from the editors of *Social Text*, and a series of letters written to *Lingua Franca*. Part 3 charts the spread of the story from the *New York Times* to op-ed columns and editorials across the country. Part 4 presents a sampling of press accounts and editorials from Europe and South America—introducing arguments and observations that have received little attention in the United States. The longer and more philosophical essays appear in part 5. And part 6 offers the remarks inspired by two live discussions: the first, a forum at New York University which brought Sokal and Ross face-to-face (and subsequently published elsewhere); and the second, an informal conversation among three scholars, who try to assess the lessons of the Sokal hoax. On some occasions, when one text in the book refers to another, a cross reference is noted in square brackets.

Several worthwhile pieces have been omitted because they addressed issues that were covered elsewhere in the anthology. At the same time, many short news reports have been included to convey a sense of how the spin varied from source to source. No doubt, the discussion will continue. Though the Sokal affair is already four years old, physicists and nonphysicists agree on one thing: It has not yet reached its half-life.

Notes

1 Three early classics of cultural studies were Richard Hoggart's *The Uses of Literacy: Aspects of Working-Class Life with Special References to Publications and Entertainment* (Chatto and Windus, 1957), and Raymond Williams's *Culture and Society: 1780–1950* (Columbia University Press, 1983) and *The Long Revolution* (Columbia University Press, 1961). E. P. Thompson and Stuart Hall, who directed the Centre from 1968 to 1979, were also major influences. In the 1970s and 1980s, some of the best-known Birmingham studies addressed youth subcultures and trends (Stuart Hall and Tony Jefferson, *Resistance through Rituals: Youth Subcultures in Postwar Britain* [Hutchinson, 1976]), the bonding rituals of disaffected working-class teenagers (Paul E. Willis, *Learning to Labour: How Working Class Kids Get Working Class Jobs* [Saxon House, 1977]), and the audience of a long-running BBC news program (David Morley, *The "Nationwide" Audience: Structure and Decoding* [British Film Institute, 1980]).

2 The early, more "epistemological" phase of science studies is often associated with the work of Thomas Kuhn (*The Structure of Scientific Revolutions* [University of Chicago Press, 1962]), and Paul Feyerabend (*Against Method: Outline of an Anarchistic Theory of Knowledge* [NLB, 1975]); and a later phase with the "social" critiques of Bruno Latour (Bruno Latour and Steve Woolgar, *Laboratory Life: The Social Construction of Scientific Facts* [Sage, 1979]), Evelyn Fox Keller (*Reflections on Gender and Science* [Yale University Press, 1985]), and Donna Haraway (*Simians, Cyborgs, and Women: The Reinvention of Nature* [Routledge, 1990]).

3   Alan Sokal, personal e-mail.

4   In the interval between the publication of Sokal's article and the revelation of the hoax in *Lingua Franca*, Roger Kimball apparently put his inside knowledge to use in writing a scathing assessment of the *Social Text* issue in *The New Criterion:* "All of the contributions in this issue of *Social Text* are bad; but without doubt the most egregious effort is the concluding essay . . . by Alan D. Sokal."

5   For other responses to the Sokal hoax see the responses printed in *Social Text* 50, vol. 15, no. 1, spring 1997, as well as Noretta Koertge, ed., *A House Built on Sand: Exposing Postmodernist Myths about Science* (Oxford, 1998). Alan Sokal has collaborated with the physicist Jean Bricmont on a book expanding upon his hoax, *Fashionable Nonsense: Postmodern Intellectuals' Abuse of Science* (St. Martin's, 1998).

6   This version of the article differs from the version published in *Social Text* in that seventy-five of the endnotes that appeared in the original article and that were source citations only have been included here in the body of the text.

1

The Article

✱

ALAN SOKAL

Transgressing the Boundaries: Toward a Transformative
Hermeneutics of Quantum Gravity

Social Text, Spring–Summer 1996

Transgressing disciplinary boundaries . . . [is] a subversive undertaking since it is likely
to violate the sanctuaries of accepted ways of perceiving. Among the most fortified
boundaries have been those between the natural sciences and the humanities.—Valerie
Greenberg, *Transgressive Readings*

The struggle for the transformation of ideology into critical science . . . proceeds on the
foundation that the critique of all presuppositions of science and ideology must be the
only absolute principle of science.—Stanley Aronowitz, *Science as Power*

There are many natural scientists, and especially physicists, who continue to
reject the notion that the disciplines concerned with social and cultural criticism can have anything to contribute, except perhaps peripherally, to their
research. Still less are they receptive to the idea that the very foundations of
their worldview must be revised or rebuilt in the light of such criticism.
Rather, they cling to the dogma imposed by the long post-Enlightenment
hegemony over the Western intellectual outlook, which can be summarized
briefly as follows: that there exists an external world, whose properties are
independent of any individual human being and indeed of humanity as a
whole; that these properties are encoded in "eternal" physical laws; and that
human beings can obtain reliable, albeit imperfect and tentative, knowledge
of these laws by hewing to the "objective" procedures and epistemological
strictures prescribed by the (so-called) scientific method.

But deep conceptual shifts within twentieth-century science have undermined this Cartesian-Newtonian metaphysics (Heisenberg 1958; Bohr 1963);
revisionist studies in the history and philosophy of science have cast further
doubt on its credibility (Kuhn 1970; Feyerabend 1975; Latour 1987; Aronowitz 1988b; Bloor 1991); and, most recently, feminist and poststructuralist
critiques have demystified the substantive content of mainstream Western
scientific practice, revealing the ideology of domination concealed behind

the facade of "objectivity" (Merchant 1980; Keller 1985; Harding 1986, 1991; Haraway 1989, 1991; Best 1991). It has thus become increasingly apparent that physical "reality," no less than social "reality," is at bottom a social and linguistic construct; that scientific "knowledge," far from being objective, reflects and encodes the dominant ideologies and power relations of the culture that produced it; that the truth claims of science are inherently theory-laden and self-referential; and consequently, that the discourse of the scientific community, for all its undeniable value, cannot assert a privileged epistemological status with respect to counterhegemonic narratives emanating from dissident or marginalized communities. These themes can be traced, despite some differences of emphasis, in Aronowitz's analysis of the cultural fabric that produced quantum mechanics (1988b, esp. chaps. 9 and 12); in Ross's discussion of oppositional discourses in post-quantum science (1991, intro. and chap. 1); in Irigaray's and Hayles's exegeses of gender encoding in fluid mechanics (Irigaray 1985; Hayles 1992); and in Harding's comprehensive critique of the gender ideology underlying the natural sciences in general and physics in particular (1986, esp. chaps. 2 and 10; 1991, esp. chap. 4).

Here my aim is to carry these deep analyses one step further, by taking account of recent developments in quantum gravity: the emerging branch of physics in which Heisenberg's quantum mechanics and Einstein's general relativity are at once synthesized and superseded. In quantum gravity, as we shall see, the space-time manifold ceases to exist as an objective physical reality; geometry becomes relational and contextual; and the foundational conceptual categories of prior science—among them, existence itself—become problematized and relativized. This conceptual revolution, I will argue, has profound implications for the content of a future postmodern and liberatory science.

My approach will be as follows. First, I will review very briefly some of the philosophical and ideological issues raised by quantum mechanics and by classical general relativity. Next, I will sketch the outlines of the emerging theory of quantum gravity and discuss some of the conceptual issues it raises. Finally, I will comment on the cultural and political implications of these scientific developments. It should be emphasized that this essay is of necessity tentative and preliminary; I do not pretend to answer all the questions that I raise. My aim is, rather, to draw the attention of readers to these important developments in physical science and to sketch as best I can their philosophical and political implications. I have endeavored here to keep mathematics to a bare minimum; but I have taken care to provide references where interested readers can find all requisite details.

[1] Quantum Mechanics: Uncertainty, Complementarity, Discontinuity, and Interconnectedness

It is not my intention to enter here into the extensive debate on the conceptual foundations of quantum mechanics.[1] Suffice it to say that anyone who has seriously studied the equations of quantum mechanics will assent to Heisenberg's measured (pardon the pun) summary of his celebrated *uncertainty principle*:

> We can no longer speak of the behaviour of the particle independently of the process of observation. As a final consequence, the natural laws formulated mathematically in quantum theory no longer deal with the elementary particles themselves but with our knowledge of them. Nor is it any longer possible to ask whether or not these particles exist in space and time objectively . . .
>
> When we speak of the picture of nature in the exact science of our age, we do not mean a picture of nature so much as a *picture of our relationships with nature*. . . . Science no longer confronts nature as an objective observer, but sees itself as an actor in this interplay between man [*sic*] and nature. The scientific method of analysing, explaining and classifying has become conscious of its limitations, which arise out of the fact that by its intervention science alters and refashions the object of investigation. In other words, method and object can no longer be separated. (Heisenberg 1958, 28–29; emphasis in original)[2]

Along the same lines, Niels Bohr (1928; cited in Pais 1991, 314) wrote: "An independent reality in the ordinary physical sense can . . . neither be ascribed to the phenomena nor to the agencies of observation." Stanley Aronowitz (1988b, 251–56) has convincingly traced this worldview to the crisis of liberal hegemony in Central Europe in the years prior and subsequent to World War I.[3]

A second important aspect of quantum mechanics is its principle of complementarity, or dialecticism. Is light a particle or a wave? Complementarity "is the realization that particle and wave behavior are mutually exclusive, yet that both are necessary for a complete description of all phenomena" (Pais 1991, 23).[4] More generally, notes Heisenberg,

> the different intuitive pictures which we use to describe atomic systems, although fully adequate for given experiments, are nevertheless mutually exclusive. Thus, for instance, the Bohr atom can be described as a small-scale planetary system, having a central atomic nucleus about which the external electrons revolve. For other experiments, however, it might be more convenient to imagine that the atomic nucleus is sur-

rounded by a system of stationary waves whose frequency is characteristic of the radiation emanating from the atom. Finally, we can consider the atom chemically. . . . Each picture is legitimate when used in the right place, but the different pictures are contradictory and therefore we call them mutually complementary. (1958, 40–41)

And once again Bohr (1934; cited in Jammer 1974, 102): "A complete elucidation of one and the same object may require diverse points of view which defy a unique description. Indeed, strictly speaking, the conscious analysis of any concept stands in a relation of exclusion to its immediate application."[5] This foreshadowing of postmodernist epistemology is by no means coincidental. The profound connections between complementarity and deconstruction have recently been elucidated by Froula (1985) and Honner (1994), and, in great depth, by Plotnitsky (1994).[6,7]

A third aspect of quantum physics is discontinuity, or rupture: as Bohr (1928; cited in Jammer 1974, 90) explained, "[the] essence [of the quantum theory] may be expressed in the so-called quantum postulate, which attributes to any atomic process an essential discontinuity, or rather individuality, completely foreign to the classical theories and symbolized by Planck's quantum of action." A half century later, the expression "quantum leap" has so entered our everyday vocabulary that we are likely to use it without any consciousness of its origins in physical theory.

Finally, Bell's theorem[8] and its recent generalizations[9] show that an act of observation here and now can affect not only the object being observed—as Heisenberg told us—but also an object arbitrarily far away (say, on Andromeda galaxy). This phenomenon—which Einstein termed "spooky"—imposes a radical reevaluation of the traditional mechanistic concepts of space, object, and causality,[10] and suggests an alternative worldview in which the universe is characterized by interconnectedness and (w)holism: what physicist David Bohm (1980) has called "implicate order."[11] New Age interpretations of these insights from quantum physics have often gone overboard in unwarranted speculation, but the general soundness of the argument is undeniable.[12] In Bohr's words, "Planck's discovery of the *elementary quantum of action* . . . revealed a feature of *wholeness* inherent in atomic physics, going far beyond the ancient idea of the limited divisibility of matter" (Bohr 1963, 2; emphasis in original).

[2] Hermeneutics of Classical General Relativity

In the Newtonian mechanistic worldview, space and time are distinct and absolute.[13] In Einstein's special theory of relativity (1905), the distinction between space and time dissolves: there is only a new unity, four-dimensional space-time, and the observer's perception of "space" and "time" depends on her state of motion.[14] In Hermann Minkowski's famous words (1908): "Henceforth space by itself, and time by itself, are doomed to fade away into mere shadows, and only a kind of union of the two will preserve an independent reality" (translated in Lorentz *et al.* 1952, 75). Nevertheless, the underlying geometry of Minkowskian space-time remains absolute.[15]

It is in Einstein's general theory of relativity (1915) that the radical conceptual break occurs: the space-time geometry becomes contingent and dynamical, encoding in itself the gravitational field. Mathematically, Einstein breaks with the tradition dating back to Euclid (which is inflicted on highschool students even today!), and employs instead the non-Euclidean geometry developed by Riemann. Einstein's equations are highly nonlinear, which is why traditionally trained mathematicians find them so difficult to solve.[16] Newton's gravitational theory corresponds to the crude (and conceptually misleading) truncation of Einstein's equations in which the nonlinearity is simply ignored. Einstein's general relativity therefore subsumes all the putative successes of Newton's theory, while going beyond Newton to predict radically new phenomena that arise directly from the nonlinearity: the bending of starlight by the sun, the precession of the perihelion of Mercury, and the gravitational collapse of stars into black holes.

General relativity is so weird that some of its consequences—deduced by impeccable mathematics, and increasingly confirmed by astrophysical observation—read like science fiction. Black holes are by now well known, and wormholes are beginning to make the charts. Perhaps less familiar is Gödel's construction of an Einstein space-time admitting closed timelike curves: that is, a universe in which it is possible to travel *into one's own past!*[17]

Thus, general relativity forces upon us radically new and counterintuitive notions of space, time, and causality;[18] so it is not surprising that it has had a profound impact not only on the natural sciences but also on philosophy, literary criticism, and the human sciences. For example, in a celebrated symposium three decades ago on *Les Langages critiques et les sciences de l'homme*, Jean Hyppolite raised an incisive question about Jacques Derrida's theory of structure and sign in scientific discourse:

> When I take, for example, the structure of certain algebraic constructions [ensembles], where is the center? Is the center the knowledge of general rules which, after a fashion, allow us to understand the interplay of the elements? Or is the center certain elements which enjoy a particular privilege within the ensemble? . . . With Einstein, for example, we see the end of a kind of privilege of empiric evidence. And in

that connection we see a constant appear, a constant which is a combination of space-time, which does not belong to any of the experimenters who live the experience, but which, in a way, dominates the whole construct; and this notion of the constant—is this the center?[19]

Derrida's perceptive reply went to the heart of classical general relativity:

> The Einsteinian constant is not a constant, is not a center. It is the very concept of variability—it is, finally, the concept of the game. In other words, it is not the concept of something—of a center starting from which an observer could master the field—but the very concept of the game.[20]

In mathematical terms, Derrida's observation relates to the invariance of the Einstein field equation $G\mu\nu = 8\pi G T\mu\nu$ under nonlinear space-time diffeomorphisms (self-mappings of the space-time manifold that are infinitely differentiable but not necessarily analytic). The key point is that this invariance group "acts transitively": this means that any space-time point, if it exists at all, can be transformed into any other. In this way the infinite-dimensional invariance group erodes the distinction between observer and observed; the π of Euclid and the G of Newton, formerly thought to be constant and universal, are now perceived in their ineluctable historicity; and the putative observer becomes fatally de-centered, disconnected from any epistemic link to a space-time point that can no longer be defined by geometry alone.

[3] Quantum Gravity: String, Weave, or Morphogenetic Field?

However, this interpretation, while adequate within classical general relativity, becomes incomplete within the emerging postmodern view of quantum gravity. When even the gravitational field—geometry incarnate—becomes a noncommuting (and hence nonlinear) operator, how can the classical interpretation of $G\mu\nu$ as a geometric entity be sustained? Now not only the observer, but the very concept of geometry, becomes relational and contextual.

The synthesis of quantum theory and general relativity is thus the central unsolved problem of theoretical physics;[21] no one today can predict with confidence what will be the language and ontology, much less the content, of this synthesis, when and if it comes. It is, nevertheless, useful to examine historically the metaphors and imagery that theoretical physicists have employed in their attempts to understand quantum gravity.

The earliest attempts, dating back to the early 1960s, to visualize geometry on the Planck scale (about 10^{-33} centimeters) portrayed it as "space-time foam": bubbles of space-time curvature, sharing a complex and ever-changing topology of interconnections (Wheeler 1964). But physicists were unable to carry this approach further, perhaps because of the inadequate development at that time of topology and manifold theory (see below).

In the 1970s physicists tried an even more conventional approach: simplify the Einstein equations by pretending that they are *almost linear*, and then apply the standard methods of quantum field theory to the thus oversimplified equations. But this method, too, failed: it turned out that Einstein's general relativity is, in technical language, "perturbatively nonrenormalizable" (Isham 1991, sec. 3.1.4). This means that the strong nonlinearities of Einstein's general relativity are intrinsic to the theory; any attempt to pretend that the nonlinearities are weak is simply self-contradictory. (This is not surprising: the almost-linear approach destroys the most characteristic features of general relativity, such as black holes.)

In the 1980s a very different approach, known as string theory, became popular: here the fundamental constituents of matter are not pointlike particles but rather tiny (Planck-scale) closed and open strings (Green *et al.* 1987). In this theory, the space-time manifold does not exist as an objective physical reality; rather, space-time is a derived concept, an approximation valid only on large length scales (where "large" means "much larger than 10^{-33} centimeters"!). For a while many enthusiasts of string theory thought they were closing in on a Theory of Everything—modesty is not one of their virtues— and some still think so. But the mathematical difficulties in string theory are formidable, and it is far from clear that they will be resolved any time soon.

More recently, a small group of physicists has returned to the full nonlinearities of Einstein's general relativity, and—using a new mathematical symbolism invented by Abhay Ashtekar—they have attempted to visualize the structure of the corresponding quantum theory (Ashtekar *et al.* 1992; Smolin 1992). The picture they obtain is intriguing: as in string theory, the space-time manifold is only an approximation valid at large distances, not an objective reality; at small (Planck-scale) distances, the geometry of space-time is a *weave*—a complex interconnection of threads.

Finally, an exciting proposal has been taking shape over the past few years in the hands of an interdisciplinary collaboration of mathematicians, astrophysicists, and biologists: this is the theory of the morphogenetic field.[22] Since the mid-1980s evidence has been accumulating that this field, first conceptualized by developmental biologists (Waddington 1965; Corner 1966; Gierer *et al.* 1978), is in fact closely linked to the quantum *gravitational* field:[23] (a) it pervades all space; (b) it interacts with all matter and energy, irrespective of whether or not that matter/energy is magnetically charged; and, most significantly, (c) it is what is known mathematically as a "symmetric second-rank tensor." All three properties are characteristic of gravity; and it was proved some years ago that the only self-consistent *nonlinear* theory of a symmetric second-rank tensor field is, at least at low energies, precisely Einstein's general relativity (Boulware and Deser 1975). Thus, if the evidence for (a), (b), and (c) holds up, we can infer that the morphogenetic field is the quantum counterpart of Einstein's gravitational field. Until recently this theory has been ignored or even scorned by the high-energy-physics establishment, which has traditionally resented the encroachment of biologists (not to mention humanists) on its "turf."[24] However, some theoretical physicists have recently begun to give this theory a second look, and there are good prospects for progress in the near future.[25]

It is still too soon to say whether string theory, the space-time weave, or morphogenetic fields will be confirmed in the laboratory: the experiments are not easy to perform. But it is intriguing that all three theories have similar conceptual characteristics: strong nonlinearity, subjective space-time, inexorable flux, and a stress on the topology of interconnectedness.

[4] Differential Topology and Homology

Unbeknownst to most outsiders, theoretical physics underwent a significant transformation—albeit not yet a true Kuhnian paradigm shift—in the 1970s and 1980s: the traditional tools of mathematical physics (real and complex analysis), which deal with the space-time manifold only locally, were supplemented by topological approaches (more precisely, methods from differential topology[26]) that account for the global (holistic) structure of the universe. This trend was seen in the analysis of anomalies in gauge theories (Alvarez-Gaumé 1985);[27] in the theory of vortex-mediated phase transitions (Kosterlitz and Thouless 1973);[28] and in string and superstring theories (Green et al. 1987). Numerous books and review articles on "topology for physicists" were published during these years (e.g., Nash and Sen 1983).

At about the same time, in the social and psychological sciences Jacques Lacan pointed out the key role played by differential topology:

> This diagram [the Möbius strip] can be considered the basis of a sort of essential inscription at the origin, in the knot which constitutes the subject. This goes much further than you may think at first, because you can search for the sort of surface able to receive such inscriptions. You can perhaps see that the sphere, that old symbol for totality, is unsuitable. A torus, a Klein bottle, a cross-cut surface, are able to receive such a cut. And this diversity is very important as it explains many things about the structure of mental disease. If one can symbolize the

subject by this fundamental cut, in the same way one can show that a cut on a torus corresponds to the neurotic subject, and on a cross-cut surface to another sort of mental disease. (Lacan 1970, 192–93; lecture given in 1966)[29]

As Althusser (1993, 50) rightly commented, "Lacan finally gives Freud's thinking the scientific concepts that it requires."[30] More recently, Lacan's *topologie du sujet* has been applied fruitfully to cinema criticism (Miller 1977–78, esp. 24–25)[31] and to the psychoanalysis of AIDS (Dean 1993, esp. 107–8). In mathematical terms, Lacan is here pointing out that the first homology group[32] of the sphere is trivial, while those of the other surfaces are profound; and this homology is linked with the connectedness or disconnectedness of the surface after one or more cuts.[33] Furthermore, as Lacan suspected, there is an intimate connection between the external structure of the physical world and its inner psychological representation qua knot theory: this hypothesis has recently been confirmed by Witten's derivation of knot invariants (in particular the Jones polynomial [Jones 1985]) from three-dimensional Chern-Simons quantum field theory (Witten 1989).

Analogous topological structures arise in quantum gravity, but inasmuch as the manifolds involved are multidimensional rather than two-dimensional, higher homology groups play a role as well. These multidimensional manifolds are no longer amenable to visualization in conventional three-dimensional Cartesian space: for example, the projective space RP^3, which arises from the ordinary 3-sphere by identification of antipodes, would require a Euclidean embedding space of dimension at least 5 (James 1991, 271–72).[34] Nevertheless, the higher homology groups can be perceived, at least approximately, via a suitable multidimensional (nonlinear) logic (Kosko 1993).[35]

[5] Manifold Theory: (W)holes and Boundaries

Luce Irigaray (1987, 76–77), in her famous article "Is the Subject of Science Sexed?" pointed out that

> the mathematical sciences, in the theory of wholes [*théorie des ensembles*], concern themselves with closed and open spaces . . . They concern themselves very little with the question of the partially open, with wholes that are not clearly delineated [*ensembles flous*], with any analysis of the problem of borders [*bords*] . . .[36]

In 1982, when Irigaray's essay first appeared, this was an incisive criticism: differential topology has traditionally privileged the study of what are known technically as "manifolds without boundary." However, in the past decade, under the impetus of the feminist critique, some mathematicians have given renewed attention to the theory of "manifolds with boundary" [Fr. *variétés à bord*] (see, for example, Hamza 1990; McAvity and Osborn 1991; Alexander *et al.* 1993). Perhaps not coincidentally, it is precisely these manifolds that arise in the new physics of conformal field theory, super-string theory, and quantum gravity.

In string theory, the quantum-mechanical amplitude for the interaction of n closed or open strings is represented by a functional integral (basically, a sum) over fields living on a two-dimensional manifold with boundary (Green *et al.* 1987). In quantum gravity, we may expect that a similar representation will hold, except that the two-dimensional manifold with boundary will be replaced by a multidimensional one. Unfortunately, multidimensionality goes against the grain of conventional linear mathematical thought, and despite a recent broadening of attitudes (notably associated with the study of multidimensional nonlinear phenomena in chaos theory), the theory of multidimensional manifolds with boundary remains somewhat underdeveloped. Nevertheless, physicists' work on the functional-integral approach to quantum gravity continues apace (Hamber 1992; Nabu-tosky and Ben-Av 1993; Kontsevich 1994), and this work is likely to stimulate the attention of mathematicians.[37]

As Irigaray anticipated, an important question in all of these theories is: can the boundary be transgressed (crossed), and if so, what happens then? Technically, this is known as the problem of boundary conditions (b.c.). At a purely mathematical level, the most salient aspect of boundary conditions is the great diversity of possibilities: for example, "free b.c." (no obstacle to crossing), "reflecting b.c." (specular reflection as in a mirror), "periodic b.c." (re-entrance in another part of the manifold), and "antiperiodic b.c." (re-entrance with 180-degree twist). The question posed by physicists is: of all these conceivable boundary conditions, which ones actually occur in the representation of quantum gravity? Or perhaps, do *all* of them occur simultaneously and on an equal footing, as suggested by the complementarity principle?[38]

At this point my summary of developments in physics must stop, for the simple reason that the answers to these questions—if indeed they have univocal answers—are not yet known. In the remainder of this essay, I propose to take as my starting point those features of the theory of quantum gravity which are relatively well established (at least by the standards of conventional science), and attempt to draw out their philosophical and political implications.

[6] Transgressing the Boundaries: Toward a Liberatory Science

Over the past two decades there has been extensive discussion among critical theorists with regard to the characteristics of modernist versus postmodernist culture; and in recent years these dialogues have begun to devote detailed attention to the specific problems posed by the natural sciences (see especially Merchant 1980; Keller 1985; Harding 1986; Aronowitz 1988b; Haraway 1991; and Ross 1991). In particular, Madsen and Madsen have recently given a very clear summary of the characteristics of modernist versus postmodernist science. They posit two criteria for a postmodern science: "A simple criterion for science to qualify as postmodern is that it be free from any dependence on the concept of objective truth. By this criterion, for example, the complementarity interpretation of quantum physics due to Niels Bohr and the Copenhagen school is seen as postmodernist" (1990, 471).[39] Clearly, quantum gravity is in this respect an archetypal postmodernist science. Second, "The other concept which can be taken as being fundamental to postmodern science is that of *essentiality*. Postmodern scientific theories are constructed from those theoretical elements which are essential for the consistency and utility of the theory" (1990, 471–72). Thus quantities or objects which are in principle unobservable—such as space-time points, exact particle positions, or quarks and gluons—ought not to be introduced into the theory.[40] While much of modern physics is excluded by this criterion, quantum gravity again qualifies: in the passage from classical general relativity to the quantized theory, space-time points (and indeed the space-time manifold itself) have disappeared from the theory.

However, these criteria, admirable as they are, are insufficient for a *liberatory* postmodern science: they liberate human beings from the tyranny of "absolute truth" and "objective reality," but not necessarily from the tyranny of other human beings. In Andrew Ross's words, we need a science "that will be publicly answerable and of some service to progressive interests" (1991, 29).[41] From a feminist standpoint, Kelly Oliver (1989, 146) makes a similar argument:

> In order to be revolutionary, feminist theory cannot claim to describe what exists, or, "natural facts." Rather, feminist theories should be political tools, strategies for overcoming oppression in specific concrete situations. The goal, then, of feminist theory, should be to develop *strategic* theories—not true theories, not false theories, but strategic theories.

How, then, is this to be done?

In what follows, I would like to discuss the outlines of a liberatory postmodern science on two levels: first, with regard to general themes and attitudes; and second, with regard to political goals and strategies.

One characteristic of the emerging postmodern science is its stress on nonlinearity and discontinuity: this is evident, for example, in chaos theory and the theory of phase transitions as well as in quantum gravity.[42] At the same time, feminist thinkers have pointed out the need for an adequate analysis of fluidity, in particular turbulent fluidity (Irigaray 1985; Hayles 1992).[43] These two themes are not as contradictory as it might at first appear: turbulence connects with strong nonlinearity, and smoothness/fluidity is sometimes associated with discontinuity (e.g., in catastrophe theory [Thom 1975, 1990; Arnol'd 1992]); so a synthesis is by no means out of the question.

Second, the postmodern sciences deconstruct and transcend the Cartesian metaphysical distinctions between humankind and Nature, observer and observed, Subject and Object. Already quantum mechanics, earlier in this century, shattered the ingenuous Newtonian faith in an objective, pre-linguistic world of material objects "out there"; no longer could we ask, as Heisenberg put it, whether "particles exist in space and time objectively." But Heisenberg's formulation still presupposes the objective existence of space and time as the neutral, unproblematic arena in which quantized particle-waves interact (albeit indeterministically); and it is precisely this would-be arena that quantum gravity problematizes. Just as quantum mechanics informs us that the position and momentum of a particle are brought into being only by the act of observation, so quantum gravity informs us that space and time themselves are contextual, their meaning defined only relative to the mode of observation.[44]

Third, the postmodern sciences overthrow the static ontological categories and hierarchies characteristic of modernist science. In place of atomism and reductionism, the new sciences stress the dynamic web of relationships between the whole and the part; in place of fixed individual essences (e.g., Newtonian particles), they conceptualize interactions and flows (e.g., quantum fields). Intriguingly, these homologous features arise in numerous seemingly disparate areas of science, from quantum gravity to chaos theory to the biophysics of self-organizing systems. In this way, the postmodern sciences appear to be converging on a new epistemological paradigm, one that may be termed an ecological perspective, broadly understood as "recogniz[ing] the fundamental interdependence of all phenomena and the embeddedness of individuals and societies in the cyclical patterns of nature" (Capra 1988, 145).[45]

A fourth aspect of postmodern science is its self-conscious stress on symbolism and representation. As Robert Markley (1992, 264) points out, the postmodern sciences are increasingly transgressing disciplinary boundaries, taking on characteristics that had heretofore been the province of the humanities:

> Quantum physics, hadron bootstrap theory, complex number theory, and chaos theory share the basic assumption that reality cannot be described in linear terms, that nonlinear—and unsolvable—equations are the only means possible to describe a complex, chaotic, and non-deterministic reality. These postmodern theories are—significantly—all metacritical in the sense that they foreground themselves as metaphors rather than as "accurate" descriptions of reality. In terms that are more familiar to literary theorists than to theoretical physicists, we might say that these attempts by scientists to develop new strategies of description represent notes towards a theory of theories, of how representation—mathematical, experimental, and verbal—is inherently complex and problematizing, not a solution but part of the semiotics of investigating the universe.[46]

From a different starting point, Aronowitz (1988b, 344) likewise suggests that a liberatory science may arise from interdisciplinary sharing of epistemologies:

> Natural objects are also socially constructed. It is not a question of whether these natural objects, or, to be more precise, the objects of natural scientific knowledge, exist independently of the act of knowing. This question is answered by the assumption of "real" time as opposed to the presupposition, common among neo-Kantians, that time always has a referent, that temporality is therefore a relative, not an unconditioned, category. Surely, the earth evolved long before life on earth. The question is whether objects of natural scientific knowledge are constituted outside the social field. If this is possible, we can assume that science or art may develop procedures that effectively neutralize the effects emanating from the means by which we produce knowledge/art. Performance art may be such an attempt.

Finally, postmodern science provides a powerful refutation of the authoritarianism and elitism inherent in traditional science, as well as an empirical basis for a democratic approach to scientific work. For, as Bohr noted, "a complete elucidation of one and the same object may require diverse points of view which defy a unique description"; this is quite simply a fact about the world, much as the self-proclaimed empiricists of modernist science might prefer to deny it. In such a situation, how can a self-perpetuating secular priesthood of credentialed "scientists" purport to maintain a monopoly on the production of scientific knowledge? (Let me emphasize that I am in no way opposed to specialized scientific training; I object only when an elite caste seeks to impose its canon of "high science," with the aim of excluding *a priori* alternative forms of scientific production by nonmembers.)[47]

The content and methodology of postmodern science thus provide powerful intellectual support for the progressive political project, understood in its broadest sense: the transgressing of boundaries, the breaking down of barriers, the radical democratization of all aspects of social, economic, political, and cultural life (see, for example, Aronowitz 1994). Conversely, one part of this project must involve the construction of a new and truly progressive science that can serve the needs of such a democratized society-to-be. As Markley observes, there seem to be two more-or-less mutually exclusive choices available to the progressive community:

> On the one hand, politically progressive scientists can try to recuperate existing practices for moral values they uphold, arguing that their right-wing enemies are defacing nature and that they, the countermovement, have access to the truth. [But] the state of the biosphere—air pollution, water pollution, disappearing rain forests, thousands of species on the verge of extinction, large areas of land burdened far beyond their carrying capacity, nuclear power plants, nuclear weapons, clearcuts where there used to be forests, starvation, malnutrition, disappearing wetlands, nonexistent grass lands, and a rash of environmentally caused diseases—suggests that the realist dream of scientific progress, of recapturing rather than revolutionizing existing methodologies and technologies, is, at worst, irrelevant to a political struggle that seeks something more than a reenactment of state socialism. (Markley 1992, 271)

The alternative is a profound reconception of science as well as politics:

> The dialogical move towards redefining systems, of seeing the world not only as an ecological whole but as a set of competing systems—a world held together by the tensions among various natural and human interests—offers the possibility of redefining what science is and what it does, of restructuring deterministic schemes of scientific education in favor of ongoing dialogues about how we intervene in our environment. (Markley 1992, 271)[48]

It goes without saying that postmodernist science unequivocally favors the latter, deeper approach.

In addition to redefining the content of science, it is imperative to restructure and redefine the institutional loci in which scientific labor takes place—universities, government labs, and corporations—and reframe the reward system that pushes scientists to become, often against their own better instincts, the hired guns of capitalists and the military. As Aronowitz (1988b, 351) has noted, "One-third of the 11,000 physics graduate students in the United States are in the single subfield of solid state physics, and all of them will be able to get jobs in that subfield." (Although this observation appeared in 1988, it is all the more true today.) By contrast, there are few jobs available in either quantum gravity or environmental physics.

But all this is only a first step: the fundamental goal of any emancipatory movement must be to demystify and democratize the production of scientific knowledge, to break down the artificial barriers that separate "scientists" from "the public." Realistically, this task must start with the younger generation, through a profound reform of the educational system (Freire 1970; Aronowitz and Giroux 1991, 1993). The teaching of science and mathematics must be purged of its authoritarian and elitist characteristics,[49] and the content of these subjects enriched by incorporating the insights of the feminist, queer, multiculturalist, and ecological critiques.[50]

Finally, the content of any science is profoundly constrained by the language within which its discourses are formulated; and mainstream Western physical science has, since Galileo, been formulated in the language of mathematics.[51] But *whose* mathematics? The question is fundamental, for, as Aronowitz has observed, "neither logic nor mathematics escapes the 'contamination' of the social" (Aronowitz 1988b, 346).[52] And as feminist thinkers have repeatedly pointed out, in the present culture this contamination is overwhelmingly capitalist, patriarchal, and militaristic: "Mathematics is portrayed as a woman whose nature desires to be the conquered Other" (Campbell and Campbell-Wright 1995, 135).[53] Thus, a liberatory science cannot be complete without a profound revision of the canon of mathematics.[54] As yet no such emancipatory mathematics exists, and we can only speculate upon its eventual content. We can see hints of it in the multidimensional and nonlinear logic of fuzzy systems theory (Kosko 1993); but this approach is still heavily marked by its origins in the crisis of late-capitalist production relations.[55] Catastrophe theory (Thom 1975, 1990; Arnol'd 1992), with its dialectical emphases on smoothness/discontinuity and metamorphosis/unfolding, will indubitably play a major role in the future mathematics; but much theoretical work remains to be done before this approach can become a concrete tool of progressive political praxis (see Schubert 1989 for an interesting start). Finally, chaos theory—which provides our deepest insights into the ubiquitous yet mysterious phenomenon of nonlinearity— will be central to all future mathematics. And yet, these images of the future mathematics must remain but the haziest glimmer: for, alongside these three young branches in the tree of science, there will arise new trunks and branches—entire new theoretical frameworks—of which we, with our present ideological blinders, cannot yet even conceive.

Notes

I thank Giacomo Caracciolo, Lucía Fernández-Santoro, Lia Gutiérrez, and Elizabeth Meiklejohn for enjoyable discussions which have contributed greatly to this essay. Needless to say, these people should not be assumed to be in total agreement with the scientific and political views expressed here, nor are they responsible for any errors or obscurities which may inadvertently remain. [Source citations from the original article (seventy-five notes) have been included in the body of the text. *Ed.*]

1   For a sampling of views, see Jammer 1974; Bell 1987; Albert 1992; Dürr *et al*. 1992; Weinberg 1992 (chap. 4); Coleman 1993; Maudlin 1994; Bricmont 1994. [The subheads in this article have been numbered for the purpose of internal cross-referencing. The numbering did not appear in the original publication. *Ed.*]

2   See also Overstreet 1980; Craige 1982; Hayles 1984; Booker 1990; Greenberg 1990; and Porter 1990 for examples of cross-fertilization of ideas between relativistic quantum theory and literary criticism.

   Unfortunately, Heisenberg's uncertainty principle has frequently been misinterpreted by amateur philosophers. As Gilles Deleuze and Félix Guattari (1994, 129–30) lucidly point out,

> in quantum physics, Heisenberg's demon does not express the impossibility of measuring both the speed and the position of a particle on the grounds of a subjective interference of the measure with the measured, but it measures exactly an objective state of affairs that leaves the respective position of two of its particles outside of the field of its actualization, the number of independent variables being reduced and the values of the coordinates having the same probability. . . . Perspectivisim, or scientific relativism, is never relative to a subject: it constitutes not a relativity of truth but, on the contrary, a truth of the relative, that is to say, of variables whose cases it orders according to the values it extracts from them in its system of coordinates.

3   See also Porush (1989) for a fascinating account of how a second group of scientists and engineers—cyberneticists—contrived, with considerable success, to subvert the most revolutionary implications of quantum physics. The main limitation of Porush's critique is that it remains solely on a cultural and philosophical plane; his conclusions would be immeasurably strengthened by an analysis of economic and political factors. (For example, Porush fails to mention that engineer-cyberneticist Claude Shannon worked for the then telephone monopoly AT&T.) A careful analysis would show, I think, that the victory of cybernetics over quantum physics in the 1940s and 1950s can be explained in large part by the centrality of cybernetics to the ongoing capitalist drive for automation of industrial production, compared with the marginal industrial relevance of quantum mechanics.

4   Aronowitz (1981, 28) has noted that wave-particle duality renders the "will to totality in modern science" severely problematic:

> The differences within physics between wave and particle theories of matter, the indeterminacy principle discovered by Heisenberg, Einstein's relativity theory, all are accommodations to the impossibility of arriving at a unified field theory, one in which the "anomaly" of difference for a theory which posits identity may be resolved without challenging the presuppositions of science itself.

For further development of these ideas, see Aronowitz 1988a, 524–25, 533.

5   Bohr's analysis of the complementarity principle also led him to a social outlook that was, for its time and place, notably progressive. Consider the following excerpt from a 1938 lecture (Bohr 1958, 30):

> I may perhaps here remind you of the extent to which in certain societies the roles of men and women are reversed, not only regarding domestic and social duties but also regarding behaviour and mentality. Even if many of us, in such a situation, might perhaps at first shrink from admitting the possibility that it is entirely a caprice of fate that the people concerned have their specific culture and not ours, and we not theirs instead of our own, it is clear that even the slightest suspicion in this respect implies a betrayal of the national complacency inherent in any human culture resting in itself.

6   This impressive work also explains the intimate connections with Gödel's proof of the incompleteness of formal systems and with Skolem's construction of nonstandard models of arithmetic, as well as with Bataille's general economy. For further discussion of Bataille's physics see Hochroth 1995.

Numerous other examples could be adduced. For instance, Barbara Johnson (1989, 12) makes no specific reference to quantum physics; but her description of deconstruction is an eerily exact summary of the complementarity principle: "Instead of a simple either/or structure, deconstruction attempts to elaborate a discourse that says *neither* 'either/or', *nor* 'both/and' nor even 'neither/nor' while at the same time not totally abandoning these logics either." See also McCarthy 1992 for a thought-provoking analysis that raises disturbing questions about the "complicity" between (nonrelativistic) quantum physics and deconstruction.

7   Permit me in this regard a personal recollection: Fifteen years ago, when I was a graduate student, my research in relativistic quantum field theory led me to an approach that I called "de[con]structive quantum field theory" (Sokal 1982). Of course, at that time I was completely ignorant of Jacques Derrida's work on deconstruction in philosophy and literary theory. In retrospect, however, there is a striking affinity: my work can be read as an exploration of how the orthodox discourse (e.g., Itzykson and Zuber 1980) on scalar quantum field theory in four-dimensional space-time (in technical terms, "renormalized perturbation theory" for the φ_4^4 theory) can be seen to assert its own unreliability and thereby to undermine its own affirmations. Since then, my work has shifted to other questions, mostly connected with phase transitions; but subtle homologies between the two fields can be discerned, notably the theme of discontinuity (see n.42). For further examples of deconstruction in quantum field theory, see Merz and Knorr Cetina 1994.

8   Bell 1987, especially chaps. 10 and 16. See also Maudlin 1994 (chap. 1) for a clear account presupposing no specialized knowledge beyond high-school algebra.

9   Greenberger *et al.* 1989, 1990; Mermin 1990, 1993.

10 Aronowitz (1988b, 331) has made a provocative observation concerning nonlinear causality in quantum mechanics and its relation to the social construction of time:

> Linear causality assumes that the relation of cause and effect can be expressed as a function of temporal succession. Owing to recent developments in quantum mechanics, we can postulate that it is possible to know the effects of absent causes; that is, speaking metaphorically, effects may anticipate causes so that our perception of them may precede the physical occurrence of a "cause." The hypothesis that challenges our conventional conception of linear time and causality and that asserts the possibility of time's reversal also raises the question of the degree to which the concept of "time's arrow" is inherent in all scientific theory. If these experiments are successful, the conclusions about the way time as "clock-time" has been constituted

historically will be open to question. We will have "proved" by means of experiment what has long been suspected by philosophers, literary and social critics: that time is, in part, a conventional construction, its segmentation into hours and minutes a product of the need for industrial discipline, for rational organization of social labor in the early bourgeois epoch.

The theoretical analyses of Greenberger *et al.* (1989, 1990) and Mermin (1990, 1993) provide a striking example of this phenomenon; see Maudlin 1994 for a detailed analysis of the implications for concepts of causality and temporality. An experimental test, extending the work of Aspect *et al.* (1982), will likely be forthcoming within the next few years.

11   The intimate relations between quantum mechanics and the mind-body problem are discussed in Goldstein 1983, chaps. 7 and 8.

12   Among the voluminous literature, Capra 1975 can be recommended for its scientific accuracy and its accessibility to nonspecialists. In addition, Sheldrake 1981, while occasionally speculative, is in general sound. For a sympathetic but critical analysis of New Age theories, see Ross 1991, chap. 1. For a critique of Capra's work from a Third World perspective, see Alvares 1992, chap. 6.

13   Newtonian atomism treats particles as hyperseparated in space and time, backgrounding their interconnectedness (Plumwood 1993a, 125); indeed, "the only 'force' allowed within the mechanistic framework is that of kinetic energy—the energy of motion by contact—all other purported forces, including action at a distance, being regarded as occult" (Mathews 1991, 17). For critical analyses of the Newtonian mechanistic worldview, see Weil 1968, esp. chap. 1; Merchant 1980; Berman 1981; Keller 1985, chaps. 2 and 3; Mathews 1991, chap. 1; and Plumwood 1993a, chap. 5.

14   According to the traditional textbook account, special relativity is concerned with the coordinate transformations relating *two* frames of reference in uniform relative motion. But this is a misleading oversimplification, as Bruno Latour has pointed out:

> How can one decide whether an observation made in a train about the behaviour of a falling stone can be made to coincide with the observation made of the same falling stone from the embankment? If there are only one, or even *two*, frames of reference, no solution can be found since the man in the train claims he observes a straight line and the man on the embankment a parabola. . . . Einstein's solution is to consider *three* actors: one in the train, one on the embankment and a third one, the author [enunciator] or one of its representants, who tries to superimpose the coded observations sent back by the two others. . . . Without the enunciator's position (hidden in Einstein's account), and without the notion of centres of calculation, Einstein's own technical argument is ununderstandable. (1988, 10–11, 35; emphasis in original)

In the end, as Latour wittily but accurately observes, special relativity boils down to the proposition that "more frames of reference with less privilege can be accessed, reduced, accumulated and combined, observers can be delegated to a few more places in the infinitely large (the cosmos) and the infinitely small (electrons), and the readings they send will be understandable. His [Einstein's] book could well be titled: "New Instructions for Bringing Back Long-Distance Scientific Travellers"" (22–23). Latour's critical analysis of Einstein's logic provides an eminently accessible introduction to special relativity for non-scientists.

15   It goes without saying that special relativity proposes new concepts not only of space and time but also of mechanics. In special relativity, as Virilio (1991, 136) has noted, "the dromospheric space, space-speed, is physically described by what is called the 'logistic equation,' the result of the product of the mass displaced by the speed of its displacement,

MxV." This radical alteration of the Newtonian formula has profound consequences, particularly in the quantum theory; see Lorentz *et al.* 1952 and Weinberg 1992 for further discussion.

16 Steven Best (1991, 225) has put his finger on the crux of the difficulty, which is that "unlike the linear equations used in Newtonian and even quantum mechanics, nonlinear equations do [not] have the simple additive property whereby chains of solutions can be constructed out of simple, independent parts." For this reason, the strategies of atomization, reductionism, and context-stripping that underlie the Newtonian scientific methodology simply do not work in general relativity.

17 Gödel 1949. For a summary of recent work in this area, see 't Hooft 1993.

18 These new notions of space, time, and causality are *in part* foreshadowed already in special relativity. Thus, Alexander Argyros (1991, 137) has noted that "in a universe dominated by photons, gravitons, and neutrinos, that is, in the very early universe, the theory of special relativity suggests that any distinction between before and after is impossible. For a particle traveling at the speed of light, or one traversing a distance that is in the order of the Planck length, all events are simultaneous." However, I cannot agree with Argyros's conclusion that Derridean deconstruction is therefore inapplicable to the hermeneutics of early-universe cosmology: Argyros's argument to this effect is based on an impermissibly totalizing use of special relativity (in technical terms, "light-cone coordinates") in a context where *general* relativity is inescapable. (For a similar but less innocent error, see n.20.)

Jean-François Lyotard (1989, 5–6) has also pointed out that not only general relativity, but also modern elementary-particle physics, imposes new notions of time:

> In contemporary physics and astrophysics . . . a particle has a sort of elementary memory and consequently a temporal filter. This is why contemporary physicists tend to think that time emanates from matter itself, and that it is not an entity outside or inside the universe whose function it would be to gather all different times into universal history. It is only in certain regions that such—only partial—syntheses could be detected. There would on this view be areas of determinism where complexity is increasing.

Furthermore, Michel Serres (1992, 89–91) has noted that chaos theory (Gleick 1987) and percolation theory (Stauffer 1985) have contested the traditional linear concept of time:

> Time does not always flow along a line . . . or a plane, but along an extraordinarily complex manifold, as if it showed stopping points, ruptures, sinks [*puits*], funnels of overwhelming acceleration [*cheminées d'accélération foudroyante*], rips, lacunae, all sown randomly. . . . Time flows in a turbulent and chaotic manner; it percolates. (Translation mine. Note that in the theory of dynamical systems, "*puits*" is a technical term meaning "sink," i.e. the opposite of "source.")

These multiple insights into the nature of time, provided by different branches of physics, are a further illustration of the complementarity principle.

General relativity can arguably be read as corroborating the Nietzschean deconstruction of causality (see, e.g., Culler 1982, 86–88), although some relativists find this interpretation problematic. In quantum mechanics, by contrast, this phenomenon is rather firmly established (see n.10). General relativity is also, of course, the starting point for contemporary astrophysics and physical cosmology. See Mathews 1991 (59–90, 109–16, 142–63) for a detailed analysis of the connections between general relativity (and its generalizations called "geometrodynamics") and an ecological worldview. For an astrophysicist's speculations along similar lines, see Primack and Abrams 1995.

19 Discussion of Derrida (1970, 265–66).

20 Right-wing critics Gross and Levitt (1994, 79) have ridiculed this statement, willfully misinterpreting it as an assertion about *special* relativity, in which the Einsteinian constant *c* (the speed of light in vacuum) is of course constant. No reader even minimally conversant with modern physics—except an ideologically biased one—could fail to understand Derrida's unequivocal reference to general relativity.

21 Luce Irigaray (1987, 77–78) has pointed out that the contradictions between quantum theory and field theory are in fact the culmination of a historical process that began with Newtonian mechanics:

> The Newtonian break has ushered scientific enterprise into a world where sense perception is worth little, a world which can lead to the annihilation of the very stakes of physics' object: the matter (whatever the predicates) of the universe and of the bodies that constitute it. In this very science, moreover [*d'ailleurs*], cleavages exist: quantum theory/field theory, mechanics of solids/dynamics of fluids, for example. But the imperceptibility of the matter under study often brings with it the paradoxical privilege of *solidity* in discoveries and a delay, even an abandoning of the analysis of the infinity [*l'in-fini*] of the fields of force.

I have here corrected the translation of *d'ailleurs*, which means "moreover" or "besides" (not "however").

22 Sheldrake 1981, 1991; Briggs and Peat 1984, chap. 4; Granero-Porati and Porati 1984; Kazarinoff 1985; Schiffmann 1989; Psarev 1990; Brooks and Castor 1990; Heinonen *et al.* 1992; Rensing 1993. For an in-depth treatment of the mathematical background to this theory, see Thom 1975, 1990; and for a brief but insightful analysis of the philosophical underpinnings of this and related approaches, see Ross 1991 (40–42, 253 n.20).

23 Some early workers thought that the morphogenetic field might be related to the electromagnetic field, but it is now understood that this is merely a suggestive analogy: see Sheldrake 1981 (77, 90) for a clear exposition. Note also point (b) below.

24 For another example of the "turf" effect, see Chomsky 1979 (6–7).

25 To be fair to the high-energy-physics establishment, I should mention that there is also an honest intellectual reason for their opposition to this theory: inasmuch as it posits a subquantum interaction linking patterns throughout the universe, it is, in physicists' terminology, a "nonlocal field theory." Now, the history of classical theoretical physics since the early 1800s, from Maxwell's electrodynamics to Einstein's general relativity, can be read in a very deep sense as a trend away from action-at-a-distance theories and toward *local field theories*: in technical terms, theories expressible by partial differential equations (Einstein and Infeld 1961; Hayles 1984). So a nonlocal field theory definitely goes against the grain. On the other hand, as Bell (1987) and others have convincingly argued, the key property of quantum mechanics is precisely its *non-locality*, as expressed in Bell's theorem and its generalizations (see nn. 8 and 9). Therefore, a nonlocal field theory, although jarring to physicists' classical intuition, is not only natural but in fact *preferred* (and possibly even *mandatory?*) in the quantum context. This is why classical general relativity is a local field theory, while quantum gravity (whether string, weave, or morphogenetic field) is inherently nonlocal.

26 Differential topology is the branch of mathematics concerned with those properties of surfaces (and higher-dimensional manifolds) that are unaffected by smooth deformations. The properties it studies are therefore primarily qualitative rather than quantitative, and its methods are holistic rather than Cartesian.

27 The alert reader will notice that anomalies in "normal science" are the usual harbinger of a future paradigm shift (Kuhn 1970).

28 The flowering of the theory of phase transitions in the 1970s probably reflects an increased emphasis on discontinuity and rupture in the wider culture (see n. 42).

29 For an in-depth analysis of Lacan's use of ideas from mathematical topology, see Juranville 1984 (chap. 7); Granon-Lafont 1985, 1990; Vappereau 1985; and Nasio 1987, 1992; a brief summary is given by Leupin 1991. See Hayles 1990 (80) for an intriguing connection between Lacanian topology and chaos theory; unfortunately she does not pursue it. See also Žižek 1991 (38–39, 45–47) for some further homologies between Lacanian theory and contemporary physics. Lacan also made extensive use of concepts from set-theoretic number theory: see, for example, Miller 1977/78 and Ragland-Sullivan 1990.

   In bourgeois social psychology, topological ideas had been employed by Kurt Lewin as early as the 1930s, but this work foundered for two reasons: first, because of its individual-ist ideological preconceptions; and second, because it relied on old-fashioned point-set topology rather than modern differential topology and catastrophe theory. Regarding the second point, see Back 1992.

30 "Il suffit, à cette fin, reconnaître que Lacan confère enfin à la pensée de Freud, les concepts scientifiques qu'elle exige." This famous essay on "Freud and Lacan" was first published in 1964, before Lacan's work had reached its highest level of mathematical rigor. It was reprinted in English translation in Althusser 1969.

31 This article has become quite influential in film theory: see, for example, Jameson 1982 (27–28) and the references cited there. As Strathausen (1994, 69) indicates, Miller's article is tough going for the reader not well versed in the mathematics of set theory. But it is well worth the effort. For a gentle introduction to set theory, see Bourbaki 1970.

32 Homology theory is one of the two main branches of the mathematical field called *algebraic topology*. For an excellent introduction to homology theory, see Munkres 1984; or for a more popular account, see Eilenberg and Steenrod 1952. A fully relativistic homology theory is discussed, for example, in Eilenberg and Moore 1965. For a dialectical approach to homology theory and its dual, cohomology theory, see Massey 1978. For a cybernetic approach to homology, see Saludes i Closa 1984.

33 For the relation of homology to cuts, see Hirsch 1976 (205–8); and for an application to collective movements in quantum field theory, see Caracciolo *et al.* 1993 (especially Appendix A.1).

34 It is, however, worth noting that the space RP^3 is homeomorphic to the group $SO(3)$ of rotational symmetries of conventional three-dimensional Euclidean space. Thus, some aspects of three-dimensional Euclidicity are preserved (albeit in modified form) in the postmodern physics, just as some aspects of Newtonian mechanics were preserved in modified form in Einsteinian physics.

35 See also Johnson 1977 (481–82) for an analysis of Derrida's and Lacan's efforts toward transcending the Euclidean spatial logic.

   Along related lines, Eve Seguin (1994, 61) has noted that "logic says nothing about the world and attributes to the world properties that are but constructs of theoretical thought. This explains why physics since Einstein has relied on alternative logics, such as trivalent logic which rejects the principle of the excluded middle." A pioneering (and unjustly forgotten) work in this direction, likewise inspired by quantum mechanics, is Lupasco 1951. See also Plumwood 1993b (453–59) for a specifically feminist perspective on non-classical logics. For a critical analysis of one nonclassical logic ("boundary logic") and its relation to the ideology of cyberspace, see Markley 1994.

36 This essay originally appeared in French in Irigaray 1982. Irigaray's phrase *théorie des ensembles* can also be rendered as "theory of sets," and bords is usually translated in the

mathematical context as "boundaries." Her phrase *ensembles flous* may refer to the new mathematical field of "fuzzy sets" (Kaufmann 1973; Kosko 1993).

37 In the history of mathematics there has been a long-standing dialectic between the development of its "pure" and "applied" branches (Struik 1987). Of course, the "applications" traditionally privileged in this context have been those profitable to capitalists or useful to their military forces: for example, number theory has been developed largely for its applications in cryptography (Loxton 1990). See also Hardy 1967 (120–21, 131–32).

38 The equal representation of all boundary conditions is also suggested by Chew's bootstrap theory of "subatomic democracy": see Chew 1977 for an introduction, and see Morris 1988 and Markley 1992 for philosophical analysis.

39 The main limitation of the Madsen-Madsen analysis is that it is essentially apolitical; and it hardly needs to be pointed out that disputes over what is *true* can have a profound effect on, and are in turn profoundly affected by, disputes over *political projects*. Thus Markley (1992, 270) makes a point similar to that of Madsen-Madsen, but rightly situates it in its political context:

> Radical critiques of science that seek to escape the constraints of deterministic dialectics must also give over narrowly conceived debates about realism and truth to investigate what kind of realities—political realities—might be engendered by a dialogical bootstrapping. Within a dialogically agitated environment, debates about reality become, in practical terms, irrelevant. "Reality," finally, is a historical construct.

See Markley 1992 (266–72) and Hobsbawm 1993 (63–64) for further discussion of the political implications.

40 Aronowitz (1988b, 292–93) makes a slightly different, but equally cogent, criticism of quantum chromodynamics (the currently hegemonic theory representing nucleons as permanently bound states of quarks and gluons): drawing on the work of Pickering (1984), he notes that

> in his [Pickering's] account, quarks are the name assigned to (absent) phenomena that cohere with particle rather than field theories, which, in each case, offer different, although equally plausible, explanations for the same (inferred) observation. That the majority of the scientific community chose one over another is a function of scientists' preference for the tradition rather than the validity of explanation.
>
> However, Pickering does not reach back far enough into the history of physics to find the basis of the research tradition from which the quark explanation emanates. It may not be found inside the tradition but in the ideology of science, in the differences behind field versus particle theories, simple versus complex explanations, the bias toward certainty rather than indeterminateness.

Along very similar lines, Markley (1992, 269) observes that physicists' preference for quantum chromodynamics over Chew's bootstrap theory of "subatomic democracy" (Chew 1977) is a result of ideology rather than data:

> It is not surprising, in this regard, that bootstrap theory has fallen into relative disfavor among physicists seeking a GUT (Grand Unified Theory) or TOE (Theory of Everything) to explain the structure of the universe. Comprehensive theories that explain "everything" are products of the privileging of coherence and order in western science. The choice between bootstrap theory and theories of everything that confronts physicists does *not* have to do primarily with the truth-value offered by these accounts of available data but with the narrative structures—indeterminate or deterministic—into which these data are placed and by which they are interpreted.

Unfortunately, the vast majority of physicists are not yet aware of these incisive critiques of one of their most fervently held dogmas.

For another critique of the hidden ideology of contemporary particle physics, see Kroker *et al.* 1989 (158–62, 204–7). The style of this critique is rather too Baudrillardian for my staid taste, but the content is (except for a few minor inaccuracies) right on target.

41 For an amusing example of how this modest demand has driven right-wing scientists into fits of apoplexy ("frighteningly Stalinist" is the chosen epithet), see Gross and Levitt 1994 (91).

42 While chaos theory has been deeply studied by cultural analysts—see, for example, Hayles 1990, 1991; Argyros 1991; Best 1991; Young 1991, 1992; Assad 1993 among many others—the theory of phase transitions has passed largely unremarked. (One exception is the discussion of the renormalization group in Hayles 1990 [154–58].) This is a pity, because discontinuity and the emergence of multiple scales are central features in this theory; and it would be interesting to know how the development of these themes in the 1970s and afterwards is connected to trends in the wider culture. I therefore suggest this theory as a fruitful field for future research by cultural analysts. Some theorems on discontinuity which may be relevant to this analysis can be found in Van Enter *et al.* 1993.

43 See, however, Schor 1989 for a critique of Irigaray's undue deference toward conventional (male) science, particularly physics.

44 Concerning the Cartesian/Baconian metaphysics, Robert Markley (1991, 6) has observed that

> Narratives of scientific progress depend upon imposing binary oppositions—true/false, right/wrong—on theoretical and experimental knowledge, privileging meaning over noise, metonymy over metaphor, monological authority over dialogical contention. . . . These attempts to fix nature are ideologically coercive as well as descriptively limited. They focus attention only on the small range of phenomena—say, linear dynamics—which seem to offer easy, often idealized ways of modeling and interpreting humankind's relationship to the universe.

While this observation is informed primarily by chaos theory—and secondarily by non-relativistic quantum mechanics—it in fact summarizes beautifully the radical challenge to modernist metaphysics posed by quantum gravity.

45 One caveat: I have strong reservations about Capra's use here of the word cyclical, which if interpreted too literally could promote a politically regressive quietism. For further analyses of these issues, see Bohm 1980; Merchant 1980, 1992; Berman 1981; Prigogine and Stengers 1984; Bowen 1985; Griffin 1988; Kitchener 1988; Callicott 1989 (chaps. 6 and 9); Shiva 1990; Best 1991; Haraway 1991, 1994; Mathews 1991; Morin 1992; Santos 1992; and Wright 1992.

46 A minor quibble: it is not clear to me that complex number theory, which is a new and still quite speculative branch of mathematical physics, ought to be accorded the same epistemological status as the three firmly established sciences cited by Markley.

See Wallerstein 1993 (17–20) for an incisive and closely analogous account of how the postmodern physics is beginning to borrow ideas from the historical social sciences; and see Santos 1989 and 1992 for a more detailed development.

47 At this point, the traditional scientist's response is that work not conforming to the evidentiary standards of conventional science is fundamentally *irrational*, that is, logically flawed and therefore not worthy of credence. But this refutation is insufficient: for, as Porush (1993) has lucidly observed, modern mathematics and physics have *themselves* admitted a

powerful "intrusion of the irrational" in quantum mechanics and Gödel's theorem—although, understandably, like the Pythagoreans twenty-four centuries ago, modernist scientists have attempted to exorcise this unwanted irrational element as best they could. Porush makes a powerful plea for a "post-rational epistemology" that would retain the best of conventional Western science while validating alternative ways of knowing.

Note also that Jacques Lacan, from a quite different starting point, came long ago to a similar appreciation of the inevitable role of irrationality in modern mathematics:

> If you'll permit me to use one of those formulas which come to me as I write my notes, human life could be defined as a calculus in which zero was irrational. This formula is just an image, a mathematical metaphor. When I say "irrational," I'm referring not to some unfathomable emotional state but precisely to what is called an imaginary number. The square root of minus one doesn't correspond to anything that is subject to our intuition, anything real—in the mathematical sense of the term—and yet, it must be conserved, along with its full function. (Lacan 1977, 28–29; seminar originally given in 1959)

For further reflections on irrationality in modern mathematics, see Solomon 1988 (76) and Bloor 1991 (122–25).

48 Along parallel lines, Donna Haraway (1991, 191–92) has argued eloquently for a democratic science comprising "partial, locatable, critical knowledges sustaining the possibility of webs of connections called solidarity in politics and shared conversations in epistemology" and founded on "a doctrine and practice of objectivity that privileges contestation, deconstruction, passionate construction, webbed connections, and hope for transformation of systems of knowledge and ways of seeing." These ideas are further developed in Haraway 1994 and Doyle 1994.

49 For an example in the context of the Sandinista revolution, see Sokal 1987.

50 For feminist critiques, see Merchant 1980; Easlea 1981; Keller 1985, 1992; Harding 1986, 1991; Haraway 1989, 1991; Plumwood 1993a. See Wylie *et al.* 1990 for an extensive bibliography. The feminist critique of science has, not surprisingly, been the object of a bitter right-wing counterattack. For a sampling, see Levin 1988; Haack 1992, 1993; Sommers 1994; Gross and Levitt 1994 (chap. 5); and Patai and Koertge 1994.

For queer critiques, see Trebilcot 1988 and Hamill 1994.

For multiculturalist critiques, see Ezeabasili 1977; Van Sertima 1983; Frye 1987; Sardar 1988; Adams 1990; Nandy 1990; Alvares 1992; Harding 1994. As with the feminist critique, the multiculturalist perspective has been ridiculed by right-wing critics, with a condescension that in some cases borders on racism. See, for example, Ortiz de Montellano 1991; Martel 1991/92; Hughes 1993 (chap. 2); and Gross and Levitt 1994 (203–14).

For ecological critiques, see Merchant 1980, 1992; Berman 1981; Callicott 1989 (chaps. 6 and 9); Mathews 1991; Wright 1992; Plumwood 1993a; Ross 1994.

51 See Wojciehowski 1991 for a deconstruction of Galileo's rhetoric, in particular his claim that the mathematico-scientific method can lead to direct and reliable knowledge of "reality."

A very recent but important contribution to the philosophy of mathematics can be found in the work of Deleuze and Guattari (1994, chap. 5). Here they introduce the philosophically fruitful notion of a "functive" [Fr. *fonctif*], which is neither a function [Fr. *fonction*] nor a functional [Fr. *fonctionnelle*] but rather a more basic conceptual entity: "The object of science is not concepts but rather functions that are presented as propositions in discursive systems. The elements of functions are called *functives*" (117). This apparently simple idea has surprisingly subtle and far-reaching consequences; its elucidation requires a detour into chaos theory (see also Rosenberg 1993 and Canning 1994):

> The first difference between science and philosophy is their respective attitudes toward chaos. Chaos is defined not so much by its disorder as by the infinite speed with which every form taking shape in it vanishes. It is a void that is not a nothingness but a *virtual*, containing all possible particles and drawing out all possible forms, which spring up only to disappear immediately, without consistency or reference, without consequence. Chaos is an infinite speed of birth and disappearance. (117–18)

But science, unlike philosophy, cannot cope with infinite speeds:

> It is by slowing down that matter, as well as the scientific thought able to penetrate it [*sic*] with propositions, is actualized. A function is a Slow-motion. Of course, science constantly advances accelerations, not only in catalysis but in particle accelerators and expansions that move galaxies apart. However, the primordial slowing down is not for these phenomena a zero-instant with which they break but rather a condition coextensive with their whole development. To slow down is to set a limit in chaos to which all speeds are subject, so that they form a variable determined as abscissa, at the same time as the limit forms a universal constant that cannot be gone beyond (for example, a maximum degree of contraction). *The first functives are therefore the limit and the variable*, and reference is a relationship between values of the variable or, more profoundly, the relationship of the variable, as abscissa of speeds, with the limit. (118–19; emphasis mine)

A rather intricate further analysis (too lengthy to quote here) leads to a conclusion of profound methodological importance for those sciences based on mathematical modeling: "The respective independence of variables appears in mathematics when one of them is at a higher power than the first. That is why Hegel shows that variability in the function is not confined to values that can be changed (2/3 and 4/6) or are left undetermined (a = 2b) but requires one of the variables to be at a higher power ($y^{2/x} = P$)" (122). (Note that the English translation inadvertently writes $y^2/x = P$, an amusing error that thoroughly mangles the logic of the argument.)

Surprisingly for a technical philosophical work, this book (*Qu'est-ce que la philosophie?*) was a best-seller in France in 1991. It has recently appeared in English translation, but is, alas, unlikely to compete successfully with Rush Limbaugh and Howard Stern for the best-seller lists in this country.

52   For a vicious right-wing attack on this proposition, see Gross and Levitt 1994 (52–54). See Ginzberg 1989; Cope-Kasten 1989; Nye 1990; and Plumwood 1993b for lucid feminist critiques of conventional (masculinist) mathematical logic, in particular the *modus ponens* and the syllogism. Concerning the *modus ponens*, see also Woolgar 1988 (45–46) and Bloor 1991 (182); and concerning the syllogism, see also Woolgar 1988 (47–48) and Bloor 1991 (131–35). For an analysis of the social images underlying mathematical conceptions of infinity, see Harding 1986 (50). For a demonstration of the social contextuality of mathematical statements, see Woolgar 1988 (43) and Bloor 1991 (107–30).

53   See Merchant 1980 for a detailed analysis of the themes of control and domination in Western mathematics and science.

Let me mention in passing two other examples of sexism and militarism in mathematics that to my knowledge have not been noticed previously. The first concerns the theory of branching processes, which arose in Victorian England from the "problem of the extinction of families" and which now plays a key role *inter alia* in the analysis of nuclear chain reactions (Harris 1963). In the seminal (and this sexist word is apt) paper on the subject, Francis Galton and the Reverend H. W. Watson (1874) wrote:

> The decay of the families of men who occupied conspicuous positions in past times has been a subject of frequent research, and has given rise to various conjectures . . .
>
> The instances are very numerous in which surnames that were once common have since become scarce or have wholly disappeared. The tendency is universal, and, in explanation of it, the conclusion has hastily been drawn that a rise in physical comfort and intellectual capacity is necessarily accompanied by a diminution in 'fertility'. . .
>
> Let p_0, p_1, p_2, . . . be the respective probabilities that a man has 0, 1, 2, . . . sons, let each son have the same probability of sons of his own, and so on. What is the probability that the male line is extinct after r generations, and more generally what is the probability for any given number of descendants in the male line in any given generation?

One cannot fail to be charmed by the quaint implication that human males reproduce asexually; nevertheless, the classism, social-Darwinism, and sexism in this passage are obvious.

The second example is Laurent Schwartz's 1973 book *Radon Measures*. While technically quite interesting, this work is imbued, as its title makes plain, with the pro-nuclear-energy worldview that has been characteristic of French science since the early 1960s. Sadly, the French left—especially but by no means solely the PCF—has traditionally been as enthusiastic for nuclear energy as the right (see Touraine *et al.* 1980).

54 Just as liberal feminists are frequently content with a minimal agenda of legal and social equality for women and "pro-choice," so liberal (and even some socialist) mathematicians are often content to work within the hegemonic Zermelo-Fraenkel framework (which, reflecting its nineteenth-century liberal origins, already incorporates the axiom of equality) supplemented only by the axiom of choice. But this framework is grossly insufficient for a liberatory mathematics, as was proven long ago by Cohen 1966.

55 Fuzzy systems theory has been heavily developed by transnational corporations—first in Japan and later elsewhere—to solve practical problems of efficiency in labor-displacing automation.

References

Adams, Hunter Havelin III. 1990. African and African-American contributions to science and technology. In *African-American baseline essays*. Portland, Ore.: Multnomah School District 1J, Portland Public Schools.

Albert, David Z. 1992. *Quantum mechanics and experience*. Cambridge, Mass.: Harvard University Press.

Alexander, Stephanie B., I. David Berg, and Richard L. Bishop. 1993. Geometric curvature bounds in Riemannian manifolds with boundary. *Transactions of the American Mathematical Society* 339: 703–16.

Althusser, Louis. 1969. Freud and Lacan. New Left Review 55: 48–65.

——. 1993. Écrits sur la psychanalyse: Freud et Lacan. Paris: Stock/IMEC.

Alvares, Claude. 1992. *Science, development, and violence: The revolt against modernity*. Delhi: Oxford University Press.

Alvarez-Gaumé, Luis. 1985. Topology and anomalies. In *Mathematics and physics: Lectures on recent results*, vol. 2, edited by L. Streit. Singapore: World Scientific.

Argyros, Alexander J. 1991. *A blessed rage for order: Deconstruction, evolution, and chaos*. Ann Arbor: University of Michigan Press.

Arnol'd, Vladimir I. 1992. *Catastrophe theory*, 3d ed. Translated by G. S. Wassermann and R. K. Thomas. Berlin: Springer.

Aronowitz, Stanley. 1981. *The crisis in historical materialism: Class, politics, and culture in Marxist theory*. New York: Praeger.

——. 1988a. The production of scientific knowledge: Science, ideology, and Marxism. In *Marxism and the interpretation of culture*, edited by Cary Nelson and Lawrence Grossberg. Urbana: University of Illinois Press.

——. 1988b. *Science as power: Discourse and ideology in modern society*. Minneapolis: University of Minnesota Press.

——. 1994. The situation of the left in the United States. *Socialist Review* 23, no. 3: 5–79.

Aronowitz, Stanley, and Henry A. Giroux. 1991. *Postmodern education: Politics, culture, and social criticism*. Minneapolis: University of Minnesota Press.

——. 1993. *Education still under siege*. Westport, Conn.: Bergin and Garvey.

Ashtekar, Abhay, Carlo Rovelli, and Lee Smolin. 1992. Weaving a classical metric with quantum threads. *Physical Review Letters* 69: 237–40.

Aspect, Alain, Jean Dalibard, and Gérard Roger. 1982. Experimental test of Bell's inequalities using time-varying analyzers. *Physical Review Letters* 49: 1804–1807.

Assad, Maria L. 1993. Portrait of a nonlinear dynamical system: The discourse of Michel Serres. *SubStance* 71/72: 141–52.

Back, Kurt W. 1992. This business of topology. *Journal of Social Issues* 48, no. 2: 51–66.

Bell, John S. 1987. *Speakable and unspeakable in quantum mechanics: Collected papers on quantum philosophy*. New York: Cambridge University Press.

Berman, Morris. 1981. *The reenchantment of the world*. Ithaca, N.Y.: Cornell University Press.

Best, Steven. 1991. Chaos and entropy: Metaphors in postmodern science and social theory. *Science as Culture* 2(2), no. 11: 188–226.

Bloor, David. 1991. *Knowledge and social imagery*, 2d ed. Chicago: University of Chicago Press.

Bohm, David. 1980. *Wholeness and the implicate order*. London: Routledge and Kegan Paul.

Bohr, Niels. 1958. Natural philosophy and human cultures. In *The philosophical writings of Niels Bohr*, vol. 2, *Essays 1932–1957 on atomic physics and human knowledge*. New York: Wiley.

——. 1963. Quantum physics and philosophy—causality and complementarity. In *The philosophical writings of Niels Bohr*, vol. 3, *Essays 1958–1962 on atomic physics and human knowledge*. New York: Wiley.

Booker, M. Keith. 1990. Joyce, Planck, Einstein, and Heisenberg: A relativistic quantum mechanical discussion of Ulysses. *James Joyce Quarterly* 27: 577–86.

Boulware, David G. and S. Deser. 1975. Classical general relativity derived from quantum gravity. *Annals of Physics* 89: 193–240.

Bourbaki, Nicolas. 1970. *Théorie des ensembles*. Paris: Hermann.

Bowen, Margarita. 1985. The ecology of knowledge: Linking the natural and social sciences. *Geoforum* 16: 213–25.

Bricmont, Jean. 1994. Contre la philosophie de la mécanique quantique. Texte d'une communication faite au colloque "Faut-il promouvoir les échanges entre les sciences et la philosophie?" Louvain-la-Neuve (Belgium), 24–25 March 1994.

Briggs, John, and F. David Peat. 1984. *Looking glass universe: The emerging science of wholeness*. New York: Cornerstone Library.

Brooks, Roger, and David Castor. 1990. Morphisms between supersymmetric and topological quantum field theories. *Physics Letters B* 246: 99–104.

Callicott, J. Baird. 1989. *In defense of the land ethic: Essays in environmental philosophy*. Albany: State University of New York Press.

Campbell, Mary Anne, and Randall K. Campbell-Wright. 1995. Toward a feminist algebra. In *Teaching the majority: Science, mathematics, and engineering that attracts women*, edited by Sue V. Rosser. New York: Teachers College Press.

Canning, Peter. 1994. The crack of time and the ideal game. In *Gilles Deleuze and the theater of philosophy*, edited by Constantin V. Boundas and Dorothea Olkowski. New York: Routledge.

Capra, Fritjof. 1975. *The tao of physics: An exploration of the parallels between modern physics and Eastern mysticism*. Berkeley, Calif.: Shambhala.

———. 1988. The role of physics in the current change of paradigms. In *The world view of contemporary physics: Does it need a new metaphysics?*, edited by Richard F. Kitchener. Albany: State University of New York Press.

Caracciolo, Sergio, Robert G. Edwards, Andrea Pelissetto, and Alan D. Sokal. 1993. Wolff-type embedding algorithms for general nonlinear s-models. *Nuclear Physics B* 403: 475–541.

Chew, Geoffrey. 1977. Impasse for the elementary-particle concept. In *The sciences today*, edited by Robert M. Hutchins and Mortimer Adler. New York: Arno.

Chomsky, Noam. 1979. *Language and responsibility*. Translated by John Viertel. New York: Pantheon.

Cohen, Paul J. 1966. *Set theory and the continuum hypothesis*. New York: Benjamin.

Coleman, Sidney. 1993. Quantum mechanics in your face. Lecture at New York University, 12 November 1993.

Cope-Kasten, Vance. 1989. A portrait of dominating rationality. *Newsletters on Computer Use, Feminism, Law, Medicine, Teaching (American Philosophical Association)* 88, no. 2 (March): 29–34.

Corner, M. A. 1966. Morphogenetic field properties of the forebrain area of the neural plate in an anuran. *Experientia* 22: 188–89.

Craige, Betty Jean. 1982. *Literary relativity: An essay on twentieth-century narrative*. Lewisburg: Bucknell University Press.

Culler, Jonathan. 1982. *On deconstruction: Theory and criticism after structuralism*. Ithaca, N.Y.: Cornell University Press.

Dean, Tim. 1993. The psychoanalysis of AIDS. *October* 63: 83–116.

Deleuze, Gilles, and Félix Guattari. 1994. *What is philosophy?* Translated by Hugh Tomlinson and Graham Burchell. New York: Columbia University Press.

Derrida, Jacques. 1970. Structure, sign, and play in the discourse of the human sciences. In *The languages of criticism and the sciences of man: The structuralist controversy*, edited by Richard Macksey and Eugenio Donato. Baltimore, Md.: Johns Hopkins University Press.

Doyle, Richard. 1994. Dislocating knowledge, thinking out of joint: Rhizomatics, Caenorhabditis elegans and the importance of being multiple. *Configurations: A Journal of Literature, Science, and Technology* 2: 47–58.

Dürr, Detlef, Sheldon Goldstein, and Nino Zanghí. 1992. Quantum equilibrium and the origin of absolute uncertainty. *Journal of Statistical Physics* 67: 843–907.

Easlea, Brian. 1981. *Science and sexual oppression: Patriarchy's confrontation with women and nature*. London: Weidenfeld and Nicolson.

Eilenberg, Samuel, and John C. Moore. 1965. *Foundations of relative homological algebra*. Providence, R.I.: American Mathematical Society.

Eilenberg, Samuel, and Norman E. Steenrod. 1952. *Foundations of algebraic topology*. Princeton, N.J.: Princeton University Press.

Einstein, Albert, and Leopold Infeld. 1961. *The evolution of physics*. New York: Simon and Schuster.

Ezeabasili, Nwankwo. 1977. *African science: Myth or reality?* New York: Vantage.

Feyerabend, Paul K. 1975. *Against method: Outline of an anarchistic theory of knowledge*. London: New Left Books.

Freire, Paulo. 1970. *Pedagogy of the oppressed*. Translated by Myra Bergman Ramos. New York: Continuum.

Froula, Christine. 1985. Quantum physics/postmodern metaphysics: The nature of Jacques Derrida. *Western Humanities Review* 39: 287–313.

Frye, Charles A. 1987. Einstein and African religion and philosophy: The hermetic parallel. In *Einstein and the humanities*, edited by Dennis P. Ryan. New York: Greenwood.

Galton, Francis, and H. W. Watson. 1874. On the probability of the extinction of families. *Journal of the Anthropological Institute of Great Britain and Ireland* 4: 138–44.

Gierer, A., R. C. Leif, T. Maden, and J. D. Watson. 1978. Physical aspects of generation of morphogenetic fields and tissue forms. In *Differentiation and development*, edited by F. Ahmad, J. Schultz, T. R. Russell, and R. Werner. New York: Academic.

Ginzberg, Ruth. 1989. Feminism, rationality, and logic. *Newsletters on Computer Use, Feminism, Law, Medicine, Teaching (American Philosophical Association)* 88, no. 2 (March): 34–39.

Gleick, James. 1987. *Chaos: Making a new science*. New York: Viking.

Gödel, Kurt. 1949. An example of a new type of cosmological solutions of Einstein's field equations of gravitation. *Reviews of Modern Physics* 21: 447–50.

Goldstein, Rebecca. 1983. *The mind-body problem*. New York: Random House.

Granero-Porati, M. I. and A. Porati. 1984. Temporal organization in a morphogenetic field. *Journal of Mathematical Biology* 20: 153–57.

Granon-Lafont, Jeanne. 1985. *La topologie ordinaire de Jacques Lacan*. Paris: Point Hors Ligne.

———. 1990. *Topologie lacanienne et clinique analytique*. Paris: Point Hors Ligne.

Green, Michael B., John H. Schwarz, and Edward Witten. 1987. *Superstring theory*. 2 vols. New York: Cambridge University Press.

Greenberg, Valerie D. 1990. *Transgressive readings: The texts of Franz Kafka and Max Planck*. Ann Arbor: University of Michigan Press.

Greenberger, D. M., M. A. Horne, and Z. Zeilinger. 1989. Going beyond Bell's theorem. In *Bell's theorem, quantum theory, and conceptions of the universe*, edited by M. Kafatos. Dordrecht: Kluwer.

Greenberger, D. M., M. A. Horne, A. Shimony, and Z. Zeilinger. 1990. Bell's theorem without inequalities. *American Journal of Physics* 58: 1131–43.

Griffin, David Ray, ed. 1988. *The reenchantment of science: Postmodern proposals*. Albany.: State University of New York Press.

Gross, Paul R,. and Norman Levitt. 1994. *Higher superstition: The academic left and its quarrels with science*. Baltimore, Md.: Johns Hopkins University Press.

Haack, Susan. 1992. Science "from a feminist perspective." *Philosophy* 67: 5–18.

———. 1993. Epistemological reflections of an old feminist. *Reason Papers* 18 (fall): 31–43.

Hamber, Herbert W. 1992. Phases of four-dimensional simplicial quantum gravity. *Physical Review D* 45: 507–12.

Hamill, Graham. 1994. The epistemology of expurgation: Bacon and The Masculine Birth of Time. In *Queering the renaissance*, edited by Jonathan Goldberg. Durham, N.C.: Duke University Press.

Hamza, Hichem. 1990. Sur les transformations conformes des variétés riemanniennes à bord. *Journal of Functional Analysis* 92: 403–47.

Haraway, Donna J. 1989. *Primate visions: Gender, race, and nature in the world of modern science*. New York: Routledge.

——. 1991. *Simians, cyborgs, and women: The reinvention of nature*. New York: Routledge.

——. 1994. A game of cat's cradle: Science studies, feminist theory, cultural studies. *Configurations: A Journal of Literature, Science, and Technology* 2: 59–71.

Harding, Sandra. 1986. *The science question in feminism*. Ithaca, N.Y.: Cornell University Press.

——. 1991. *Whose science? Whose knowledge? Thinking from women's lives*. Ithaca, N.Y.: Cornell University Press.

——. 1994. Is science multicultural? Challenges, resources, opportunities, uncertainties. *Configurations: A Journal of Literature, Science, and Technology* 2: 301–30.

Hardy, G. H. 1967. *A mathematician's apology*. Cambridge: Cambridge University Press.

Harris, Theodore E. 1963. *The theory of branching processes*. Berlin: Springer.

Hayles, N. Katherine. 1984. *The cosmic web: Scientific field models and literary strategies in the twentieth century*. Ithaca, N.Y.: Cornell University Press.

——. 1990. *Chaos bound: Orderly disorder in contemporary literature and science*. Ithaca, N.Y.: Cornell University Press.

——. 1992. Gender encoding in fluid mechanics: Masculine channels and feminine flows. *Differences: A Journal of Feminist Cultural Studies* 4, no. 2: 16–44.

——, ed. 1991. *Chaos and order: Complex dynamics in literature and science*. Chicago: University of Chicago Press.

Heinonen, J., T. Kilpelinen, and O. Martio. 1992. Harmonic morphisms in nonlinear potential theory. *Nagoya Mathematical Journal* 125: 115–40.

Heisenberg, Werner. 1958. *The physicist's conception of nature*, translated by Arnold J. Pomerans. New York: Harcourt Brace.

Hirsch, Morris W. 1976. *Differential topology*. New York: Springer.

Hobsbawm, Eric. 1993. *The new threat to history*. New York Review of Books, 16 December, 62–64.

Hochroth, Lysa. 1995. The scientific imperative: Improductive expenditure and energeticism. *Configurations: A Journal of Literature, Science, and Technology* 3: 47–77.

Honner, John. 1994. Description and deconstruction: Niels Bohr and modern philosophy. In *Niels Bohr and contemporary philosophy. Boston Studies in the Philosophy of Science 153*, edited by Jan Faye and Henry J. Folse. Dordrecht: Kluwer.

Hughes, Robert. 1993. *Culture of complaint: The fraying of America*. New York: Oxford University Press.

Irigaray, Luce. 1982. Le sujet de la science est-il sexué? *Les Temps Modernes* 9, no. 436 (November): 960–74.

——. 1985. The "mechanics" of fluids. In *This sex which is not one*, translated by Catherine Porter with Carolyn Burke. Ithaca, N.Y.: Cornell University Press.

——. 1987. Le sujet de la science est-il sexué? / Is the subject of science sexed? Translated by Carol Mastrangelo Bové. *Hypatia* 2, no. 3: 65–87.

Isham, C. J. 1991. Conceptual and geometrical problems in quantum gravity. In *Recent aspects of quantum fields. Lecture Notes in Physics 396*, edited by H. Mitter and H. Gausterer. Berlin: Springer.

Itzykson, Claude, and Jean-Bernard Zuber. 1980. *Quantum field theory*. New York: McGraw-Hill International.

James, I. M. 1971. Euclidean models of projective spaces. *Bulletin of the London Mathematical Society* 3: 257–76.

Jameson, Fredric. 1982. Reading Hitchcock. *October* 23: 15–42.

Jammer, Max. 1974. *The philosophy of quantum mechanics*. New York: Wiley.

Johnson, Barbara. 1977. The frame of reference: Poe, Lacan, Derrida. *Yale French Studies* 55/56: 457–505.

———. 1989. *A world of difference*. Baltimore, Md.: Johns Hopkins University Press.

Jones, V. F. R. 1985. A polynomial invariant for links via Von Neumann algebras. *Bulletin of the American Mathematical Society* 12: 103–12.

Juranville, Alain. 1984. *Lacan et la philosophie*. Paris: Presses Universitaires de France.

Kaufmann, Arnold. 1973. *Introduction à la théorie des sous-ensembles flous à l'usage des ingénieurs*. Paris: Masson.

Kazarinoff, N. D. 1985. Pattern formation and morphogenetic fields. In *Mathematical essays on growth and the emergence of form*, edited by Peter L. Antonelli. Edmonton: University of Alberta Press.

Keller, Evelyn Fox. 1985. *Reflections on gender and science*. New Haven, Conn.: Yale University Press.

———. 1992. *Secrets of life, secrets of death: Essays on language, gender, and science*. New York: Routledge.

Kitchener, Richard F., ed. 1988. *The world view of contemporary physics: Does it need a new metaphysics?* Albany: State University of New York Press.

Kontsevich, M. 1994. Résultats rigoureux pour modèles sigma topologiques. Conférence au XIème Congrès International de Physique Mathématique, Paris, 18–23 juillet 1994. Edité par Daniel Iagolnitzer et Jacques Toubon. À paraître.

Kosko, Bart. 1993. *Fuzzy thinking: The new science of fuzzy logic*. New York: Hyperion.

Kosterlitz, J. M., and D. J. Thouless. 1973. Ordering, metastability and phase transitions in two-dimensional systems. *Journal of Physics C* 6: 1181–1203.

Kroker, Arthur, Marilouise Kroker, and David Cook. 1989. *Panic encyclopedia: The definitive guide to the postmodern scene*. New York: St. Martin's.

Kuhn, Thomas S. 1970. *The structure of scientific revolutions*, 2d ed. Chicago: University of Chicago Press.

Lacan, Jacques. 1970. Of structure as an inmixing of an otherness prerequisite to any subject whatever. In *The languages of criticism and the sciences of man*, edited by Richard Macksey and Eugenio Donato. Baltimore, Md.: Johns Hopkins University Press.

———. 1977. Desire and the interpretation of desire in Hamlet. Translated by James Hulbert. *Yale French Studies* 55/56: 11–52.

Latour, Bruno. 1987. *Science in action: How to follow scientists and engineers through society*. Cambridge, Mass.: Harvard University Press.

———. 1988. A relativistic account of Einstein's relativity. *Social Studies of Science* 18: 3–44.

Leupin, Alexandre. 1991. Introduction: Voids and knots in knowledge and truth. In *Lacan and the human sciences*, edited by Alexandre Leupin. Lincoln: University of Nebraska Press.

Levin, Margarita. 1988. Caring new world: Feminism and science. *American Scholar* 57: 100–6.

Lorentz, H. A., A. Einstein, H. Minkowski, and H. Weyl. 1952. *The principle of relativity*, translated by W. Perrett and G. B. Jeffery. New York: Dover.

Loxton, J. H., ed. 1990. *Number theory and cryptography*. Cambridge: Cambridge University Press.

Lupasco, Stéphane. 1951. *Le principe d'antagonisme et la logique de l'énergie*. Actualités Scientifiques et Industrielles no. 1133. Paris: Hermann.

Lyotard, Jean-François. 1989. *Time today*. Translated by Geoffrey Bennington and Rachel Bowlby. Oxford Literary Review 11: 3–20.

Madsen, Mark, and Deborah Madsen. 1990. Structuring postmodern science. *Science and Culture* 56: 467–72.

Markley, Robert. 1991. What now? An introduction to interphysics. *New Orleans Review* 18, no. 1: 5–8.

———. 1992. The irrelevance of reality: Science, ideology, and the postmodern universe. *Genre* 25: 249–76.

———. 1994. Boundaries: Mathematics, alienation, and the metaphysics of cyberspace. *Configurations: A Journal of Literature, Science, and Technology* 2: 485–507.

Martel, Erich. 1991/92. How valid are the Portland baseline essays? *Educational Leadership* 49, no. 4: 20–23.

Massey, William S. 1978. *Homology and cohomology theory*. New York: Marcel Dekker.

Mathews, Freya. 1991. *The ecological self*. London: Routledge.

Maudlin, Tim. 1994. *Quantum non-locality and relativity: Metaphysical intimations of modern physics*. Aristotelian Society Series, vol. 13. Oxford: Blackwell.

McAvity, D. M., and H. Osborn. 1991. A DeWitt expansion of the heat kernel for manifolds with a boundary. *Classical and Quantum Gravity* 8: 603–38.

McCarthy, Paul. 1992. Postmodern pleasure and perversity: Scientism and sadism. *Postmodern Culture* 2, no. 3. Available as *mccarthy.592* from *listserv@listserv.ncsu.edu* or *http://jefferson.village.virginia.edu/pmc* (Internet). Also reprinted in *Essays in postmodern culture*, edited by Eyal Amiran and John Unsworth. New York: Oxford University Press, 1993.

Merchant, Carolyn. 1980. *The death of nature: Women, ecology, and the scientific revolution*. New York: Harper and Row.

———. 1992. *Radical ecology: The search for a livable world*. New York: Routledge.

Mermin, N. David. 1990. Quantum mysteries revisited. *American Journal of Physics* 58: 731–34.

———. 1993. Hidden variables and the two theorems of John Bell. *Reviews of Modern Physics* 65: 803–15.

Merz, Martina, and Karin Knorr Cetina. 1994. *Deconstruction in a 'thinking' science: Theoretical physicists at work*. Geneva: European Laboratory for Particle Physics (CERN), preprint CERN-TH.7152/94.

Miller, Jacques-Alain. 1977/78. Suture (elements of the logic of the signifier). *Screen* 18, no. 4: 24–34.

Morin, Edgar. 1992. Method: Towards a Study of Humankind, vol. 1, *The nature of nature*, translated by J. L. Roland Bélanger. New York: Peter Lang.

Morris, David B. 1988. Bootstrap theory: Pope, physics, and interpretation. *The Eighteenth Century: Theory and Interpretation* 29: 101–21.

Munkres, James R. 1984. *Elements of algebraic topology*. Menlo Park, Calif.: Addison-Wesley.

Nabutosky, A, and R. Ben-Av. 1993. Noncomputability arising in dynamical triangulation model of four-dimensional quantum gravity. *Communications in Mathematical Physics* 157: 93–98.

Nandy, Ashis, ed. 1990. *Science, hegemony, and violence: A requiem for modernity*. Delhi: Oxford University Press.

Nash, Charles, and Siddhartha Sen. 1983. *Topology and geometry for physicists*. London: Academic.

Nasio, Juan-David. 1987. *Les yeux de Laure: Le concept d'objet a dans la théorie de J. Lacan. Suivi d'une introduction à la topologie psychanalytique*. Paris: Aubier.

———. 1992. Le concept de sujet de l'inconscient. Texte d'une intervention realisée dans le cadre du séminaire de Jacques Lacan "La topologie et le temps," le mardi 15 mai 1979. In *Cinq lecons sur la théorie de Jacques Lacan*. Paris: Éditions Rivages.

Nye, Andrea. 1990. *Words of power: A feminist reading of the history of logic*. New York: Routledge.

Oliver, Kelly. 1989. Keller's gender/science system: Is the philosophy of science to science as science is to nature? *Hypatia* 3, no. 3: 137–48.

Ortiz de Montellano, Bernard. 1991. Multicultural pseudoscience: Spreading scientific illiteracy among minorities: Part I. *Skeptical Inquirer* 16, no. 2: 46–50.

Overstreet, David. 1980. Oxymoronic language and logic in quantum mechanics and James Joyce. *Sub-Stance* 28: 37–59.

Pais, Abraham. 1991. Niels Bohr's times: *In physics, philosophy, and polity*. New York: Oxford University Press.

Patai, Daphne, and Noretta Koertge. 1994. *Professing feminism: Cautionary tales from the strange world of women's studies*. New York: Basic Books.

Pickering, Andrew. 1984. *Constructing quarks: A sociological history of particle physics*. Chicago: University of Chicago Press.

Plotnitsky, Arkady. 1994. *Complementarity: Anti-epistemology after Bohr and Derrida*. Durham, N.C.: Duke University Press.

Plumwood, Val. 1993a. *Feminism and the mastery of nature*. London: Routledge.

——. 1993b. The politics of reason: Towards a feminist logic. *Australasian Journal of Philosophy* 71: 436–62.

Porter, Jeffrey. 1990. "Three quarks for Muster Mark": Quantum wordplay and nuclear discourse in Russell Hoban's Riddley Walker. *Contemporary Literature* 21: 448–69.

Porush, David. 1989. Cybernetic fiction and postmodern science. *New Literary History* 20: 373–96.

——. 1993. Voyage to Eudoxia: The emergence of a post-rational epistemology in literature and science. *SubStance* 71/72: 38–49.

Prigogine, Ilya, and Isabelle Stengers. 1984. *Order out of chaos: Man's new dialogue with nature*. New York: Bantam.

Primack, Joel R., and Nancy Ellen Abrams. 1995. "In a beginning . . .": Quantum cosmology and Kabbalah. *Tikkun* 10, no. 1 (January/February): 66–73.

Psarev, V. I. 1990. Morphogenesis of distributions of microparticles by dimensions in the coarsening of dispersed systems. *Soviet Physics Journal* 33: 1028–33.

Ragland-Sullivan, Ellie. 1990. Counting from 0 to 6: Lacan, "suture," and the imaginary order. In *Criticism and Lacan: Essays and dialogue on language, structure, and the unconscious*, edited by Patrick Colm Hogan and Lalita Pandit. Athens: University of Georgia Press.

Rensing, Ludger, ed. 1993. Oscillatory signals in morphogenetic fields. Part 2 of *Oscillations and morphogenesis*. New York: Marcel Dekker.

Rosenberg, Martin E. 1993. Dynamic and thermodynamic tropes of the subject in Freud and in Deleuze and Guattari. *Postmodern Culture* 4, no. 1. Available as *rosenber.993* from *listserv@listserv.ncsu.edu* or *http://jefferson.village. virginia.edu/pmc* (Internet).

Ross, Andrew. 1991. *Strange weather: Culture, science, and technology in the age of limits*. London: Verso.

——. 1994. *The Chicago gangster theory of life: Nature's debt to society*. London: Verso.

Saludes i Closa, Jordi. 1984. Un programa per a calcular l'homologia simplicial. *Butlletí de la Societat Catalana de Ciències (segona època)* 3: 127–46.

Santos, Boaventura de Sousa. 1989. *Introdução a uma ciência pós-moderna*. Porto: Edições Afrontamento.

——. 1992. A discourse on the sciences. *Review (Fernand Braudel Center)* 15, no. 1: 9–47.

Sardar, Ziauddin, ed. 1988. *The revenge of Athena: Science, exploitation, and the third world*. London: Mansell.

Schiffmann, Yoram. 1989. The second messenger system as the morphogenetic field. Biochemical and Biophysical Research Communications 165: 1267–71.

Schor, Naomi. 1989. This essentialism which is not one: Coming to grips with Irigaray. *Differences: A Journal of Feminist Cultural Studies* 1, no. 2: 38–58.

Schubert, G. 1989. Catastrophe theory, evolutionary extinction, and revolutionary politics. *Journal of Social and Biological Structures* 12: 259–79.

Schwartz, Laurent. 1973. *Radon measures on arbitrary topological spaces and cylindrical measures*. London: Oxford University Press.

Seguin, Eve. 1994. A modest reason. *Theory, Culture, and Society* 11, no. 3: 55–75.

Serres, Michel. 1992. *Éclaircissements: Cinq entretiens avec Bruno Latour*. Paris: François Bourin.

Sheldrake, Rupert. 1981. *A new science of life: The hypothesis of formative causation*. Los Angeles: J. P. Tarcher.

——. 1991. *The rebirth of nature*. New York: Bantam.

Shiva, Vandana. 1990. Reductionist science as epistemological violence. In *Science, hegemony, and violence: A requiem for modernity*, edited by Ashis Nandy. Delhi: Oxford University Press.

Smolin, Lee. 1992. Recent developments in nonperturbative quantum gravity. In *Quantum gravity and cosmology* (Proceedings 1991, Sant Felíu de Guixols, Estat Lliure de Catalunya), ed. J. Pérez-Mercader, J. Sola, and E. Verdaguer. Singapore: World Scientific.

Sokal, Alan D. 1982. An alternate constructive approach to the φ_3^4 quantum field theory, and a possible destructive approach to φ_4^4. *Annales de l'Institut Henri Poincaré* A 37: 317–98.

——. 1987. Informe sobre el plan de estudios de las carreras de Matemática, Estadística y Computación. Report to the Universidad Nacional Autónoma de Nicaragua, Managua, unpublished manuscript.

Solomon, J. Fisher. 1988. *Discourse and reference in the nuclear age*. Oklahoma Project for Discourse and Theory, vol. 2. Norman: University of Oklahoma Press.

Sommers, Christina Hoff. 1994. *Who stole feminism? How women have betrayed women*. New York: Simon and Schuster.

Stauffer, Dietrich. 1985. *Introduction to percolation theory*. London: Taylor and Francis.

Strathausen, Carsten. 1994. Althusser's mirror. *Studies in Twentieth Century Literature* 18: 61–73.

Struik, Dirk Jan. 1987. *A concise history of mathematics*, 4th rev. ed. New York: Dover.

Thom, René. 1975. *Structural stability and morphogenesis*, translated by D. H. Fowler. Reading, Mass.: Benjamin.

——. 1990. *Semio physics: A sketch*. Translated by Vendla Meyer. Redwood City, Calif.: Addison-Wesley.

't Hooft, G. 1993. Cosmology in 2+1 dimensions. *Nuclear Physics B* (*Proceedings Supplement*) 30: 200–3.

Touraine, Alain, Zsuzsa Hegedus, François Dubet, and Michel Wievorka. 1980. *La prophétie anti-nucléaire*. Paris: Seuil.

Trebilcot, Joyce. 1988. Dyke methods, or Principles for the discovery/creation of the withstanding. *Hypatia* 3, no. 2: 1–13.

Van Enter, Aernout C. D., Roberto Fernández, and Alan D. Sokal. 1993. Regularity properties and pathologies of position-space renormalization-group transformations: Scope and limitations of Gibbsian theory. *Journal of Statistical Physics* 72: 879–1167.

Van Sertima, Ivan, ed. 1983. *Blacks in science: Ancient and modern*. New Brunswick, N.J.: Transaction Books.

Vappereau, Jean Michel. 1985. *Essaim: Le groupe fondamental du noeud. Psychanalyse et Topologie du Sujet*. Paris: Point Hors Ligne.

Virilio, Paul. 1991. *The lost dimension*. Translation of *L'espace critique*, translated by Daniel Moshenberg. New York: Semiotext(e).

Waddington, C. H. 1965. Autogenous cellular periodicities as (a) temporal templates and (b) basis of 'morphogenetic fields.' *Journal of Theoretical Biology* 8: 367–69.

Wallerstein, Immanuel. 1993. The TimeSpace of world-systems analysis: A philosophical essay. *Historical Geography* 23, no. 1/2: 5–22.

Weil, Simone. 1968. *On science, necessity, and the love of God*, translated and edited by Richard Rees. London: Oxford University Press.

Weinberg, Steven. 1992. *Dreams of a final theory*. New York: Pantheon.

Wheeler, John A. 1964. Geometrodynamics and the issue of the final state. In *Relativity, groups, and topology*, edited by Cecile M. DeWitt and Bryce S. DeWitt. New York: Gordon and Breach.

Witten, Edward. 1989. Quantum field theory and the Jones polynomial. *Communications in Mathematical Physics* 121: 351–99.

Wojciehowski, Dolora Ann. 1991. Galileo's two chief word systems. *Stanford Italian Review* 10: 61–80.

Woolgar, Steve. 1988. *Science: The very idea*. Chichester, U.K.: Ellis Horwood.

Wright, Will. 1992. *Wild knowledge: Science, language, and social life in a fragile environment*. Minneapolis: University of Minnesota Press.

Wylie, Alison, Kathleen Okruhlik, Sandra Morton, and Leslie Thielen-Wilson. 1990. Philosophical feminism: A bibliographic guide to critiques of science. *Resources for Feminist Research/Documentation sur la Recherche Féministe* 19, no. 2 (June): 2–36.

Young, T. R. 1991. Chaos theory and symbolic interaction theory: Poetics for the postmodern sociologist. *Symbolic Interaction* 14: 321–34.

———. 1992. Chaos theory and human agency: Humanist sociology in a postmodern era. *Humanity and Society* 16: 441–60.

Žižek, Slavoj. 1991. *Looking awry: An introduction to Jacques Lacan through popular culture*. Cambridge, Mass.: MIT Press.

2

Revelation and Response

ALAN SOKAL

Revelation: A Physicist Experiments with Cultural Studies

Lingua Franca, May–June 1996

The displacement of the idea that facts and evidence matter by the idea that everything boils down to subjective interests and perspectives is—second only to American political campaigns—the most prominent and pernicious manifestation of anti-intellectualism in our time.—Larry Laudan, *Science and Relativism* (1990)

For some years I've been troubled by an apparent decline in the standards of rigor in certain precincts of the academic humanities. But I'm a mere physicist: If I find myself unable to make heads or tails of *jouissance* and *différance*, perhaps that just reflects my own inadequacy.

So, to test the prevailing intellectual standards, I decided to try a modest (though admittedly uncontrolled) experiment: Would a leading North American journal of cultural studies—whose editorial collective includes such luminaries as Fredric Jameson and Andrew Ross—publish an article liberally salted with nonsense if (a) it sounded good and (b) it flattered the editors' ideological preconceptions?

The answer, unfortunately, is yes. Interested readers can find my article, "Transgressing the Boundaries: Toward a Transformative Hermeneutics of Quantum Gravity," in the Spring/Summer 1996 issue of *Social Text*. It appears in a special number of the magazine devoted to the "Science Wars" [see pt. 1].

What's going on here? Could the editors really not have realized that my article was written as a parody?

In the first paragraph I deride "the dogma imposed by the long post-Enlightenment hegemony over the Western intellectual outlook":

> that there exists an external world, whose properties are independent of any individual human being and indeed of humanity as a whole; that these properties are encoded in "eternal" physical laws; and that human beings can obtain reliable, albeit imperfect and tentative, knowledge of these laws by hewing to the "objective" procedures and epistemological strictures prescribed by the (so-called) scientific method.

Is it now dogma in cultural studies that there exists no external world? Or that there exists an external world but science obtains no knowledge of it?

In the second paragraph I declare, without the slightest evidence or argument, that "physical 'reality' [note the scare quotes] . . . is at bottom a social and linguistic construct." Not our *theories* of physical reality, mind you, but the reality itself. Fair enough: Anyone who believes that the laws of physics are mere social conventions is invited to try transgressing those conventions from the windows of my apartment. (I live on the twenty-first floor.)

Throughout the article, I employ scientific and mathematical concepts in ways that few scientists or mathematicians could possibly take seriously. For example, I suggest that the "morphogenetic field"—a bizarre New Age idea proposed by Rupert Sheldrake—constitutes a cutting-edge theory of quantum gravity. This connection is pure invention; even Sheldrake makes no such claim. I assert that Lacan's psychoanalytic speculations have been confirmed by recent work in quantum field theory. Even nonscientist readers might well wonder what in heaven's name quantum field theory has to do with psychoanalysis; certainly my article gives no reasoned argument to support such a link.

Later in the article I propose that the axiom of equality in mathematical set theory is somehow analogous to the homonymous concept in feminist politics. In reality, all the axiom of equality states is that two sets are identical if and only if they have the same elements. Even readers without mathematical training might well be suspicious of the claim that the axiom of equality reflects set theory's "nineteenth-century liberal origins."

In sum, I intentionally wrote the article so that any competent physicist or mathematician (or undergraduate physics or math major) would realize that it is a spoof. Evidently, the editors of *Social Text* felt comfortable publishing an article on quantum physics without bothering to consult anyone knowledgeable in the subject.

The fundamental silliness of my article lies, however, not in its numerous solecisms but in the dubiousness of its central thesis and of the "reasoning" adduced to support it. Basically, I claim that quantum gravity—the still-speculative theory of space and time on scales of a millionth of a billionth of a billionth of a billionth of a centimeter—has profound political implications (which, of course, are "progressive"). In support of this improbable proposition, I proceed as follows: First, I quote some controversial philosophical pronouncements of Heisenberg and Bohr, and assert (without argument) that quantum physics is profoundly consonant with "postmodernist epistemology." Next, I assemble a pastiche—Derrida and general relativity, Lacan and topology, Irigaray and quantum gravity—held together by vague references to "nonlinearity," "flux," and "interconnectedness." Finally, I jump (again without argument) to the assertion that "postmodern science" has abolished the concept of objective reality. Nowhere in all of this is there anything resembling a logical sequence of thought; one finds only citations of authority, plays on words, strained analogies, and bald assertions.

In its concluding passages, my article becomes especially egregious. Having abolished reality as a constraint on science, I go on to suggest (once again without argument) that science, in order to be "liberatory," must be subordinated to political strategies. I finish the article by observing that "a liberatory science cannot be complete without a profound revision of the canon of mathematics." We can see hints of an "emancipatory mathematics," I suggest, "in the multidimensional and nonlinear logic of fuzzy systems theory; but this approach is still heavily marked by its origins in the crisis of late-capitalist production relations." I add that "catastrophe theory, with its dialectical emphases on smoothness/discontinuity and metamorphosis/unfolding, will indubitably play a major role in the future mathematics; but much theoretical work remains to be done before this approach can become a concrete tool of progressive political praxis."

It's understandable that the editors of *Social Text* were unable to evaluate critically the technical aspects of my article (which is exactly why they should have consulted a scientist). What's more surprising is how readily they accepted my implication that the search for truth in science must be subordinated to a political agenda, and how oblivious they were to the article's overall illogic.

Why did I do it? While my method was satirical, my motivation is utterly serious. What concerns me is the proliferation, not just of nonsense and sloppy thinking per se, but of a particular kind of nonsense and sloppy thinking: one that denies the existence of objective realities, or (when challenged) admits their existence but downplays their practical relevance. At its best, a journal like *Social Text* raises important issues that no scientist should ignore—questions, for example, about how corporate and government funding influence scientific work. Unfortunately, epistemic relativism does little to further the discussion of these matters.

In short, my concern about the spread of subjectivist thinking is both intellectual and political. Intellectually, the problem with such doctrines is that they are false (when not simply meaningless). There *is* a real world; its properties are *not* merely social constructions; facts and evidence do matter. What sane person would contend otherwise? And yet, much contemporary academic theorizing consists precisely of attempts to blur these obvious truths.

Social Text's acceptance of my article exemplifies the intellectual arrogance of Theory—postmodernist *literary* theory, that is—carried to its logical extreme. No wonder they didn't bother to consult a physicist. If all is discourse and "text," then knowledge of the real world is superfluous; even physics becomes just another branch of cultural studies. If, moreover, all is rhetoric and language games, then internal logical consistency is superfluous too: a patina of theoretical sophistication serves equally well.

Incomprehensibility becomes a virtue; allusions, metaphors, and puns substitute for evidence and logic. My own article is, if anything, an extremely modest example of this well-established genre.

Politically, I'm angered because most (though not all) of this silliness is emanating from the self-proclaimed Left. We're witnessing here a profound historical volte-face. For most of the past two centuries, the Left has been identified with science and against obscurantism; we have believed that rational thought and the fearless analysis of objective reality (both natural and social) are incisive tools for combating the mystifications promoted by the powerful—not to mention being desirable human ends in their own right. The recent turn of many "progressive" or "leftist" academic humanists and social scientists toward one or another form of epistemic relativism betrays this worthy heritage and undermines the already fragile prospects for progressive social critique. Theorizing about "the social construction of reality" won't help us find an effective treatment for AIDS or devise strategies for preventing global warming. Nor can we combat false ideas in history, sociology, economics, and politics if we reject the notions of truth and falsity.

The results of my little experiment demonstrate, at the very least, that some fashionable sectors of the American academic Left have been getting intellectually lazy. The editors of *Social Text* liked my article because they liked its conclusion: that "the content and methodology of postmodern science provide powerful intellectual support for the progressive political project" [sec. 6]. They apparently felt no need to analyze the quality of the evidence, the cogency of the arguments, or even the relevance of the arguments to the purported conclusion.

Of course, I'm not oblivious to the ethical issues involved in my rather unorthodox experiment. Professional communities operate largely on trust; deception undercuts that trust. But it is important to understand exactly what I did. My article is a theoretical essay based entirely on publicly available sources, all of which I have meticulously footnoted. All works cited are real, and all quotations are rigorously accurate; none are invented. Now, it's true that the author doesn't believe his own argument. But why should that matter? The editors' duty as scholars is to judge the validity and interest of ideas, without regard for their provenance. (That is why many scholarly journals practice blind refereeing.) If the *Social Text* editors find my arguments convincing, then why should they be disconcerted simply because I don't? Or are they more deferent to the so-called "cultural authority of technoscience" than they would care to admit?

In the end, I resorted to parody for a simple pragmatic reason. The targets of my critique have by now become a self-perpetuating academic subculture that typically ignores (or disdains) reasoned criticism from the outside. In such a situation, a more direct demonstration of the subculture's intellectual standards was required. But how can one show that the emperor has no clothes? Satire is by far the best weapon; and the blow that can't be brushed off is the one that's self-inflicted. I offered the *Social Text* editors an opportunity to demonstrate their intellectual rigor. Did they meet the test? I don't think so.

I say this not in glee but in sadness. After all, I'm a leftist too (under the Sandinista government I taught mathematics at the National University of Nicaragua). On nearly all practical political issues—including many concerning science and technology—I'm on the same side as the *Social Text* editors. But I'm a leftist (and a feminist) *because* of evidence and logic, not in spite of it. Why should the right wing be allowed to monopolize the intellectual high ground?

And why should self-indulgent nonsense—whatever its professed political orientation—be lauded as the height of scholarly achievement?

BRUCE ROBBINS AND ANDREW ROSS
coeditors of *Social Text*
Response: Mystery Science Theater
Lingua Franca, July–August 1996

What were some of the initial responses of the journal's editors when we first learned about Alan Sokal's prank on *Social Text*? One suspected that Sokal's parody was nothing of the sort, and that his admission represented a change of heart, or a folding of his intellectual resolve. Another editor was unconvinced that Sokal knew very much about what he was attempting to expose. A third was pleasantly astonished to learn that our journal is taken seriously enough to be considered a target of a hoax, especially a hoax by a physicist. Others were concerned that the hoax might spark off a new round of caricature and thereby perpetuate the climate in which science studies and cultural studies have been subject recently to so much derision from conservatives in science.

All of us were distressed at the deceptive means by which Sokal chose to make his point. This breach of ethics is a serious matter in any scholarly community, and has damaging consequences when it occurs in science publishing. What is the likely result of Sokal's behavior for nonscientific journals? Less well known authors who submit unsolicited articles to journals like ours may now come under needless suspicion, and the openness of intellectual inquiry that *Social Text* has played its role in fostering will be curtailed.

However varied our responses, we all believe that Sokal took too much for granted in his account of his prank. Indeed, his claim—that our publication of his article proves that something is rotten in the state of cultural studies—is as wobbly as the article itself.

Obviously, we now regret having published Sokal's article, and apologize to our readers and to those in the science studies or cultural studies communities who might feel their work has been disparaged as a result of this affair. To give readers a clear sense of the circumstances underlying the publication of the article, we have taken the time to recount the relevant history of the editorial process. We regret that *Lingua Franca* did not provide us with such an opportunity when it decided to publish his statement.

From the first, we considered Sokal's unsolicited article to be a little hokey. It is not every day we receive a dense philosophical tract from a professional physicist. Not knowing the author or his work, we engaged in some speculation about his intentions, and concluded that the article was the earnest attempt of a professional scientist to seek some kind of affirmation from postmodern philosophy for developments in his field. Sokal's adventures in PostmodernLand were not really our cup of tea. Like other journals of our vintage that try to keep abreast of cultural studies, it has been many years since *Social Text* published direct contributions to the debate about postmodern theory, and his article would have been regarded as somewhat outdated if it had come from a humanist or a social scientist. As the work of a natural scientist it was unusual, and, we thought, plausibly symptomatic of how someone like Sokal might approach the field of postmodern epistemology, i.e., awkwardly but assertively trying to capture the "feel" of the professional language of this field, while relying upon an armada of footnotes to ease his sense of vulnerability. In other words, we read it more as an act of good faith of the sort that might be worth encouraging than as a set of arguments with which we agreed. On those grounds, the editors considered it of interest to readers as a "document" of that time-honored tradition in which modern physicists have discovered harmonic resonances with their own reasoning in the field of philosophy and metaphysics. Consequently, the article met one of the several criteria for publication which *Social Text* recognizes.

As a non-refereed journal of political opinion and cultural analysis produced by an editorial collective (and entirely self-published until its adoption four years ago by Duke University Press), *Social Text* has always seen its lineage in the "little magazine" tradition of the independent Left as much as in the academic domain, and so we often balance diverse editorial criteria when discussing the worth of submissions, whether they be works of fiction, interviews with sex workers, or essays about anticolonialism. In other words, this is an editorial milieu with criteria and aims quite remote from those of a professional scientific journal. Whether Sokal's article would have been declared substandard by a physicist peer reviewer is debatable (it is not, after all, a scholarly contribution to the discipline of physics) but not finally relevant to us—at least not according to the criteria we employed.

Having established an interest in Sokal's article, we did ask him informally to revise the piece. We requested him (a) to excise a good deal of the philosophical speculation and (b) to excise most of his footnotes. Sokal seemed resistant to any revisions, and indeed insisted on retaining almost all of his footnotes and bibliographic apparatus on the grounds that his peers, in science, expected extensive documentation of this sort. Judging from his response, it was clear that his article would appear as is, or not at all. At this point, Sokal was designated as a "difficult, uncooperative author," a category well known to journal editors. We judged his article too much trouble to publish, not yet on the reject pile, perhaps of sufficient interest to readers if published in the company of related articles.

Sometime after this impasse was reached, the editors did indeed decide to assemble a special issue on the topic of science studies. We wanted to gauge how science critics were responding to the attacks by Paul Gross and Norman Levitt and by other conservatives in science. Contributions were solicited from across the field of knowledge—from humanists, social scientists, and natural scientists. (The final lineup included many of the more significant names in the field—Sandra Harding, Steve Fuller, Emily Martin, Hilary Rose, Langdon Winner, Dorothy Nelkin, Richard Levins, George Levine, Sharon Traweek, Sarah Franklin, Ruth Hubbard, Joel Kovel, Stanley Aronowitz, and Les Levidow.) Most responded directly to the evolving controversy that some were calling the "Science Wars," while others wrote their own accounts of work in their respective fields. Here, we thought, was an appropriate and heterogeneous context in which Sokal's article might appear, providing a feasible solution to the editorial problem posed by his piece. He expressed some concern when asked if we could publish his work in this special issue (we assumed he wished to distance himself from the polemical company assembled for the issue), but reiterated his eagerness to see it in print. Our final decision to include him presumed that readers would see his article in the particular context of the Science Wars issue, as a contribution from someone unknown to the field whose views, however offbeat, might still be thought relevant to the debate. Since his article was not written for that special issue, and bears little resemblance, in tone or substance, to the commissioned articles, it was not slated to be included in the expanded book version of the issue (with additional articles by Katherine Hayles, Michael Lynch, Roger Hart, and Richard Lewontin) which will be published by Duke University Press in September.

In sum, Sokal's assumption that his parody caught the woozy editors of *Social Text* sleeping on the job is ill conceived. Its status as parody does not alter substantially our interest in the piece itself as a symptomatic document. Indeed, Sokal's conduct has quickly become an object of study for those who analyze the behavior of scientists. Our own role has also come under scrutiny, since, at the very least, the affair says something about our conception of how physicists read philosophy. As for the decision to publish his article, readers can judge for themselves whether we were right or wrong. But to construe this decision as proof of the bankruptcy of cultural studies is absurd.

What Alan Sokal's confession most altered was our perception of his own good faith as a self-declared Leftist. However we feel about his deception, we do hope that the ensuing discussion has been, and will continue to be, productive, and that interlocutors will resist the opportunity to exploit existing divisions and splits among committed people and seek instead to bridge and heal those differences. There is nothing we regret more than watching the Left eat the Left, surely one of the sorriest spectacles of the twentieth century.

Having talked to the (real) Sokal subsequently, we believe that most of the issues he intended to air are, at this point, rather well known to readers of *Social Text* and *Lingua Franca.* Indeed, they have been going the rounds in the academy since the first postmodern, social constructionist, or antifoundational critiques of positivism appeared over thirty-five years ago. That many natural scientists have only recently felt the need to respond to these critiques says something about the restricted trade routes through which knowledge is still circulated in the academy, policed, as it is, at every departmental checkpoint by disciplinary passport controls. Nor are these critiques unfamiliar to folks who have long been involved in debates about the direction of the Left, where positivism has had a long and healthy life. At this point in time, we have a vestigial stake in these critiques and debates, but much less of an interest than Sokal supposes. Like Gross and Levitt, he appears to have absorbed these critiques only at the level of caricatures and has been reissuing these caricatures in the form of otherworldly fanatics who deny the existence of facts, objective realities, and gravitational forces. We are sure Sokal knows that no such persons exist, and we have wondered why on earth he would promote this fiction. He must be aware that early proponents of quantum reality encountered similar parodies of themselves in the opposition to their ideas. Physics is not the only field where this occurred. Comparable caricatures have figured in many different scholarly controversies, from early twentieth century debates about legal realism to more recent ones about genetic reductionism. It is time to put them to rest.

On the other hand, we recognize that professional scientists like Sokal do feel that their beliefs and their intellectual integrity are threatened by the diverse work done in the field of science studies. Doubtless, there have been distorted and reductive descriptions of scientists in many aspects of that work. Over the years, many scholars in the field have responded sympathetically to this grievance, and a good deal of common ground has been established. We share Sokal's own concerns about obscurantism, for example. It is highly ironic that *Social Text* should now be associated with a kind of sectarian postmodernism that we have been at pains to discourage for many years. We would be all too happy if this episode cleared the air. Sokal has said that he agrees with many of the arguments put forth by other authors in the Science Wars issue of *Social Text*. Unfortunately, he declined to enter into a publishable dialogue with us for this issue of *Lingua Franca*. We are heartened, however, by the prospect of any levelheaded discussion about the politics of science that does not rest exclusively on claims of expertise and that is shaped by the public interest.

Our main concern is that readers new to the debates engendered by science studies are not persuaded by the Sokal stunt that this is simply an academic turf war between scientists and humanists/social scientists, with each side trying to outsmart the other. Sadly, this outcome would simply reinforce the premise that only professional scientists have the credentialed right to speak their minds on scientific matters that affect all of us. What's important to us is not so much the gulf of comprehension between "the two cultures," but rather the gulf of power between experts and lay voices, and the currently shifting relationship between science and the corporate-military state. Nor are these concerns extrinsic to the practice of science itself. Prior to deciding whether science intrinsically tells the truth, we must ask, again and again, whether it is possible, or prudent, to isolate facts from values. This is a crucial question to ask, because it bears upon the kind of progressive society we want to promote.

Why does science matter so much to us? Because its power, as a civil religion, as a social and political authority, affects our daily lives and the parlous condition of the natural world more than does any other domain of knowledge. Does it follow that nonscientists should have some say in the decision-making processes that define and shape the work of the professional scientific community? Some scientists (including Sokal, presumably) would say yes, and in some countries non-expert citizens do indeed participate in these processes. All hell breaks loose, however, when the following question is asked: Should nonexperts have anything to say about scientific methodology and epistemology? After centuries of scientific racism, scientific sexism, and scientific domination of nature, one might have thought this was a pertinent question to ask.

SELECTED LETTERS TO THE EDITOR

Lingua Franca, July–August 1996

Alan Sokal's prank was a brilliant strategy for making an extremely important point, but what exactly is this point, and for whom is it important?

First, the point. Is it that the academy houses scholars who have the audacity to question the meaning of objectivity, or to challenge the immunity of science from social forces? Or that some literary scholars have begun to write about scientific texts without first seeking the approval of scientists? Not only does Sokal seriously weaken his case with such suggestions, but he helps fuel the media's enthusiasm for the outlandish idea that a Left antiscience conspiracy is perpetrating the claim that the world is not real. I wish he had let his ruse speak for itself, for its point is quite simple: The editors of *Social Text* have been shown to be unable to distinguish a hilarious jargon-ridden spoof from real argument. Or perhaps the editors were so eager to count a physicist as one of their own that they chose to publish an article they themselves regarded as "hokey."

Now, to whom should this matter? For many scientists, this episode will only bolster their fear that postmodernism (and science studies more generally) threatens the integrity and well-being of their own disciplines. But it is not science that is threatened by the hapless publication of gibberish; it is science studies itself. And the embarrassing defense offered by Ross and Robbins (not to mention the many counterattacks) just makes the problem worse. Scholars in science studies who have turned to postmodernism have done so out of a real need: Truth and objectivity turn out to be vastly more problematic concepts than we used to think, and neither can be measured simply by the weight of scientific authority, nor even by demonstrations of efficacy. Yet surely the ability to distinguish argument from parody is a prerequisite to any attempt at understanding the complexities of truth claims, in science or elsewhere. How can we claim credibility for responsible scholarship—for the carefully reasoned and empirically founded research that makes up the bulk of science studies—if we do not recognize a problem here?

It saddens me that my scientific colleagues so readily confuse the analysis of social influence on science with radical subjectivism, mistaking challenges to the autonomy of science with the "dogma" that there exists no external world. And it alarms me to see the politicization of legitimate intellectual argument as a "Left anti-science" movement vs. a defense of traditional values mounted by the "Right." But neither condones the failure of my colleagues in science studies to acknowledge so blatant a compromise to the integrity of their own discipline.

Evelyn Fox Keller,
professor of history and philosophy of science, MIT

How did Alan Sokal fool the *Social Text* editorial collective? Simple: The members of that collective knew very little about physics (nothing wrong with that) and they didn't bother to ask an expert. They didn't do so, Ross and Robbins have told us, because "professional" standards "are not finally relevant to us, at least not according to the criteria we employed." This is a rather opaque justification, and no wonder. Basically, it means that *Social Text* doesn't care whether Sokal's work—or anybody else's—is solid or not. Nice to know, in general. But still, why did *Social Text* publish this particular article?

Because, the editors say, "[we] concluded that this article was the earnest attempt by a professional scientist to seek some kind of affirmation from postmodern philosophy for developments in his field." In plainer words: We publish Sokal not because he is interesting, but because he says we are. This a wonderful explanation, with a great hidden premise—that people in the humanities have nothing to learn from a scientist. He may be exhibited as a curious convert to theory, but we don't have to take him seriously. The *Social Text* board read and reread the article, and didn't understand a thing—yet they didn't care, because at bottom they believe that physics has nothing to teach them. In the *Social Text* cosmology, science is a socially aggressive but intellectually weak enterprise that seeks "affirmation" from postmodern philosophy. This is why they didn't check Sokal's claims out: Whether the physics made sense or not made no difference, because its value had to be in the philosophy anyway. So why bother?

This disciplinary narcissism, so typical of recent literary cultural studies, is a mystery to me. After all, the natural sciences have been quite successful with their object of study, and we probably have a lot to learn from their methods. But no: For Stanley Aronowitz (quoted in the *New York Times*), Sokal is "ill-read and half-educated." Well, then, how does it feel being duped by the half-educated?

Towards the end of his reply, Ross states that "we must ask, again and again, wherever it is possible, or prudent, to isolate facts from values." I would respond that yes, it is possible (though difficult), and certainly very prudent, because it's the only way to learn anything. If facts cannot be isolated from values, then values can never be tested, never contradicted, never changed. Research, experiment, evidence, and discussion all become useless. Only values, everywhere. A nightmare: Cardinal Bellarmino and Stanley Aronowitz, forever together.

Why Ross likes this scenario, and what makes it "progressive," is another mystery. "Science trades in knowledge," wrote Brecht at the end of Galileo, "which is the product of doubt. And this new art of doubt has enchanted the public. . . . They snatched the telescopes out of our hands and had them trained on their tormentors: prince, official, public moralist." Knowledge, doubt, enchantment, polemical unmasking: Here is the science we need; not prudence. But alas, much of the Left has lost its passion for knowledge, and *Social Text* has proved it.

So far, *Social Text* has not offered arguments, but rather invoked all sorts of Victorian pieties ("deception," "breach of ethics," "irresponsible," "good faith," "confession") in the hope of exorcising the hoax. Come on. You are a polemical journal, with an issue entitled "Science Wars." Drop the pose, accept the facts, and another, more interesting discussion may begin.

Franco Moretti,
professor of comparative literature,
Columbia University

Somewhere in this whole affair a significant element has been lost: Sokal's article masqueraded not as straight cultural criticism, not as sociology of science, and not as science, but as an interdisciplinary study. In other words, we should separate what Sokal wanted to mock (cultural criticism) from what he imitated (interdisciplinary research). As someone who works on relativity, quantum mechanics, and literary culture, I spend a great deal of time wondering what such research should look like. Sokal's piece didn't even come close.

The point of interdisciplinary endeavor is that work done in one field may be used to elucidate material in another. This idea rests on two premises: first, that certain ideas and concepts can be useful across disciplinary boundaries; and second, that their development in different disciplines may not be perfectly symmetrical. Finding commonalities between science and the humanities, then, does not mean that they have the same thing to tell us, but that concepts from one can be used to help us see new things about the other. They function as cognitive metaphors: unexpected associations that reorganize a familiar conceptual field and allow us to behave differently within it.

Interdisciplinary work, then, is always translation—from one specialized discourse into another. But a great deal of Sokal's article is incomprehensible, and he tells us now that its science is also wrong. Several respondents ask why *Social Text* didn't check the article's correctness. I also want to know why its opacity didn't bother them. Even if the physics of the article had been right, the editors should have refused it because it made no effort to be understood. The value of interdisciplinary work is precisely that it allows us to see something new—and this rests on the premise that it allows us to see, period.

So far this debate has taken the form of mutual accusation: "Those critics hate science, but they still use their toasters." Or, "Scientists think culture and politics aren't important, but I'd like to see them work without language." The truth is, without science, we'd have no toasters. But without culture, we'd never want toast. Neither the don't-touch-it-if-you-don't-have-a-Ph.D. cop-out of territorial scientists, nor the no-one-really-understands-differential-equations-anyway cop-out of some cultural theorists should be allowed to undermine the possibility of a real interdisciplinary effort. I resent Sokal's piece because he used his command of a powerful and fascinating discourse to fortify the boundaries between disciplines, and I resent the editors of *Social Text* because they let him. Science (even quantum mechanics) can be made perfectly comprehensible to non-scientists, but it takes careful translation and a lot of work.

Teri Reynolds,
Ph.D. candidate in English and comparative literature,
Columbia University

If something useful is to come from the *Social Text* furor, scientists and humanists who study science need to talk with each other openly and frankly about what we disagree about as well as what views we share. I would thus like to urge a cease-fire in what has been called the "Science Wars." Here are some points on which I think common ground might be found.

1) Scholars in the humanities have a right, and a duty, to examine what scientists do, and vice versa. Certainly, anyone who has something new to contribute to the understanding of scientific methodology and epistemology must do so. But they should be warned that issues like quantum mechanics or molecular biology must be approached with care and subtlety.

2) The key issue is democracy and how it may work in a pluralistic, global society in which everyone's future depends on decisions about scientific and technological issues. Anyone who wants to play a real role in this context must learn to communicate clearly and to listen to what people are actually

saying. If academics, with special training in reading and writing, cannot communicate with each other, they have little hope of having genuine influence outside the academy.

3) Perhaps it is time to give up the notion that knowledge is "constructed" and replace it with the more generous conception that the products of culture are the results of a negotiation with a natural world of which we are a part.

These are just a few issues whose resolution will require a dialogue between humanists and scientists. Our task, then, is not to argue further over the meaning of obscure texts; it is to invent a way of thinking about important political, philosophical, and aesthetic issues that orients us toward the problems and promises of the future.

Lee Smolin,
professor of physics,
Pennsylvania State University

There are a lot of different ways to respond to Sokal's "hoax." Perhaps the best way would be lightly, trading joke for joke. But I guess the stakes are a little too high for me to laugh a lot; my ultimate response to this prank is sadness.

In my essay in the *Social Text* volume that includes Sokal's article, I argue that for science studies to matter at all, its practitioners need to know something substantial about the scientific issues they address. One can't, for example, take a principled position on what to do to prevent the decay of forests without knowing what would in fact prevent that decay. And I argue too that it's necessary to engage scientists in discussion of the cultural issues that inescapably link the activities of science with the life of non-scientists. The key—and Paul Gross and Norman Levitt, authors of *Higher Superstition*, actually agree with Andrew Ross on this, if they would face what they have written—is that the public should have a responsible *and* intelligent relationship to science. Sokal's crusade for reality demonstrates not the slightest understanding of the complexity of anti-realist arguments (with their millennia-long genealogy); it shows no awareness that a constructionist argument does not and cannot mean that "reality" can be changed just like that. The whole enterprise is rather only another move in a self-defeating crusade to keep people who are affected by science but don't "do" science from having anything to say about it.

Why are Sokal, Gross, and Levitt so threatened by people who are just about the only intellectuals in town really interested in a responsible public relation to science? Sokal should be aware that the real threat to the supercollider or to science funding is not coming from Andrew Ross or from Stanley Aronowitz. The threat comes from a culture profoundly anti-intellectual, and now overwhelmingly preoccupied with taxes and money.

Sokal says he is on the same side as the editors of *Social Text*. But he and his colleagues are dazzlingly unaware that the very imperial mode of their intellectual stance—which they want to keep as a central aspect of the institution of science—is part of the reason people at large have so little real sense of what science does, so little understanding of its workings, so painfully meager a recognition that what happens in scientific enterprises has something to do with what happens outside them. What Sokal's hoax reveals is his anxiety as a scientist about this empire of knowledge, as well as a rather ignorant and chortlingly condescending relation to complicated philosophical, sociological, and theoretical positions. Its effect will be to further divide those who ought to be working together against the anti-intellectualism of culture at large. It will reduce to sneering condescension what ought to be a serious debate about how, precisely, the work of science reflects upon, influences, and is influenced by social, cultural, and political forces.

George Levine, director,
Center for the Critical Analysis of Contemporary Culture,
Rutgers University

The following unpublished letter was submitted to Lingua Franca.
As a co-founder and former editor of *Social Text*, I was chagrined to see the journal subjected to Alan Sokal's hoax in the recent "Science Wars" issue. I take considerable pride in having helped launch the journal and, since leaving it in 1983, have been gratified to see it thrive as a major force in cultural studies. However, I find the editors' response to the hoax disturbing and misguided.

It's time for a reality-check at *Social Text*.

In publishing Sokal's parody, "Transgressing the Boundaries: Toward a Transformative Hermeneutics of Quantum Gravity," the editors goofed—big time. It's pretty obvious that their error stemmed from three factors: first, their knowledge of various scientific and mathematical concepts was insufficient to detect Sokal's tongue-in-cheek assertions about science; second, and far more significantly, they didn't detect the utterly faulty argumentation of several of Sokal's claims—permitting him to assert, for example, that something in the theory of gravity confirms such and such a proposition in psychoanalytic theory!—quite possibly because his jargon and his worldview seemed to coincide with their own; third, they succumbed to—perhaps even craved—the very thing their commitment to critical science studies purports to demystify, namely, the surfeit of prestige that accrues to whatever a scientist has to say.

A nasty hoax by Alan Sokal, a serious error by *Social Text*. So be it. Editors are universally susceptible to hoaxes. The *Washington Post* won a Pulitzer Prize for an article on a drug-addicted child that had, it turned out, been completely fabricated by the reporter. *The Education of Little Tree*, long thought to be an authentic Native American autobiography, turned out to be written by a white writer, Forrest Carter, himself evidently a white supremacist.

The editors of *Social Text* could have admitted their error, apologized for making it, congratulated the author of the hoax, and announced that the editorial committee had emerged from a lively, twelve-hour, closed-door meeting having identified the causes of the editorial breakdown and corrected their decision-making procedures for the future.

But no such admission, apology, congratulations, or announcement has been forthcoming. (One can only hope the meeting took place.) Instead, the editors have launched a counter-attack against Sokal, compounding their original error by confusing a defense of science studies with a defense of themselves. Their own credibility crumbles with each new statement, and, far worse, they are undermining the critical study of science itself.

First there are the ad hominem arguments directed against Sokal.

Stanley Aronowitz, a co-founder of *Social Text*, current member of the Editorial Collective, and contributor to the "Science Wars" issue, tells the *New York Times* that Sokal is "ill-read and half-educated." Reality-check Number One: for the moment at least, isn't it rather obvious that Sokal has demonstrated the better grasp of science studies as well as science? He got the rhetoric just right, *Social Text* read the argument just wrong.

The Chronicle of Higher Education reports editors Bruce Robbins and Andrew Ross retorting that Sokal's action "smacked of a temper often attributed to 'unreconstructed male leftists.' " How anachronistic and ironic—since nothing quite so epitomizes male leftism of the 1990s as the editors' own rhetorical swagger, intellectual chic, and multilayered vocabularies. They haven't illuminated anything about this controversy by evoking gender, but the question of style does seem to bother them. It still sounds like boys mocking boys when Ross tells the *Chronicle*, "It seems slightly geeky to pull this thing."

So, Sokal is poorly educated, too male, too nerdy. Next come the arguments from higher ground, moral and intellectual. They are even less convincing.

Consider Aronowitz's effort at explaining to the general public the real stakes of the debate: The critics of science "never deny the real world," he tells the New York Times in rebuttal of Sokal's claims and insinuations. "They are talking about whether meaning can be derived from observation of the real world." Earth to Stanley: Has there ever been a worse sound-bite? Is Aronowitz claiming that meaning can't be derived from observation of the real world? Is he claiming that meanings can or should be derived without observation of the real world? Does he mean that the other possible sources of meaning—metaphysics, religion, ideology, whatever—are superior to observation? Or inescapably more powerful?

Robbins finds his higher ground in lamenting Sokal's focus on epistemology altogether, telling the Chronicle that his "stunt distracts attention from the real interest of our 'Science Wars' issue"—namely, "the social organization and social consequence of science." Robbins is wrong on two counts here. On the one hand, Social Text itself made epistemology and challenges to accepted understandings of scientific knowledge a key topic. In the first place, by publishing Sokal's essay, which starts right off with a large challenge to "the 'objective' procedures and epistemological strictures prescribed by the (so-called) scientific method." On the other hand, the hoax does bear directly on Social Text's claim (as several contributors to the issue maintain) to have special insight into how nonscientists in their role as citizens, politicians, and intellectuals should participate directly in determining the direction, structure, and even the procedures of scientific research.

The call to politicize scientific inquiry presupposes a scientifically informed public and a scientifically responsible nonscientific intelligentsia. Since the arguments throughout the issue do not stress—as does, for example, Carl Sagan's new book, The Demon-Haunted World: Science as a Candle in the Dark—the need for improving science education and mathematical literacy but, instead, enumerate the social harms and epistemological errors perpetrated by science, one can only conclude that Social Text believes it already commands the learning and the judgment required to intervene in science policy. It is just this stance of assumption and judgment that the hoax throws into question.

Stanley Fish makes a learned, principled foray into the debate on the op-ed page of the New York Times. Identifying himself as the executive director of Duke University Press, which publishes Social Text, he marshals his considerable learning and wit to answer Sokal's rather self-satisfied claims in Lingua Franca, which he caricatures without seriously engaging the idea of the social construction of scientific knowledge. Fish is well-known for various essays about the role of communities of inquiry in shaping what counts as knowledge or meaning, even what counts as a fact or object. He gives a spirited defense of his own understanding of the social construction of knowledge and quite successfully dispenses with Sokal's more dogmatic claims. But Fish's intervention, however principled and spirited, is ultimately wrong: it misses the point of the hoax, which was to show that a group of cultural studies folks, who claim to be in a position to judge scientific inquiry from a political and an epistemological point of view, were in fact unable to distinguish argument from gibberish in a scientist's ruminations on the politics and epistemology of scientific inquiry.

Like the editors of *Social Text*, Fish attempts to finesse this embarrassing situation by attacking Sokal's motives and ethics. Having built up a little picture of the ethos of trust and mutual dependence among the participants in a community of inquirers, he accuses Sokal of violating this trust by writing the hoax in the first place. Hoaxes are intrinsically bad? Parody is immoral? In addition to being poorly educated, too male, too nerdy, Sokal is apparently also naughty.

All these gestures are an effort to save face, which undoubtedly reflects the editors' and publisher's realization that this scandal will have ramifications. I worry about academic committee meetings on tenure, fellowships, and promotions filled with snide remarks questioning what it means that so-and-so's article made it through that journal's editorial committee. *Social Text* and its defenders only make things worse, however, by posturing as though they didn't make a mistake and don't need to re-examine any of their own assumptions and procedures.

When we started *Social Text*, we made a straightforward choice not to have manuscripts refereed blindly in a peer-review process. Like the great "tendency" journals in France at that time, *Les Temps Modernes*, *Tel Quel*, *Nouvelle Critique*, or our counterparts in the United States, *Telos*, *New German Critique*, *Radical History*, we organized very active editorial committees that read manuscripts, argued whether to accept or reject, hammered out editorial suggestions, and so on. *PMLA* or *Critical Inquiry* use peer-review to create a very different kind of journal, one which publishes a forum or representative sampling of quality work in the field across a range of methodological, intellectual, and political orientations. *Social Text* represents, by contrast, a shared political and intellectual project intent on foregrounding particular methods, topics, and debates. It has flourished in the academic world because it also maintains high standards. Publishing Alan Sokal's essay amounted to a glitch in that editorial process. But the editors' steadfast refusal to publicly take stock of the significance of the editorial breakdown raises the stakes and deepens skepticism about their foray into science studies.

John Brenkman, editor,
Venue, New York

3

Press Reactions

LINDA SEEBACH

Scientist Takes Academia for a Ride with Parody

Contra Costa (Calif.) Times, 12 May 1996

Physicist Alan Sokal of New York University meticulously observed all the rules of the academic game when he constructed his article on postmodern physics and submitted it to a prestigious journal of cultural studies called *Social Text.*

The people he cites as authorities are the superluminaries of the field, the quotations he uses to illustrate his argument are strictly accurate and the text is bristling with footnotes.

All the rules but one, that is: Sokal's article is a parody. Under the grandiloquent title "Transgressing the Boundaries: Toward a Transformative Hermeneutics of Quantum Gravity," it appeared in the Spring/Summer 1996 special issue of the magazine, one entirely devoted to "the science wars," as the editors term the tension between people who actually do science and the critics who merely theorize about it.

Many scientists believe that the emperors of cultural studies have no clothes. But Sokal captured the whole royal court parading around in naked ignorance and persuaded the palace chroniclers to publish the portrait as a centerfold.

Once the article was safely in print, Sokal revealed his modest experiment. "Would a leading North American journal of cultural studies," he wrote in the May/June issue of *Lingua Franca,* "publish an article liberally salted with nonsense if (a) it sounded good and (b) it flattered the editors' ideological preconceptions?" [pt. 2, "Revelation"].

Unfortunately yes, and Sokal's deliberate nonsense is anything but subtle. Translated into plain English from the high-flown language he borrowed for the occasion, his first paragraph says that scientists "cling to the dogma" that the external world exists and its properties are independent of what human beings think.

But nobody believes that old stuff any more, right? Now we all know that physical reality is "at bottom a social and linguistic construct."

Is there a sound when a tree falls in the forest and no one hears it? Under the theory of social construction, there's not even a tree.

There are so many red flags planted throughout the paper that even non-scientists should have spotted at least one and started laughing, Sokal said Thursday. "Either this is a parody or the author is off his rocker." Sokal was prompted into parody by a 1994 book, *Higher Superstition: The Academic Left and Its Quarrels with Science*, by Paul Gross and Norman Levitt, which ruffled a lot of postmodernist feathers.

"I'm an academic leftist and I have no quarrel with science," Sokal said, "so the first thing I did was go to the library and check their references, to see whether (Gross and Levitt) were being fair" and they were. In fact, he found even more examples of scientific illiteracy, some of them even worse.

"It would be so boring to refute them," Sokal said. "I picked the silliest quotes from the most prominent people, and I made up an argument for how they were linked together."

Was Sokal's experiment ethical? "It's true the author doesn't believe his own arguments," he wrote in *Lingua Franca*. "But why should that matter? If the *Social Text* editors find my arguments convincing, then why should they be disconcerted simply because I don't?"

They are disconcerted, of course, and for reasons that transcend their private embarrassment at being taken in. Sokal's successful spoof calls into question the intellectual standards of the whole field.

If you're chuckling, but inclined to think it's just professors doing their usual angels-on-a-pinhead thing, please do think again. Tuition and fees at the priciest private universities run nearly $1,000 for each week of class. Taxpayers pick up a big chunk of the bill for public universities. Many of those classes are being taught, it appears, by professors who deny the distinction between truth and falsity and consequently can't distinguish double-talk from rational argument.

Maybe some of the junior professors and the graduate students do know what they're hearing is nonsense, but think it would be harmful to their careers to speak out. Living with such deception, possibly for a lifetime, is profoundly corrupting. Honest people just get out, leaving the field to those who don't mind deception or don't recognize it. It's hard to say which is worse.

It's easy to see why Sokal's spoof was enticing to editors desperate for the imprimatur of a working scientist on their critical enterprise, and he even inserted the evidence by quoting Andrew Ross, who edited the special issue.

The kind of science that's needed, Ross said, is one "that will be publicly answerable and of some service to progressive interests."

So that's the kind of science Sokal claimed to be writing about.

"A liberatory science cannot be complete without a profound revision of the canon of mathematics," he concludes. "We can see hints of (such emancipatory mathematics) in the multidimensional and nonlinear logic of fuzzy systems theory; but this approach is still heavily marked by its origins in the crisis of late-capitalist production relations" [pt. 1, sec. 6]. He drags in catastrophe theory and chaos theory, too.

There is a political point to Sokal's demonstration, but it's not the right-wing one he's sure will be attributed to him. He's proud to call himself a leftist, and his resume includes a stint teaching mathematics at the National University of Nicaragua under the Sandinistas.

"If you take up crazy philosophies you undermine your ability to tackle questions of public policy, like ecology," he said. "It really matters whether the world is warming up."

I don't remotely share Sokal's political views, but I agree with him that the corruption of clear thought and clear language is dangerous. And corruption has to be exposed before it can be cleaned up.

MITCHELL LANDSBERG

Is It Gibberish or Merely Obscure?
Scientist Hoaxes Academic Journal

Associated Press, 16 May 1996

Alan Sokal, a physicist at New York University, conducted a little experiment recently. He wrote an article that was close to pure gibberish and sent it off to a respected social science journal.

Then he sat back and waited to see if it would be published.

It was.

The article, an impenetrable bramble of physics and philosophy that appears to argue that the physical world does not exist, landed in the pages of the spring-summer issue of *Social Text*, a leftist journal of cultural studies published by Duke University Press.

Then Sokal, adding insult to injury, wrote a gloating article about his hoax for *Lingua Franca*, a magazine about academia.

"What's going on here?" he wrote in the follow-up article. "Could the editors really not have realized that my article was written as a parody?" [pt. 2, "Revelation"].

Well, no, the editors of *Social Text* concede.

In fact, editor Andrew Ross said Thursday, he thought the Sokal article was simply a bad attempt at philosophy by a scientist. He included it in the journal's new issue—which is devoted to a rift between scientists and cultural critics of science—as a "curio" intended to reflect the scientists' side of the debate.

But why would anyone publish something that appeared to be nonsense?

"Physics is obscure enough as it is, and philosophy is obscure enough as it is," Ross said, "and when you have physicists who are writing in that genre, then what they write is obscure. But there's a difference between obscurity and gibberish, right?"

Well, yes, sometimes. But consider what Sokal wrote.

In the opening paragraph, he lays out his basic theme: There are scientists, he asserts, who "cling to the dogma imposed by the long post-Enlightenment hegemony over the Western intellectual outlook, which can be summarized briefly as follows: that there exists an external world, whose properties are independent of any individual human being and indeed of humanity as a whole."

In other words, some dumb scientists actually believe that the world exists.

There follow many pages of impossibly dense scientific mumbo-jumbo, all supported by lengthy footnotes. From time to time, Sokal slips in little parenthetical zingers.

"Mathematically, Einstein breaks with the tradition dating back to Euclid (which is inflicted on high-school students even today!)," he writes [pt. 1, sec. 2]. It's not hard to imagine him chuckling over his keyboard.

In his post-mortem in *Lingua Franca*, Sokal talks about how, at another point in his article, "I suggest that the 'morphogenetic field'—a bizarre New Age idea proposed by Rupert Sheldrake—constitutes a cutting-edge theory of quantum gravity."

Not quite. Morphogenesis is defined as the structural changes occurring during the development of an organism.

"In sum," he says, "I intentionally wrote the article so that any competent physicist or mathematician (or undergraduate physics or math major) would realize that it is a spoof" [pt. 2, "Revelation"].

But not the editors of *Social Text*.

"I think Andrew (Ross) made a mistake, that's all," said Stanley Aronowitz, a professor of sociology at the City University of New York's Graduate Center and a founder of *Social Text*. Sokal's article, he said, "borders on gibberish and shouldn't have been published."

Still, Aronowitz and Ross insist that while Sokal may have succeeded in his prank, he failed in his larger aim of spoofing their work, which attempts to analyze science from a cultural perspective, much as postmodern critics have been deconstructing literature for years.

"It was a bad parody," Aronowitz said. "He just doesn't get it."

Sokal was out of town Thursday and couldn't be reached for comment. But he wrote in *Lingua Franca* that he decided to write the hoax out of a concern, heightened by his own left-wing politics, that leftist social scientists were spreading "nonsense and sloppy thinking" about science.

"*Social Text*'s acceptance of my article exemplifies the intellectual arrogance of Theory—postmodernist literary theory, that is—carried to its logical extreme," he wrote [pt. 2, "Revelation"].

Ross said Sokal's prank reflects the arrogance of scientists who resent anyone outside their field attempting to critique it. That, he said, was the basic point of *Social Text*'s special issue. So, in a sense, the Sokal hoax fit right in.

"I cannot really say I feel snakebit," he said. And then he paused.

"Well," he conceded, "I suppose I can."

JANNY SCOTT
Postmodern Gravity Deconstructed, Slyly
New York Times, 18 May 1996

A New York University physicist, fed up with what he sees as the excesses of the academic left, hoodwinked a well-known journal into publishing a parody thick with gibberish as though it were serious scholarly work.

The article, entitled "Transgressing the Boundaries: Toward a Transformative Hermeneutics of Quantum Gravity," appeared this month in *Social Text*, a journal that helped invent the trendy, sometimes baffling field of cultural studies.

Now the physicist, Alan Sokal, is gloating. And the editorial collective that publishes the journal says it sorely regrets its mistake. But the journal's co-founder says Professor Sokal is confused.

"He says we're epistemic relativists," complained Stanley Aronowitz, the co-founder and a professor at CUNY. "We're not. He got it wrong. One of the reasons he got it wrong is he's ill-read and half-educated."

The dispute over the article—which was read by several editors at the journal before it was published—goes to the heart of the public debate over left-wing scholarship, and particularly over the belief that social, cultural and political conditions influence and may even determine knowledge and ideas about what is truth.

In this case, Professor Sokal, 41, intended to attack some of the work of social scientists and humanists in the field of cultural studies, the exploration of culture—and, in recent years, science—for coded ideological meaning.

In a way, this is one more skirmish in the culture wars, the battles over multiculturalism and college curriculums and whether there is a single objective truth or just many differing points of view.

Conservatives have argued that there is truth, or at least an approach to truth, and that scholars have a responsibility to pursue it. They have accused the academic left of debasing scholarship for political ends.

"While my method was satirical, my motivation is utterly serious," Professor Sokal wrote in a separate article in the current issue of the magazine

Lingua Franca, in which he revealed the hoax and detailed his "intellectual and political" motivations.

"What concerns me is the proliferation, not just of nonsense and sloppy thinking per se, but of a particular kind of nonsense and sloppy thinking: one that denies the existence of objective realities," he wrote in *Lingua Franca* [pt. 2, "Revelation"].

In an interview, Professor Sokal, who describes himself as "a leftist in the old-fashioned sense," said he worried that the trendy disciplines and obscure jargon could end up hurting the leftist cause. "By losing contact with the real world, you undermine the prospect for progressive social critique," he said.

Norman Levitt, a professor of mathematics at Rutgers University and an author of a book on science and the academic left that first brought the new critique of science to Professor Sokal's attention, yesterday called the hoax "a lot of fun and a source of a certain amount of personal satisfaction."

"I don't want to claim that it proves that all social scientists or all English professors are complete idiots, but it does betray a certain arrogance and a certain out-of-touchness on the part of a certain clique inside academic life," he said.

Professor Sokal, who describes himself as "a leftist and a feminist" who once spent his summers teaching mathematics in Nicaragua, said he became concerned several years ago about what academics in cultural studies were saying about science.

"I didn't know people were using deconstructive literary criticism not only to study Jane Austen but to study quantum mechanics," he said yesterday. Then, he said, he read *Higher Superstition: The Academic Left and its Quarrel With Science* by Professor Levitt and Paul R. Gross.

Professor Sokal said the book, which analyzes the critique of science, prompted him to begin reading work by the critics themselves. "I realized it would be boring to write a detailed refutation of these people," he said. So, he said, he decided to parody them.

"I structured the article around the silliest quotes about mathematics and physics from the most prominent academics, and I invented an argument praising them and linking them together," he said. "All this was very easy to carry off because my argument wasn't obliged to respect any standards of evidence or logic."

To a lay person, the article appears to be an impenetrable hodgepodge of jargon, buzzwords, footnotes and other references to the work of the likes of Jacques Derrida and Professor Aronowitz. Words like hegemony, counterhegemonic and epistemological abound.

In it, Professor Sokal wrote: "It has thus become increasingly apparent that physical 'reality,' no less than social 'reality,' is at bottom a social and linguistic construct; that scientific 'knowledge,' far from being objective, reflects and encodes the dominant ideologies and power relations of the culture that produced it" [pt. 1, intro.].

Andrew Ross, a co-editor of *Social Text* who also happens to be a professor at NYU, said yesterday that about a half-dozen editors at the journal dealt with Professor Sokal's unsolicited manuscript. While it appeared "a little hokey," they decided to publish it in a special issue they called "Science Wars," he said.

"We read it as the earnest attempt of a professional scientist to seek some sort of philosophical justification for his work," said Professor Ross, director of the American studies program at NYU. "In other words, it was about the relationship between philosophy and physics."

Now Professor Ross says he regrets having published the article. But he said Professor Sokal misunderstood the ideas of the people he was trying to expose. "These are caricatures of complex scholarship," he said.

Professor Aronowitz, a sociologist and director of the Center for Cultural Studies at CUNY, said Professor Sokal seems to believe that the people he is parodying deny the existence of the real world. "They never deny the real world," Professor Aronowitz said. "They are talking about whether meaning can be derived from observation of the real world."

Professor Ross said it would be a shame if the hoax obscured the broader issues his journal sought to address, "that scientific knowledge is affected by social and cultural conditions and is not a version of some universal truth that is the same in all times and places."

Coiled Gibberish in a Thicket of Prose

An excerpt from "Transgressing the Boundaries," a parody by Prof. Alan D. Sokal of New York University that was published in the social science journal *Social Text* as if it were a serious article.

Here my aim is to carry these deep analyses one step further, by taking account of recent developments in quantum gravity: the emerging branch of physics in which Heisenberg's quantum mechanics and Einstein's general relativity are at once synthesized and superseded. In quantum gravity, as we shall see, the space-time manifold ceases to exist as an objective physical reality; geometry becomes relational and contextual; and the foundational conceptual categories of prior science—among them, existence itself—become problematized and relativized. This conceptual revolution, I will argue, has profound implications for the content of a future postmodern and liberatory science. [Pt. 1, intro.]

JOHN YEMMA

Hokum for High-Brows

Boston Globe, 18 May 1996

Academia isn't the real world. But then the real world may not be real either.

That's what physicist Alan Sokal of New York University convincingly argued in a recent footnote-packed article in a scholarly journal.

The article was a hoax that suckered the editors of *Social Text*, a left-wing "critical studies" publication based in New York, and created a sensation in academia.

"Physical reality is at bottom a social and linguistic construct," [pt. 1, intro.] Sokal wrote, citing quantum mechanics, deconstructionist theory and "the multidimensional and non-linear logic of fuzzy systems" to make his case [pt. 1, sec. 6].

Such jargon is common in academic journals and papers. In exposing his spoof in the May issue of *Lingua Franca*, an academic-issues monthly, Sokal said he figured any "competent physicist or mathematician" would see he was blowing smoke.

While there are people who believe the physical world doesn't exist, they tend to be mystics, saints or swamis, not scientists.

"Anyone who believes that the laws of physics are mere social conventions is invited to try transgressing those conventions from the windows of my apartment," Sokal said.

In his *Social Text* article, Sokal claimed that the "dogma" about the external world was simply a product of "the long, post-Enlightenment hegemony over the Western intellectual outlook."

The editor of *Social Text*, Andrew Ross, didn't find that unusual. Such assertions are often made by academics who practice "critical theory," an ideologically charged movement that questions basic assumptions and points out biases that are supposed to be embedded in Western philosophy and science.

Besides, Ross told the Associated Press, these articles aren't supposed to be easy reads.

"Physics is obscure enough as it is, and philosophy is obscure enough as it is," Ross said. "And when you have physicists who are writing in that genre, then what they write is obscure."

Sokal, who could not be reached for comment, wrote in *Lingua Franca* that he concocted his spoof to "test prevailing academic standards."

"Sounds like what would have happened if Theodore Kaczynski had stayed at Berkeley," said Greg Petsko, a professor of biochemistry at Brandeis, referring to the man suspected of being the Unabomber.

Sokal's method also raised questions among scholars about whether hoaxing doesn't simply sully scholarship and undermine the public's trust in academic institutions.

"It's like bilking an elderly couple of their money to show that there is fraud in the investment industry," said David Cutts, a physics professor at Brown University.

But Marc Abrahams, editor of the *Annals of Improbable Research*, a Cambridge journal that skewers shoddy science, said *Social Text* was simply done in by its own gullibility.

"Because it said what they wanted to hear, they didn't read it," he said. "They just published it—without peer review or fact checking."

As Sokal put it: "I offered the *Social Text* editors an opportunity to demonstrate their intellectual rigor. Did they meet the test? I don't think so."

STANLEY FISH

Professor Sokal's Bad Joke

New York Times, 21 May 1996

When the editors of *Social Text* accepted an essay purporting to link developments in quantum mechanics with the formulations of postmodern thought, they could not have anticipated that on the day of its publication the author, Alan Sokal, a physicist at New York University, would be announcing in the pages of another journal, *Lingua Franca*, that the whole thing had been an elaborate hoax.

He had made it all up, he said, and gloated that his "prank" proved that sociologists and humanists who spoke of science as a "social construction" didn't know what they were talking about. Acknowledging the ethical issues raised by his deception, Professor Sokal declared it justified by the importance of the truths he was defending from postmodernist attack: "There is a real world; its properties are not merely social constructions; facts and evidence do matter. What sane person would contend otherwise?" [pt. 2, "Revelation"].

Exactly! Professor Sokal's question should alert us to the improbability of the scenario he conjures up: Scholars with impeccable credentials making statements no sane person could credit. The truth is that none of his targets would ever make such statements.

What sociologists of science say is that of course the world is real and independent of our observations but that accounts of the world are produced by observers and are therefore relative to their capacities, education, training, etc. It is not the world or its properties but the vocabularies in whose terms we know them that are socially constructed—fashioned by human beings—which is why our understanding of those properties is continually changing.

Distinguishing fact from fiction is surely the business of science, but the means of doing so are not perspicuous in nature—for if they were, there would be no work to be done. Consequently, the history of science is a record of controversies about what counts as evidence and how facts are to be established.

Those who concern themselves with this history neither dispute the accomplishments of science nor deny the existence or power of scientific procedure. They just maintain and demonstrate that the nature of scientific procedure is a question continually debated in its own precincts. What results is an incredibly complex and rich story, full of honor for scientists, and this is the story sociologists of science are trying to tell and get right.

Why then does Professor Sokal attack them? The answer lies in two misunderstandings. First, Professor Sokal takes "socially constructed" to mean "not real," whereas for workers in the field "socially constructed" is a compliment paid to a fact or a procedure that has emerged from the welter of disciplinary competition into a real and productive life where it can be cited, invoked and perhaps challenged. It is no contradiction to say that something is socially constructed and also real.

Perhaps a humble example from the world of baseball will help make the point. Consider the following little catechism:

Are there balls and strikes in the world? Yes.

Are there balls and strikes in nature (if by nature you understand physical reality independent of human actors)? No.

Are balls and strikes socially constructed? Yes.

Are balls and strikes real? Yes.

Do some people get $3.5 million either for producing balls and strikes or for preventing their production? Yes.

So balls and strikes are both socially constructed and real, socially constructed and consequential. The facts about ball and strikes are also real but they can change, as they would, for example, if baseball's rule makers were to vote tomorrow that from now on it's four strikes and you're out.

But that's just the point, someone might object. "Sure the facts of baseball, a human institution that didn't exist until the 19th century, are socially constructed. But scientists are concerned with facts that were there before anyone looked through a microscope. And besides, even if scientific accounts of facts can change, they don't change by majority vote."

This appears to make sense, but the distinction between baseball and science is not finally so firm. On the baseball side, the social construction of the game assumes and depends on a set of established scientific facts. That is why the pitcher's mound is not 400 feet from the plate. Both the shape in which we have the game and the shapes in which we couldn't have it are strongly related to the world's properties.

On the science side, although scientists don't take formal votes to decide what facts will be considered credible, neither do they present their competing accounts to nature and receive from her an immediate and legible verdict. Rather they hazard hypotheses that are then tested by other workers in the field in the context of evidentiary rules, which may themselves be altered in the process. Verdicts are then given by publications and research centers whose judgments and monies will determine the way the game goes for a while.

Both science and baseball then are mixtures of adventuresome inventiveness and reliance on established norms and mechanisms of validation, and the facts yielded by both will be social constructions and be real.

Baseball and science may be both social constructions, but not all social constructions are the same. First, there is the difference in purpose—to refine physical skills and entertain, on the one hand, and to solve problems of a theoretical and practical kind, on the other. From this difference flow all the other differences, in the nature of the skills involved, the quality of the attention required, the measurements of accomplishment, the system of reward, and on and on.

Even if two activities are alike social constructions, if you want to take the measure of either, it is the differences you must keep in mind.

This is what Professor Sokal does not do, and this is his second mistake. He thinks that the sociology of science is in competition with mainstream science—wants either to replace it or debunk it—and he doesn't understand that it is a distinct enterprise, with objects of study, criteria, procedures and goals all of its own.

Sociologists of science aren't trying to do science; they are trying to come up with a rich and powerful explanation of what it means to do it. Their question is, "What are the conditions that make scientific accomplishments possible?" and answers to that question are not intended to be either substitutes for scientific work or arguments against it.

When Professor Sokal declares that "theorizing about 'the social construction of reality' won't help us find an effective treatment for AIDS," he is at once right and wrong. He is right that sociologists will never do the job assigned properly to scientists. He is wrong to imply that the failure of the sociology of science to do something it never set out to do is a mark against it.

My point is finally a simple one: A research project that takes the practice of science as an object of study is not a threat to that practice because, committed as it is to its own goals and protocols, it doesn't reach into, and therefore doesn't pose a danger to, the goals and protocols it studies. Just as the criteria of an enterprise will be internal to its own history, so will the threat to its integrity be internal, posed not by presumptuous outsiders but by insiders who decide not to play by the rules or to put the rules in the service of a devious purpose.

This means that it is Alan Sokal, not his targets, who threatens to undermine the intellectual standards he vows to protect. Remember, science is above all a communal effort. No scientist (and for that matter, no sociologist or literary critic) begins his task by inventing anew the facts he will assume, the models he will regard as exemplary and the standards he tries to be faithful to.

They are all given by the tradition of inquiry he has joined, and for the most part he must take them on faith. And he must take on faith, too, the reports offered to him by colleagues, all of whom are in the same position, unable to start from scratch and therefore dependent on the information they receive from fellow researchers. (Indeed, some professional physicists who take Professor Sokal on faith report finding his arguments plausible.)

The large word for all this is "trust," and in his *A Social History of Truth*, Steven Shapin poses the relevant (rhetorical) question: "How could coordinated activity of any kind be possible if people could not rely upon others' undertakings?"

Alan Sokal put forward his own undertakings as reliable, and he took care, as he boasts, to surround his deception with all the marks of authenticity, including dozens of "real" footnotes and an introductory section that enlists a roster of the century's greatest scientists in support of a line of argument he says he never believed in. He carefully packaged his deception so as not to be detected except by someone who began with a deep and corrosive attitude of suspicion that may now be in full flower in the offices of learned journals because of what he has done.

In a 1989 report published in *The Proceedings of the National Academy of Science*, fraud is said to go "beyond error to erode the foundation of trust on which science is built." That is Professor Sokal's legacy, one likely to be longer lasting than the brief fame he now enjoys for having successfully pretended to be himself.

SCOTT MCCONNELL
When Pretension Reigns Supreme
New York Post, 22 May 1996

The successful joke that New York University physicist Alan Sokal was able to have at the expense of the editors of *Social Text* highlights an issue more serious than the fact that obtuse pretentiousness reigns at that particular academic journal.

Sokal, who describes himself as a man of the Left (he spent several summers as a volunteer math teacher in revolutionary Nicaragua), was disturbed by a growing fad among American academics to ignore—and even deny—the existence of objective truth.

He observed that in the new field of "cultural studies" there was a move about to use deconstructive literary techniques not only on Jane Austen, but on quantum mechanics; Sokal was concerned not only "by nonsense and sloppy thinking" but by a tendency to engage in exercises which "den[y] the existence of objective realities."

Sokal worried that "by losing contact with the real world, you undermine the prospect for progressive social critique." So he contributed an essay. And the latest issue of *Social Text*—edited by the deconstructionist superstar Andrew Ross (he was featured in a cover story in *The New York Times Magazine*, a plum which doesn't often fall to college English teachers)—printed it.

But Sokal's essay was neither a regular contribution, nor a rebuttal, but a parody—designed to make fun of the kind of work that Ross and the other "cultural studies" mavens carry out.

As he later explained it, "I structured the article around the silliest quotes about mathematics and physics from the most prominent academics, and I invented an argument praising them and linking them together . . . All this was very easy to carry off because my argument wasn't obliged to respect any standards of evidence and logic."

In his parody, Sokal wrote: "It has thus become increasingly apparent that physical 'reality,' no less than social 'reality' is at bottom a social and linguistic construct" and that "scientific 'knowledge,' far from being objective, reflects and encodes the dominant ideologies of the culture that produced it" [pt. 1, intro.].

He pillowed his analysis with 13 pages of footnotes, praising some of the seminal icons of cultural studies, and another ten pages of references. Six editors of *Social Text* read the manuscript before publication.

When six prestigious academics, working at their scholarly leisure, are unable to discern that an essay is intentional gibberish, it says quite a lot about the turn that advanced areas of academic life has taken in the U.S.

If this sort of nonsense were confined only to an isolated corner of American academic life, it would be a problem mainly for the students who waste their precious college years being taught by such professors, and the parents who foot the bills.

But the basic idea underlying "cultural studies"—that there is no such thing as objective knowledge or scholarship—has metastasized into several areas. A close cousin of "cultural studies" is Afrocentric scholarship, which attempts to fashion a heroic past for black people, even as it is based on a rather remote relationship with the actual discipline of history.

Mary Lefkowitz, a professor of classics at Wellesley, conducts a polite polemic with the new discipline of [*sic*] in her book *Not Out of Africa*. Lefkowitz notes that she was astonished several years ago to discover that a number of courses in her university and others were devoted to teaching things that were simply not true.

Among the dubious factoids in the Afrocentric canon: that Socrates and Cleopatra were both black; that Greek philosophy and science were stolen from Africa; and that Aristotle stole his philosophy from the library at Alexandria.

None of these assertions was based on any new scholarship—not on discoveries in Egypt or in Greece. These claims were part and parcel of Marcus Garvey's Harlem stem-winders in the 1930s. But they are now being taught as fact in places like Wellesley.

Lefkowitz wades patiently through the assertions—some of them, like Cleopatra's origins, at least worthy of debate; others, like Aristotle's "theft," plainly preposterous—and disposes of them.

But what is most interesting here is that Afrocentrism continues to thrive at prestigious universities, even though administrators acknowledge privately that it is a crock.

One reason why (though Lefkowitz doesn't delve into this) presumably is that it provides employment opportunities for pseudo-scholars (like Leonard Jeffries) so that universities can tout the diversity of their faculty.

Afrocentrism is clearly a variant of the kind of thought Alan Sokal was mocking with his *Social Text* parody—the idea that, at bottom, all social truth is ideologically constructed.

But pseudohistory is not limited to the Afrocentrists. In the National Endowment for the Humanities' inital draft for national history standards, it was proposed to teach all American students that the Founding Fathers relied on ideas they learned from Native Americans and Africans, though of course there is no real historical evidence for such a claim.

Some might argue that pseudohistory is acceptable if the intent is noble—i.e., greater self-esteem for America's minorities. But the intent isn't always benign. In the nether reaches of the far Right there exists the pseudo-history of Holocaust revisionism—dedicated to propagating the idea that the Nazi war against the Jews did not take place in anything like the manner and degree which historical evidence tells us it did.

It has not made nearly the dent into mainstream culture that Afrocentrism has (and the motivation—presumably to buff up the historical image of the Third Reich—is far more sinister). But once we are willing to allow one kind of pseudo-scholarship a foothold, the main rationale for closing the gates to others must logically come from judging the motivation behind them—a potentially dicey proposition.

That's why the little joke that Alan Sokal had at the expense of *Social Text* is so delightful. American society as a whole has a tremendous stake in the integrity of intellectual discourse in which facts are facts, and can't be "deconstructed" or made up at will.

RUTH ROSEN

A Physics Prof Drops a Bomb on the Faux Left

Los Angeles Times, 23 May 1996

When I was a child, my favorite story was "The Emperor's New Clothes." A chorus of adults praises the Emperor's new wardrobe, but a child blurts out the truth: The Emperor is in fact stark naked. From this tale, I learned that adults could be intimidated into endorsing all kinds of flummery. The longer I teach at the university, the more I return to this story for consolation.

Last week, a little known academic scandal made its way to the front page of the *New York Times*. The scandal actually began about a decade ago, when a growing cadre of Academic Emperors began empire-building within American universities. They claimed that their scholarship, shielded from outsiders by impenetrable theory and incomprehensible prose, constituted a radical political movement and that they were the true theorists of the "academic left."

It took a New York University physicist named Alan Sokal to expose the unearned prestige that the Academic Emperors have heaped upon themselves. A self-described progressive and feminist (to which I can attest; I helped with his exposé), Sokal became fed up with certain trendy academic theorists who have created a mystique around the (hardly new) idea that truth is subjective and that objective reality is fundamentally unknowable. To Sokal, the denial of known reality seemed destructive of progressive goals.

To his credit, he didn't just sit and fume. After immersing himself in the theorists' arcane literature, Sokal wrote a brilliant parody titled "Transgressing the Boundaries: Toward a Transformative Hermeneutics of Quantum Gravity." Penned in unintelligible prose, heavily documented with lengthy footnotes, Sokal's article basically argued against the "Enlightenment idea" that there exists an external and knowable world. Physics, the physicist implied, was simply another field of cultural criticism.

When I first obtained a copy of Sokal's still unpublished parody, it seemed no worse than much of the dense writing that passes for cutting-edge theoretical criticism. I delighted in his ability to mimic the imponderable syntax and jargon of contemporary theoretical academic writing:

In quantum gravity, as we shall see, the space-time manifold ceases to exist as an objective physical reality; geometry becomes relational and contextual; and the foundational conceptual categories of prior science—among them, existence itself—become problematized and relativized. This conceptual revolution, I will argue, has profound implications for the content of a future post-modern and liberatory science. [Pt. 1, intro.]

Sokal decided to submit his gibberish to *Social Text*, a prestigious academic journal that has promoted the new cultural criticism as a radical political movement. Without soliciting a scientific opinion from an outside reader, the *Social Text* editors published Sokal's article in a special spring issue devoted to the "Science Wars," the quarrel between social theorists and actual scientists.

Sokal disclosed his deception in the current issue of the academic magazine *Lingua Franca*. He explained that he had been disturbed "by the decline in intellectual rigor in the trendier precincts of the American academic humanities" and had "decided to try an admittedly uncontrolled experiment: Would the leading North American journal of cultural studies . . . publish an article consisting of utter nonsense if it sounded good and flattered the editors' ideological preconceptions? . . . The answer, unfortunately, is yes."[1]

Satire is often the best way of revealing the truth (recall Jonathan Swift's "A Modest Proposal"). Sokal's spoof exposed the hypocrisy practiced by these so-called cultural revolutionaries. They claim to be democratizing thought, but they purposely write in tongues for an initiated elite. They claim that their work is transformative and subversive, but they focus obsessively on the linguistic and social construction of human consciousness, not on the hard reality of people's lives. Their claim to originality is particularly offensive to historians who have always known that social structure and cultural meaning change over time. With few exceptions, their pretensions obscure their nakedness.

Yes, I know that the conservative right may use Sokal's parody to further attack "tenured radicals." But if the progressive left is to survive and be credible, it must withstand the glare of public scrutiny and be worthy of people's respect.

We shall soon see which ideas can pass the giggle test.

Notes

1   This quote was altered. A phrasing consistent with Sokal's original piece would read as follows: he was disturbed "by an apparent decline in the standards of rigor in certain

precincts of the academic humanities" and "had decided to try a modest (though admittedly uncontrolled) experiment: Would a leading North American journal of cultural studies . . . publish an article liberally salted with nonsense if (a) it sounded good and (b) it flattered the editors' ideological preconceptions? . . . The answer, unfortunately, is 'yes' " (pt. 2, "Revelation"). *Ed.*

GEORGE F. WILL

Smitten with Gibberish

Washington Post, 30 May 1996

Novelist Walker Percy defined a "deconstructionist" as an academic who claims that the meaning of all communication is radically indeterminate but who leaves a message on his wife's answering machine requesting pepperoni pizza for dinner. Deconstructionists read things like *Social Text*, which will never again be called a "learned journal."

In it Alan Sokal, a New York University physicist, has perpetrated a hilarious hoax that reveals the gaudy silliness of some academics. He submitted to *Social Text* for publication an essay that was a tissue of pseudoscientific solecisms and gaseous philosophical rhetoric, flecked with the political jargon that causes leftists' pulses to race. *Social Text* published his parody as serious scholarship, thereby proving that any nonsense, however prolix and preposterous, can win academic approval if it includes "progressive" murmurings about feminism and the baneful effects of "the Western intellectual outlook."

Sokal's essay was intellectual cotton candy—the mere appearance of nourishment—spun from the patois by which certain charlatans disguise their lack of learning. He laid down a fog about "liberatory" this and "postmodernist" that, "nonlinearity" and "emancipatory mathematics" and "transformative hermeneutics" and the "morphogenic field," and did not neglect that old reliable, "the crisis of late-capitalist production relations." All this supposedly pertained to physics.

Any competent undergraduate physics or math major would, Sokal says, recognize the essay as a spoof. So what, beyond ignorance, explains why *Social Text*'s editors swallowed it? Arrogance, for starters, the arrogance of what Sokal calls a "self-perpetuating academic subculture." It is defined by its ideology, which holds that ideology permeates everything, so there is no truth, only "sublimated" power relations "encoded" in various "texts."

Social Text's editors never thought to ask scientists to review Sokal's "argument" because to do so would be to "privilege" a point of view and concede the existence of objective truths. After all, the editors were smitten by Sokal's ridicule of the "Western" notion that "there exists an external world" the physical laws of which can be discovered by the "so-called" scientific method. And the editors surely liked the political tone of Sokal's exhortation "to demystify and democratize the production of scientific knowledge."

He is indeed a leftist, having taught mathematics for Nicaragua's Sandinistas. But as he says in *Lingua Franca*, the magazine of academic affairs in which he revealed his spoof, the left has become hospitable to intellectual sloppiness.

Actually, he is too kind. Something more sinister than sloth is involved. The lumpen Marxists and other theory-mongers begin with Nietzsche's assertion that there are no facts, only interpretations. They proceed to belabor certain banalities, such as that developments in science are influenced by political and social forces, and that literature is conditioned by writers' contexts. And they arrive at an encompassing relativism, by which they justify seeing everything through the lens of politics.

Everything, they assert, from science to sexuality, is a "social construction," and thus arbitrary. The issue of *Social Text* containing Sokal's parody includes excruciatingly serious essays that read like parodies, such as "Gender and Genitals: Constructs of Sex and Gender," which reports that "transgender theorists and activists" are refuting the "Western assumption that there are only two sexes" and are promoting "increased fluidity" and "a 'rainbow' of gender" purged of "the binary male/female model." No wonder *Social Text*'s editors nodded approvingly even as Sokal strained to be, as he says, "especially egregious" in his conclusion concerning "the dialectical emphases" of "catastrophe theory" becoming a "concrete tool of progressive political praxis."

Well, if, as academics who read things like *Social Text* like to say, we are all captives of racial, sexual and class conditioning, and if any "text," properly "interrogated" (sorry, but they talk this way), reveals not the writer's intention but power relations and the hidden agenda of our phallocentric society's dominant cliques, then let's get on with the agenda of academic victimology. That agenda involves using higher education's curricula to dole out reparations to "underrepresented cultures."

Sokal's spoof became still more entertaining when Prof. Stanley Fish shoved his oar in. Fish is professor of English and executive director of the Duke University Press, which publishes *Social Text*. Sokal having demonstrated the comic potential of *Social Text*'s poverty of intellectual standards, Fish denounced Sokal as a threat to, of all things, "intellectual standards."

Say what? Science, says Fish, is a "communal effort" but because of Sokal, communal efforts may be more difficult because there may be "a deep and corrosive attitude of suspicion" in the offices of learned journals.

Learned people hope so, and hope especially for suspicion of the likes of Fish.

JOHN OMICINSKI

Hoax Article Yanks Academics' Legs

Gannett News Service, 3 June 1996

The academic world won't soon recover from the literary hoax perpetrated by New York University physicist Alan Sokal. Sokal unmasked the foolishness that masquerades as higher education in many ivy-covered corners of America by submitting a bogus article that sounded like the real thing to an influential academic magazine called *Social Text*. What Sokal did was absolutely delicious.

Sokal camouflaged his essay with purposely ponderous, pompous, tendentious, and prolix prose, lushly footnoted and elaborately bibliographed. He made it look like any other tangled testament to tenure, and the editors became his unwilling prey.

His complicated paragraphs, wandering through ess-curves of commas and parentheses, are difficult to read, like much of that slow water flowing through the stagnant academic swamp of the 1990s.

Its priceless title—"Transgressing the Boundaries: Toward a Transformative Hermeneutics of Quantum Gravity"—is appropriately soporific, even monastic, so elegant that it must be true, right?

His article posed the central thesis that there is no such thing as physical or social "reality." In other words, the real world isn't really real.

Many natural scientists, wrote Sokal, "cling to the dogma imposed by the long post-Enlightenment hegemony over the Western intellectual outlook . . . that there exists an external world, whose properties are independent of any individual human being and indeed of humanity as a whole; that these properties are encoded in 'eternal' physical laws" [pt. 1, intro.].

But cool academics in the know, he said, are aware that these things we see and touch and feel around us every day are "at bottom a social and linguistic construct." There is a "gender ideology underlying the natural sciences," he declared. There are no real and absolute laws of science, he suggested, just those that some old male tyrants made up to subjugate succeeding generations.

What is needed, he said, is a "liberatory postmodern science" to "liberate human beings from the tyranny of 'absolute truth' and 'objective reality'" [pt. 1, sec. 6].

Despite a jumble of footnotes and backup quotes (all accurate), Sokal offered no real proof for his declaration that science is errant tyranny, that there is no provable real world, no essential truth. What's real is in our imagination.

While he didn't believe a world of what he was writing, he knew it would ring true with academics seeking to release themselves from the rigors of study and free themselves to make up their own stuff as they go along.

And he was oh so right. The editors, needless to say, ate it up.

Social Text printed Sokal's essay without question, not bothering to check it back with Sokal or to run it past physics authorities or those familiar with the history of science.

Sokal's baloney sailed proudly into print. His article was sheer gobbledygook, but it was a big hit with the *Social Text* staff.

A little later, Sokal revealed the hoax in *Lingua Franca*, an academic news magazine. His observations are enlightening.

"I offered the *Social Text* editors an opportunity to demonstrate their intellectual rigor," he wrote. "Did they meet the test? I don't think so" [pt. 2, "Revelation"].

Sokal proved that post-modern American academia is a banana republic, pledging allegiance to an ever-changing panoply of trendy ideas that make little sense except that they require little previous knowledge or study. The only requirement seems to be that they attack the thousand-year heritage of scholarship that is the modern world's foundation.

People who couldn't pass Physics 101 now want to set the agenda for science on many campuses. People who don't know Kant or Spinoza or Aquinas are writing philosophy curricula. People who can't do long division denounce the tyranny of mathematics.

We are threatened with the triumph of the dodo on college campuses in the name of political correctness and the dangerous postmodern view that no one knows the real truth, and Sokal knows it.

"Nowhere in all of this," wrote Sokal in *Lingua Franca*, "is there anything resembling a logical sequence of thought; one finds only citations of authority, plays on words, strained analogies, and bald assertions" [pt. 2, "Revelation"].

What's more surprising, says Sokal, "is how readily they accepted my implication that the search for truth in science must be subordinated to a political agenda, and how oblivious they were to the article's overall illogic" [pt. 2, "Revelation"].

Anyone interested in truth should be applauding Sokal.

He is a real academic guerrilla who won a crucial battle without firing a shot. Indeed, he is still inflicting casualties. Being an editor at an academic magazine is going to be a real nightmare for a while.

KATHA POLLITT

Pomolotov Cocktail, and selected responses

The Nation, 10 June 1996

You've got to hand it to Alan Sokal, the New York University physicist who tricked *Social Text*, the cultural studies journal, into publishing in its special "Science Wars" issue—as a straight academic article—his over-the-top parody of postmodern science critique. "Transgressing the Boundaries: Toward a Transformative Hermeneutics of Quantum Gravity" is a hilarious compilation of pomo gibberish, studded with worshipful quotations from all the trendy thinkers—Derrida, Lacan, Lyotard, Irigaray, *Social Text* board member Stanley Aronowitz (cited thirteen times) and issue editor Andrew Ross (four times). Its thesis, barely discernible through the smoke and fog of jargon, is that the theory of quantum gravity has important affinities with assorted New Age and postmodern ideas; it concludes with a call for "emancipatory mathematics." The whole production was rigged so that anyone who knew physics would realize how preposterous it was. I tried it out on the Last Marxist and had to leave the room, he was laughing so hard. To judge by the gleeful e-mail that's been zipping around academia since Sokal revealed his prank in the current issue of *Lingua Franca*, the L.M. is far from alone.

When one has been duped so incontrovertibly and so publicly there's only one thing to say: Is my face red! Instead, Ross has circulated an editorial response that stakes out some very dubious turf, much of it seeded with land mines. "A breach of professional ethics"? Talk about the transgressor transgressed! A "hokey" article, "not really our cup of tea"? And yet they published it. *Social Text* not a peer-reviewed journal? Maybe it should be.

Certainly Ross's claim (see "Science Backlash on Technoskeptics," *The Nation*, October 2, 1995) that people need no expertise in science to direct its social uses has been done no favors by this rather spectacular display of credulity. And surely it does not help matters to impugn Sokal's motives, as Ross did when I spoke with him—to insist that this self-described leftist and feminist who taught math in Nicaragua under the Sandinistas (more than I ever did) is not on the level. Equally foolish is his attempt to play the gender card—calling the parody a "boy stunt" and urging responses from "women's voices, since this affair, at least as it has been presented in the press so far, has been a boy debate." It's chicks up front all over again.

It's hard not to enjoy the way this incident has made certain humanities profs look self-infatuated and silly—most recently, Stanley Fish, who defended *Social Text* on the *Times* Op-Ed page by comparing scientific laws to the rules of baseball. Sokal's demonstration of the high hot-air quotient in cultural studies—how it combines covert slavishness to authority with the most outlandish radical posturing—is, if anything, long overdue. Unfortunately, another effect of his prank will be to feed the anti-intellectualism of the media and the public. Now people who have been doing brilliant, useful work for years in the social construction of science—some of whom (Dorothy Nelkin, Hilary Rose, Ruth Hubbard) are represented in that same issue of *Social Text*—will have to suffer, for a while, the slings and arrows of journalists like the *Times*'s Janny Scott, who thinks "epistemological" is a funny word, and who portrays the debate over science studies as being between "conservatives" who "have argued that there is truth, or at least an approach to truth, and that scholars have a responsibility to pursue it" and academic leftists who, since they believe nothing is real, can just make up any old damn thing. No light can come from a discussion whose premises are so fundamentally misconstrued (including by Sokal, who in his *Lingua Franca* piece cites as ridiculous postmodern "dogma" the argument that the world is real but unknowable, a position put forward by Kant in 1781, and that I have to say exactly accords with my everyday experience).

And the biggest misconstruction, of course, is that "the academic left," a.k.a. postmodernists and deconstructionists, is the left, even on campus. When I think of scholars who are doing important and valuable intellectual work on the left I think of Noam Chomsky and Adolph Reed, of historians like Linda Gordon and Eric Foner and Rickie Solinger and Natalie Zemon Davis; I think of scientists like Richard C. Lewontin, Stephen Jay Gould; feminists like Ann Snitow and Susan Bordo. None of these people—and the many others like them—dismiss reason, logic, evidence and other Enlightenment watchwords. All write clearly, some extremely well. All build carefully on previous scholarly work—the sociology and history of science, for example, goes back to the 1930s—to approach that "truth" that has somehow become the right's possession. As if Charles Murray is a disinterested scholar!

How "the left" came to be identified as the pomo left would make an interesting Ph.D. thesis. I suspect it has something to do with the decline of actual left-wing movements outside academia, with the development in the 1980s of an academic celebrity system that meshes in funny, glitzy ways with the worlds of art and entertainment, with careerism—the need for graduate students, in today's miserable job market, to defer to their advisers' penchant for bad puns and multiple parentheses, as well as their stranger and less investigated notions. What results is a pseudo-politics, in which everything is claimed in the name of revolution and democracy and equality and anti-authoritarianism, and nothing is risked, nothing, except maybe a bit of harmless cross-dressing, is even expected to happen outside the classroom.

How else explain how pomo leftists can talk constantly about the need to democratize knowledge and write in a way that excludes all but the initiated few? Indeed, the comedy of the Sokal incident is that it suggests that even the postmodernists don't really understand one another's writing and make their way through the text by moving from one familiar name or notion to the next like a frog jumping across a murky pond by way of lily pads. Lacan . . . performativity . . . Judith Butler . . . scandal . . . (en)gendering (w)holeness . . . Lunch!

Selected Responses
The Nation, 8 July 1996

No Teddy Bears' Picnic

New York City

It's not surprising that the Sokal hoax has generated strong feelings. When the left deceives the left, no one expects a teddy bears' picnic. But some good will come out of the science wars once folks get beyond the caricatures and look at the science studies scholarship from a public interest perspective.

The same goes for the left, although Katha Pollitt's intemperate sketch of postmodern affinities among the academic left will not get us very far along that road. Sure, there exists something like a sectarian postmodernism. Like most sectarian left tendencies, it is marginal, its influence is overestimated, its insider language is open to ridicule and its heyday is long over. That's not the whole story, however, at least if I have Pollitt right. There also exist at least two generations of committed scholars and activists who have, in some fashion, been influenced by postmodern thought. It's not so easy to dismiss this broad, and diverse, population.

They include many, myself among them, who share Pollitt's (and Sokal's) dislike of obscurantism, and who make it their business to write public journalism. They include many more who read both Michel Foucault *and* Noam Chomsky; Cornel West *and* Adolph Reed; Judith Butler *and* Cherrie Moraga; Bruno Latour *and* Ruth Hubbard; Patricia Williams *and* Manning Marable; Nancy Fraser *and* Ellen Willis; James Clifford *and* Ward Churchill;

Stuart Hall *and* Herb Schiller, just to name a few combinations. They include some who write philosophy and political economy in the tradition of Marx himself, i.e., complex, learned analysis, not readily available to the general reader but essential to the continuity of left theory. They include many more who have contributed passionately to the struggles for affirmative action, reproductive rights, sexual freedoms, environmental justice and economic equity.

Many of them already read *The Nation*. Many more should, and probably would if they discerned a little more in the way of hospitality than Pollitt offered.

Andrew Ross

Pollitt replies

New York City

If I were as "intemperate" as Andrew Ross claims, I would have quoted some of the remarkable statements he made when I spoke with him on the phone: that Sokal had possibly written his article seriously, and only now claimed it as a parody; that its being a parody was, in any case, irrelevant to its content; that "we have no corroboration" for Sokal's claim to have taught math for the Sandinistas; that leftists should support *Social Text* out of "unity and solidarity." I took exception to this phrase, and sure enough, minutes later Ross called back to say that what he had really meant was that we on the left should be "tolerant" of one another. This from the man who minutes before was suggesting that if Alan Sokal "fabricated" an article he might well have fabricated his Nicaraguan teaching too!

Of course I am well aware that many wonderful scholars make use of postmodernism—I mentioned several. The question on the table, though, is not Michel Foucault's thinking, which I find quite interesting, much less Karl Marx's prose style (a model of lucidity, actually; it's his ideas that are knotty). It's the *Social Text* flap—which does seem to me to be redolent of that in-groupish, rigid "sectarian postmodernism" Ross assures us is marginal, open to ridicule and virtually over. This whole thing, after all, would never have happened if *Social Text* had done what most magazines, peer-reviewed or not, do with an arcane submission: Send it out to someone who really knows the stuff. True, that would mean acknowledging that philosophy of science and history of science—not to mention science—are actual disciplines, not just grist for the cultural-studies deconstruction mill. Failing that, *Social Text* should cultivate the skeptical attitude toward the text that is, supposedly, the hallmark of the postmodern: Maybe, if something sounds fishy, it is. Failing *that*, they should recognize that the joke's on them, and the more they huff and puff the sillier they look.

As for Ross's suggestion that my column keeps pomo-influenced academics away from *The Nation*, I stand ready to sacrifice myself, in the name of unity, solidarity and tolerance.

JAMES TERRY

Another Dispatch from the Culture Wars

Kansas City (Mo.) New Times, 13 June 1996

A physicist, troubled by what he perceives to be the laxness of thought in "certain precincts of the . . . humanities" has perpetrated a spectacular academic hoax. Alan Sokal, a physics professor at New York University, wrote an intentionally ridiculous article called "Transgressing the Boundaries: Toward a Transformative Hermeneutics of Quantum Gravity." The article is a hodgepodge of trendy clichés and bad science. In his article Sokal calls for a "revision of the canon of mathematics"; he suggests that scientific constants are socially determined and that quantum physics foreshadows radical politics. The entire article is a brilliant joke, comical in its rhetorical excess and slavish ideological purity. It is also a brilliant parody of the worst of postmodern writing. The joke, it turns out, is on the editors of the cultural-studies journal *Social Text*, who accepted the article for publication in their recent "Science Wars" special issue.

Sokal is no William Bennett defending white patrimony from the perceived threat of modern radical scholars. His credentials as a committed leftist are in order: He taught math in Sandinista Nicaragua. In the May/June issue of *Lingua Franca*, Sokal explains his hoax. He is troubled by critiques of science emanating from non- (or even anti-) scientific quarters. He asks in the *Lingua Franca* article, "Is it now dogma in cultural studies that there exists no external world?" The notion didn't seem so outlandish to the *Social Text* editors. To them Sokal offers this retort: "Anyone who believes that the laws of physics are mere social conventions is invited to try transgressing those conventions from the windows of my apartment" [pt. 2, "Revelation"]. His invitation has a respectable antecedent. Dr. Samuel Johnson responded to Berkeley's *Principles of Human Knowledge*—which seems to deny the reality of matter—by kicking a rock and exclaiming, "I refute him thus." Sokal's response, like Johnson's, is clever but not profound.

As Johnson did before him, Sokal is attacking a caricature, in this case a popular caricature of cultural studies. In the stereotype, leftist scholars renounce objectivity, preach radical moral relativism to tender 19-year-olds and deny the utility of facts, evidence and scholarly standards. Like any caricature, it has elements of truth that are inflated well out of proportion.

Sokal's hoax has demonstrated a dearth of critical thinking among the "self-proclaimed Left" (Sokal's phrase), at least at the far reaches. The post-modernists continue the academic tradition of playing at radicalism while pursuing the standard bourgeois lifestyle common in academia. They pro-tect their turf by speaking in a dense, opaque, anti-democratic code. Sokal gives us reason to suspect that they don't know what they are talking about. As Sokal points out in *Lingua Franca*, leftists should be "combating the mystifications promoted by the powerful" and not creating mystifications of our own. Sokal says we cannot "combat false ideas in history, sociology, economics, and politics if we reject the notions of truth and falsity" [pt. 2, "Revelation"]. Sokal's hoax is an overdue victory for clear thinking.

In spite of the jargon and posturing, some very useful work is being done by these so-called Leftists. Cultural studies tell us that we are immersed in a system of ideology and power so pervasive that we scarcely notice it. The academic left is dedicated to revealing—and then changing—this system. The "science wars" are turf skirmishes between scientists—who insist on the myth of disinterestedness—and social scientists—who insist that science is a social endeavor and therefore subject to ideological constraint. It is a con-vincing argument. Scientific "objectivity" can be purchased to defend to-bacco or dioxin. Since World War II most scientists have labored either for the Pentagon or for capital. So much for disinterestedness. This point of view isn't just another manifestation of '60s radicalism. The social critique of science dates to the 1930s, when a handful of British scholars showed that the scientific developments of Newton's era were guided not so much by an objective search for truth as by the technological needs of mercantile imperialism.

After Sokal 'fessed up in *Lingua Franca*, conservatives were quick to at-tack the "tenured radicals," despite the slight ammunition. The *Washington Times* said Sokal had "saved academic standards from total destruction by the postmodern menace." A more common interpretation is that Sokal's hoax is a PR disaster for the left. Roger Kimball, managing editor of the reactionary highbrow journal the *New Criterion*, said in the *Wall Street Journal* that Sokal's leftist politics "makes his hoax all the more embarrassing for the academic left." "Hoax Turns Left's Brains a Bright Shade of Red," said the *Herald-Sun* (Durham, N.C.). The *Washington Times* wrote, "Sokal's spoof has spread panic in the . . . academic left." Actually, the only people who need feel red-faced are the editors of *Social Text*. The incident says plenty about the magazine's review process, but little about the wider leftist commitment to social justice. Sokal has scored a point for activism and against abstract theory. This will be good for the left.

Cultural conservatives may want to tend their own gardens for awhile. They have their own doctrinaire wackos and irrational ideologues. Alabama State Sen. Charles Davidson, a Republican running for the U.S. House, recently suggested that slavery is the will of God. "People who are bitter and hateful about slavery are obviously bitter and hateful against God and his word, because they reject what God says and embrace what mere humans say concerning slavery." It's in the Bible, so it must be so. The Christian right wants to subject us to a theocracy, Pat Buchanan and David Duke foment xenophobia, and in Alabama it is permissible to speak of slavery as a Christian duty. Given these idiocies, it seems a stretch for conservatives to pretend they are defending the Enlightenment against leftist irrationality. Sokal has performed some long overdue house-cleaning. But who will sweep Charles Davidson out on the right? Who will rebuke him? Probably nobody. The cultural right should remove the log from its own eye before going after the speck in the left's. It's in the Bible; look in a concordance under "hypocrite."

EDITORIAL

Scholarly Article a Fine Hoax: Social Scientists Wore No Clothes

Fort Meyers (Fla.) News-Press, 23 July 1996

Sometimes it takes utter nonsense to make a point perfectly clear.

Consider a recent scholarly article penned by Alan Sokal, a physicist at New York University, who had been critical of the impenetrability of scholarly tomes. Sokal was particularly upset by left-wing tracts that pontificate about how social, cultural and political conditions may determine ideas about what is truth.

To make his point, he constructed a piece of pure gibberish, shipped it off to such a publisher—and waited.

Sure enough, they bit.

Social Text, a leftist journal of cultural studies, published the piece, titled "Transgressing the Boundaries: Toward a Transformative Hermeneutics of Quantum Gravity."

Its chief point: There are scientists who "cling to the dogma imposed by the long post-Enlightenment hegemony over Western intellectual outlook . . . : That there exists an external world, whose properties are independent of an individual human being and indeed of humanity as a whole" [pt. 1, intro.].

Translation: Some silly scientists actually believe the physical world exists.

Social Text editors were angered by the hoax and scurried to serve up excuses to explain.

All this just confirms what many suspected: In the pursuit of ersatz erudition and increasingly impenetrable insights, many scholars—and the journals they rely on—don't have a clue what they or others are saying.

And nobody's willing to admit it.

4

Foreign Press Coverage

EUAN FERGUSON

Illogical Dons Swallow Hoaxer's Leap into Quantum Gibberish

The Observer (London), 19 May 1996

It's the kind of hoax that snaps dons awake, screaming, in the hour before dawn. An American academic has sucker-punched the world of cultural studies—often ridiculed for its obscurantist jargon—by writing a lengthy parody of an article, stiff with invented jargon and gibberish, only to see every word reproduced in good faith by the subject's leading journal.

Physicist Alan Sokal, of New York University, grew so infuriated at the "proliferation of nonsense and sloppy thinking" in cultural studies—which looks behind popular culture and, now, science for hidden ideological meaning—that he offered the magazine *Social Text* an article entitled "Transgressing the Boundaries: Toward a Transformative Hermeneutics of Quantum Gravity," thick with references to the work of Jacques Derrida and liberally peppered with meaningless footnotes on counterhegemonic epistemiology.

"I structured the article around the silliest quotes about mathematics and physics from the most prominent academics," he said yesterday, "and I invented an argument praising them and linking them together. All this was very easy to carry off because my argument wasn't obliged to respect any standards of evidence or logic."

The editorial collective that publishes the journal now says it sorely regrets its mistake. But Stanley Aronowitz, the magazine's co-founder, still appears to be missing the whole point of the parody, complaining: "He says we're epistemic relativists. We're not. He got it wrong. One of the reasons he got it wrong is he's ill-read and half-educated."

The dispute goes to the heart of the public debate over left-wing scholarship, particularly over the contention that social, cultural and political conditions influence and/or determine knowledge and ideas about what is truth, i.e., that truth, be it cultural or scientific, need not be objective.

"While my method was satirical," says Sokal, "my motivation is utterly serious."

He worries that the "trendy" disciplines and obscure jargon could end up hurting the left-wing cause; by losing contact with the real world, you undermine the prospect for progressive social critique.

Norman Levitt, a professor of mathematics at Rutgers University and an author of a book on science and the academic Left that first brought the new critique of science to Sokal's attention, calls the hoax "a lot of fun. I don't want to claim that it proves that all social scientists or all English professors are complete idiots, but it does betray a certain arrogance and a certain out-of-touchness on the part of a certain clique."

ROBERTO CAMPOS
Sokal's Prank

Folha de São Paulo (Brazil), 22 September 1996

The imbecile collective . . . is a group of people of average or above-average intelligence who are drawn together by the common desire to make one another look foolish.—Olavo de Carvalho

An amusing but timely storm is still shaking up the suburbs of American academic life. A physicist and professor at New York University, Dr. Alan Sokal, published an extremely convoluted essay entitled "Transgressing the Boundaries: Toward a Transformative Hermeneutics of Quantum Gravity" in the Spring/Summer 1996 issue of *Social Text*, a leftist journal of cultural criticism dedicated primarily to "postmodernism." Soon afterward, Sokal published another article, "A Physicist Experiments with Cultural Studies," in the magazine *Lingua Franca*. In the second piece, Sokal explains that the text sent to *Social Text* was a parody at the expense of practitioners of "science studies," nothing more than a joke full of meaningless phrases that appear to question the validity of measuring physical "reality."

What really stung is that *Social Text* had earned a certain reputation for seriousness in more obscure areas of the left-wing cultural studies camp. It had become a sort of final intellectual refuge for the remains of an academic radicalism that persists in the so-called social sciences. For quite some time, scientists of the "hard" disciplines have been experiencing increasing disgust with the facile methods, the prattle, and the intellectual pretensions of this *engagé* group.

No one has forgotten what happened in the golden years of Stalin's socialism, when the theory of relativity was "bourgeois" and "Jewish" science. Cybernetics was banned for similar reasons (which set back Soviet technology enormously), and Mendelian genetics led to the Gulag or worse (because it went against the socialist presumption of "heredity of acquired traits").

These are old stories, it's true, but the evil habit of intellectual bullying—demanding that ideas conform to ideology—is too appealing to the left, which gains some modicum of power through such practices. Here in the land of Macuna'ma, many people were watched and persecuted, often in the most vile way—all, of course, in the name of the "good cause." There are contentious ideologues: Antônio Callado, for example, in literature, and Emir Sader, in the social sciences. Callado sought to veto publication in the newspaper *Jornal do Brasil* of articles by Olavo de Carvalho, an erudite philosopher. Sader attacked Josþ Guilherme Merquior, who was undoubtedly the sociologist with the most profound cultural impact among the young Brazilian generation—as well as the most internationally renowned.

Perhaps Sokal's prank wouldn't have deserved any more than a good guffaw if the contributors to *Social Text* hadn't lost their sportsmanship and cried "breach of ethics," thus inciting a war with the so-called conservatives in science. In fact, they've confessed that they interpreted Sokal's article as a physicist's serious attempt to find support in "postmodern philosophy" for the developments in his field.

Some of the statements by the journal's publisher, Stanley Fish, of Duke University Press, ended up sounding almost as amusing as Sokal's: "The sociologists of science," he says, "aren't trying to do science; they are trying to come up with a rich and powerful explanation of what it means to do it" [pt. 3, "Professor Sokal's Bad Joke"]. This attempt at self-justification fanned the flames in academic circles around the world. But it's nothing new for serious thinkers to protest against the facile methods with which practitioners of the so-called social sciences—and of philosophy—misuse the criteria of rationality and semantics, at times in defense of immediate ideological interests. The great logician-mathematician Carnap, for example, harshly criticized meaningless assertions by philosophers then in fashion. All of this is part of the game, however, and wouldn't attract attention if it weren't for the growing lack of intellectual sensitivity by the radical chic, the *engagés*, who deny the validity of science's efforts toward objective knowledge and brazenly preach as "science" their own political and ideological biases.

The debate spread like wildfire to other fields. For example, one journalist revealed that some professors were teaching that Cleopatra and Socrates were both black, that Greek science and philosophy were taken from Africa, and that Aristotle stole his philosophy from the Alexandria library. Nonsense like this barely hides an insulting, paternalistic bias that only harms the cause of racial justice. Not without reason, the extreme radical black American leader Farrakhan, who organized the recent march in Washington and who preaches, moreover, strict separation from whites, rejects this hypocrisy and calls on his followers to engage in a "serious self-affirmation."

For us Brazilians, accustomed to much greater impudence by our radicals, the diluted repercussions of this case might seem like nothing more than

First World entertainment. But behind all this lie valid questions. Could everything be so relative that nothing objective can be affirmed about the real world? Is the scientist bound by the laws of logic and ethics of consistency, or is political commitment the priority? Is "truth" always "political" and "ideological," or can the principles of reason lead us to an ever vaster knowledge, accessible to all and verifiable by all?

There are no absolute answers to these inquiries. But we all have to maintain some relation to what we can call the "real world." Even a politically committed "sociologist of culture," no matter how involved he might be in "postmodern deconstruction," expects the light to come on when a switch is flipped, and, upon turning a car key, expects without a shadow of doubt that the "relative" laws of physics and chemistry and the mathematics in which they're formulated won't stop working at that moment.

On the other hand, the "deconstruction" effort, like all critical endeavors, can be useful to demarcate our thinking and reveal some of our limits—this is not all that new. Twenty-five centuries ago, the Greeks were pondering paradoxes not that different from those faced by the mathematicians and logicians Whitehead and Russell and, more recently, Gödel.

Economists, especially, live with a permanent headache, because they deal with subjects that belong at once to math and physics and to history and culture. That is, on the one hand, there's the risk of the black hole of an excessive degree of abstraction; on the other, there's a quagmire of facile methods of which "social science" slackers avail themselves. There are small perversities on both sides. For example, the economist Paul Krugman recently told an anecdote about a Hindu economics professor who explained reincarnation to his students as follows: "If you're sincere, apply yourselves, and do your work well, in your next incarnation you'll come back as physicists. If you're lazy and slouch off, you'll return as sociologists."

I don't intend to draw conclusions because I prefer not to take sides. I've already suffered my share of intellectual bullying. But a bit more rigor in Brazilian discourse would be very useful. There will be only gains if we begin to follow the semantics of subject-verb-predicate, instead of indulging our tropical disrespect for words and for the fact that, behind them, there has to be some meaning in things . . .

OLAVO DE CARVALHO
Sokal, a Self-Parodist
Folha de São Paulo (Brazil), 21 October 1996

After each new series of embarrassing incidents, the left emerges reinvigorated by the miracle of verbal ablution.

Having sent an article of pure nonsense written in academic jargon to a
leftist sociological journal to see if they would publish it, the physicist Alan
Sokal added the title of humorist to his resume. Having taken the bait, the
journal—*Social Text*—got into an even stickier situation trying to justify the
publication.

Beyond simple entertainment, the stunt served to reveal the intellectual
ineptitude of the academic left. In an article published in the newspaper
Folha de São Paulo (22 September 1996), Roberto Campos underscored the
importance of the experiment, which exposed the true nakedness of one of
the world's most pretentious communities [pt. 4, "Sokal's Prank"]. Surprisingly, Alan Sokal has now weighed in to say that Campos interpreted him
with "blind prejudice" (6 October 1996).

"The parody," proclaims Sokal, "was not intended to make fun of the left,
but to strengthen it by criticizing its excesses. With the exception of those
most directly affected—those caught with their pants down—the vast majority of the North American intellectual left supported my intervention." "The
bulk of the left," he suggests, has "begun to recognize its errors, to renew
itself intellectually"; Campos is the one who distorted everything by discern-
ing a global embarrassment in the case.

But this argument is a bit bizarre. An author who wished to educate a
sinner by criticizing his excesses, without making him the butt of a joke,
would make him an object of exhortation, or analysis, or something comparable—never of parody, a genre that consists precisely of exposing another to
ridicule by imitation of his gestures. As for knowing whether an object of
parody will come out strengthened or weakened, no experienced comedy
writer would try to control an effect that depends entirely on the victim's
free moral reaction. The victim can either take advantage of the stimulus to

regenerate himself or make it an occasion to expose himself to even greater ridicule, as did the editor of *Social Text*, dragging down, as Campos recognized only too well, many like-minded journals into the confusion. If the ridicule produced by Sokal wasn't premeditated, this merely shows that the novice humorist runs the risk of becoming a comic character, much like the sailor who flushed the toilet at the exact moment his ship was hit by a torpedo.

That some leftists applaud the parody ex post facto doesn't prove that they're free of the vices it denounces. It merely proves that they didn't stand by their colleagues caught in the embarrassment of a *flagrante delicto*. Handing over one's rings to save one's fingers is no intellectual novelty; it's just an old trick.

The left has effectively lived to denounce its own mistakes since the days of the French Revolution, when it recognized the usefulness of executing the executioner—an act that sent the movement's prestige soaring and gave it leave to continue executing whomever it wished. Since then, each new leftist generation has been born of the self-righteous discrediting of the previous generation. Marxism itself emerged from a crushing criticism of the errors of the left. From Robespierre to Alan Sokal, the gadflies change, but—how shall I put it?—the procession goes on. From each new series of embarrassments, horrors, and failures, the left emerges reinvigorated by the miracle of verbal ablution and imbued with a sense of its rightful trustworthiness, all the more renewable since debt always falls into the account of the previous administration. Sokal is just another celebrant in the ancient cyclical ritual in which the left feeds itself, dialectically, through self-denial.

To top it all off, Sokal seeks to minimize the scope of his own criticism, asserting that he only attacked a minority. But how do we explain that the criticism of a minority has provoked such an uproar if the part wasn't representative of the whole? Sokal admits that his article cited a list of nonsensical quotes "by prominent intellectuals"—and no one is prominent for being applauded by the minority alone. Derrida, Foucault, Lyotard, Lacan, Deleuze aren't the objects of worship of a small provincial following: They are idols of the international "intelligentsia." Mocked, they necessarily compromise the (already shaky) image of the left's intellectual respectability as a whole. There is no escape.

Sokal could have preserved at least his own respectability, had he not shown himself to share the traditional tendency of the left to judge acts solely by their alleged intentions, denying responsibility for their actual effects, predictable as they might have been. Yet he preferred to outdo—as unwilling humorist—his own gifts of parody. For the air of innocence with which the skilled parodist declares he had no intention of ridiculing only adds to the joke if we didn't know that he believes what he says and that, in Sokal's case, believing his own denial is tantamount to admitting that he does not know what he has done.

Academic Insult in Greenwich Village, and Selected Responses

Il manifesto (Rome), 6 November 1996

Alan Sokal—the NYU physics professor who devised the academic hoax of the decade—was very pleased with himself at a Roman dinner this summer with his Italian wife. But the hoax that made the front pages of newspapers from the *New York Times* to *The Observer* and set off furious debate among American intellectuals was ignored in Italy, until Nobel physicist Steven Weinberg's article appeared in the *Rivista dei Libri*. Here's the story: in its Spring/Summer 1996 issue, the prestigious journal *Social Text* publishes a ponderous essay by Sokal entitled "Transgressing the Boundaries: Toward a Transformative Hermeneutics of Quantum Gravity." *Social Text* is published by Duke University Press, and has been edited by prestigious scholars like Fredric Jameson, Andrew Ross, and Stanley Aronowitz. Sokal's essay is accompanied by an imposing array of footnotes, complete with quotations from (naturally) Aronowitz and Ross, but also Derrida, Lacan, Latour, Lyotard, Irigaray, Virilio, and physicists like Heisenberg and Bohr.

But there's a catch. On the very day *Social Text* reaches the bookstores, another academic journal, *Lingua Franca*, publishes an article by Sokal in which he declares his *Social Text* piece to be sheer nonsense. He explains that all his quotes are perfectly accurate, but that the rest, beginning with the title, is a gargantuan pastiche of senseless phrases: he maintains that "quantum gravity has profound political implications," that "quantum physics is profoundly consonant with postmodernist epistemology," and concludes with a prediction that "postmodern science" will draw strength from an "emancipatory mathematics," on whose content for the time being one can only sketch out preliminary hypotheses.

As country squires on a hunt like to say, Sokal really rubbed their noses in it. And Act Two is not hard to imagine: the bitter, embarrassed, and entirely unsportsmanlike reaction of the victims, and the academics around them who hasten to take sides for or against. But there is a political side, too. Sokal calls himself a man of the Left with the capital L—as he points out rather too often, he taught mathematics in Managua under the Sandinistas (as one might have fought in Spain in the thirties). And he calls himself a feminist.

Now, as a rule, such proclamations precede violent attacks against the left and feminism, which is indeed the case here. Sokal's target is the "academic left," the "Faux Left." He claims that, while his "method was satirical, [his] motivation is entirely serious": he wanted to show the stupidity of thinking that "physical 'reality' . . . is at bottom a social and linguistic construct . . . that scientific 'knowledge,' far from being objective, reflects and encodes the dominant ideologies and power relations of the culture that produced it" [pt. 2, "Revelation"; pt. 1, intro.]. Here Sokal reveals his nineteenth-century scientism, borrowed from positivists like Comte—even though old Auguste was French, and Sokal dislikes Frenchness (the success of his hoax has a lot to do with Anglo-Saxon distaste for gallic cultural arrogance).

Sokal is convinced that, by way of his hoax, he has refuted the idea that every human theory is a human elaboration—and as such, is linguistic, and in the end, is social. Unfortunately for him, things are a little more complex (physics, quantum or not, is itself a human creation). But if the hoax were merely an episodic comeback of good old reductionist positivism, of 24-karat scientism . . . well, there wouldn't be much to say. But in fact, although his hoax proves nothing about "the objectivity of science," it says a lot about the present practice of hermeneutics and cultural studies—and that is significant indeed.

To begin with, it shows how dependent this field is on the authority principle: people care less about *what* is said than about *who* says it. So, if a piece of nonsense has a Derrida logo, it's a deep concept. And Sokal brings to light the visceral antiscientism of this milieu. If people like him aren't exactly subtle when it comes to epistemology, deconstruction theorists and company have, for their part, a lousy relationship with science based on a similar arrogance: after all, had they asked a physicist to check Sokal's specific claims, the hoax would have been defused. But the idea didn't even cross their minds: "technical" questions are too petty for them.

What Sokal has brought to light, then, is "the specialized discourse of the anti-specialist," like politicians who make careers out of attacking politics. As Tom Frank has written in *In These Times*, "post-structuralist jargon . . . is the sacred talk of a professional group . . . But it's a jargon with a curious twist, a professional jargon that celebrates anti-professionalism, and fetishizes the subversive power of transgression."

One final reflection: the whole thing may have been philosophically unrefined, true, but it has become the object of a public debate, making the front page of the *Times*. The affair *has been taken seriously*, as if truth were at stake. And that's probably why, here in Italy, it has been picked up so late, and in such a muted way. In our *Bel Paese*, our gift for subtlety and nuance would have nipped the debate in the bud. No academic would have taken things as seriously as Sokal has done—studying text after text of Derridians, feminists, Lacanians, and setting up an imposing critical apparatus simply to execute a hoax. And if someone had published the article, no scandal would have followed, given the embarrassing superficiality of so many of our "humanities" journals, where people publish all sorts of things and no one notices. And even if the scandal had occurred, newspapers would have treated it as an amusing curiosity, out of Boccaccio or Bandello—which is the way Franco Prattico reported Weinberg's article in *La Repubblica* (the only Italian paper to have mentioned the event). How much can a question of *truth* matter when we have so many more urgent issues, like the Swiss man who has supposedly raped 1,500 children in Sri Lanka. And notice that 1,500: a nice, round, precise figure, endowed with the same aura of certainty as "postmodern quantum theory."

Selected responses
Il manifesto, 21 January 1997

Alan Sokal writes:

With some delay, I wish to thank my friend Marco D'Eramo for his article on my academic hoax and the ensuing scandal, but also feel that I have to correct some of his statements.

It is not true that "Sokal is convinced that he has refuted the idea that every human theory is a human elaboration." How could I reject such an evident tautological truth? What I deny is that the validity of a theory is a social construction, rather than an "objective property of Nature." Furthermore, Marco complains that I am "not exactly subtle when it comes to epistemology." On what grounds? My brief *Lingua Franca* article, in which I revealed the hoax, never pretended to be an epistemological treatise. Marco labels me as a "positivist," whereas I reject positivism for a moderate realism, as do most contemporary physicists that are also interested in philosophy (see for instance Steven Weinberg's book, *Dreams of a Final Theory*).

Finally, I am not attacking the "academic left," but rather its postmodern wing, which in my opinion has completely lost touch (at least in the United States) with social and economic reality. I don't claim that the publication of my parody proves much beyond the incompetence of *Social Text*'s editorial board. The lesson is to be found in the content of the parody—an annotated bibliography of nonsense by some of the best known French and American intellectuals.

Marco D'Eramo replies:

Dear Alan Sokal, I admit it, I am incapable of distinguishing between reality and perception (and theories) of physical reality. According to my senses, the sun moves around the earth: if I state that objective reality is different, and the earth moves around the sun, it is because I follow my theoretical description of reality (which, by the way, dramatically contradicts my eyesight). For millennia, objective reality was different. For two centuries, objective reality included an absolute time (Newton's), but after Einstein's relativity, absolute time disappeared from objective reality. That's why the same statement that inspires your derision—"that scientific 'knowledge,' far from being objective, reflects and encodes the dominant ideologies and power relations of the culture that produced it" [pt. 1, intro.]—seems to me perfectly meaningful and sensible. As a matter of fact, we cannot utter a single statement which is not codified and influenced by social relations, given that all we say is said through language—and language is the result of our culture, and thus of the spontaneous ideology that shapes us all. This is the reason for the tautology "every human theory is a human elaboration." All human products are social products, determined by the society that generates them. As a consequence, the belief that nature may be described mathematically, because "mathematics is the alphabet in which God has written Nature" (Galileo), is a "metaphysical" one. Couldn't God have used a different alphabet (or not have "written" Nature at all)?

Positivist prejudice equates "objective" and "true," so that what is not objective is false. But the fact that a theory is a social construction has nothing to do with its truth or falsity; rather, we must resign ourselves to an inescapable epistemological uncertainty. After Gödel and Cohen, we all know that the foundations of mathematics are problematic; and those of physics are quite shaky too. Read the whole affair of "cold fusion" as an immense—and far more devastating—joke *à la Sokal* and you'll see that the giant of high energy physics has feet of soft clay, ready to melt at room temperature.

A. N. WILSON
When Clever Men Think Rubbish, Sound the Alarm Bells
Evening Standard (London), 17 December 1996

An academic prank, played by an American physicist, Alan Sokal, has thrown into sharp relief an alarming fact about many western intellectuals of the present day. What alarms is not their having fallen for a hoax, and mistaken falsehood for truth. It is their failure to see the need to distinguish between truth and falsehood.

It is a clear demonstration of "post-modernism" in action, and when we have finished laughing at the episode, we might feel a little disturbed.

What happened was this. Sokal submitted an article to a periodical called *Social Text*: a journal which prides itself on its modishness. His article, quite deliberately, was a tissue of nonsense. He set out a case for "relativism" in physics and mathematics, claiming—in layman's speak—that there are no objective reasons for believing in empirical scientific method; that the statements of modern physicists are only relative; that mathematics is a similarly arbitrary discipline and that its set (Zermelo-Fraenkel) theories have no more validity than abracadabra.

That is putting it simply, but Sokal did not put it simply. He dressed up his argument (which he deliberately laced with many non sequiturs and untruths) in the language of post-modern gobbledygook. *Social Text* printed his article, not questioning even those paragraphs which he had set out to make as incomprehensible, and as meaningless, as possible.

When Sokal's hoax was revealed—and here lies the disturbing part of the story—the editors of *Social Text* did not seem to believe that anything untoward had happened. It did not worry them. They seem to believe that there was something "valid" about the article, even though it was meant as a joke to expose their nonsense.

In a disturbing article in the *Times Literary Supplement*, Professor Paul Boghossian of New York sees the Sokal hoax as part of a trend which has swept through American—and by extension Western—intellectual life in the last few decades. He cites the example of an English archaeologist, Roger Anyon, who considers it perfectly "valid" to accept the American Indian myth that their people rose to that continent from a subterranean spirit-world, rather than—as seems a more rational view, worked out from stray pieces of actual evidence by other archaeologists and anthropologists—having crossed the Bering Strait 10,000 years ago.

In the "post-modernist" view, one idea is just as acceptable as another; indeed the fairy stories of the Zuni tribesmen are—for obvious political reasons—in many ways more attractive than the "scientific" outlook based on all that male-dominated, westernized Aristotelian "true or false" stuff.

Several journalists have tried to puzzle out what is meant by the phrase "post-modern," and usually come to the humorous conclusion that it belongs to the "pseud's corner" end of the newspaper. But incidents like this, among the supposedly cleverest in our society, give cause for alarm.

Intellectuals are important, and it does matter what we think. It is not purely accidental that most English intellectuals of the last century (even those who reacted against it) were influenced by the empirical traditions of the 18th century, and by the rigorous liberalism of Mill. They believed (perhaps absurdly in some cases) in "not entertaining any proposition with greater assurance than the proofs it is built upon will warrant" (Locke). Even the Idealists who reacted against the materialists believed this.

For continental intellectuals it was otherwise. The ideas of Hegel, reheated and mixed about in mad laboratory conditions by Marx and Nietzsche and other visionaries, really did have an effect. Russia, having stupefied its mind with irrational religion for 1,000 years, made the switch to Leninism with pain—but they were used to the irrational. Germany, the birthplace of much brilliant nonsense, embraced Hitler because its intellectuals had been used to thinking rubbish for 100 years.

Think rubbish, and you start behaving foolishly. Educate a whole generation to think rubbish—all the cleverest young people in American and European universities are confronted with the beguiling relativism of post-modernist doctrines—and you ask for trouble.

The generation in Britain who looked to J. S. Mill as their master entered public life with a burning desire not to destroy society by Marxist revolution but to undo injustice and inequality by liberal means. The feminist movement, the growth in public education, sanitation, decent housing, moderate state socialism and welfare—the evolution of British society since the middle of the last century—happened in defiance of many politicians; it happened because of what a few intellectuals had taught.

The ideas of Marx—that change could only come about when millions of people had been killed, when peasant-owners had been conned into a revolution and then themselves slaughtered—you can read them all in the books he scribbled while living in Kentish Town. Lenin followed them to the letter.

Hitler in his different way was influenced by the same notion—that reason and decency had no place in public life; the world was not something to be viewed objectively, it was a product of Spirit, it was a plaything, which could follow fairy stories from Grimm and doom-laden operas by Wagner.

We are in a situation today in the West alarmingly like Europe 100 years ago. Many of our cleverest people are decadents. It has become fashionable to decry intellectuals, and intellectuals themselves delight in the anti-intellectualism of post-modernism. One point of view is as good as another. The dull old Anglo-Saxon empirical tradition of common sense has gone quiet. Religious revivals, when they occur, are not of a reasonable but of a fanatical kind.

It takes very little in such circumstances—a recession just a bit worse than the last one, a war slightly fiercer than the one in Bosnia—for some mastermind of nonsense, some Hitler or Lenin, to step on to the scene. As in Dostoyevsky's masterpiece on the subject, "The Devils," the intellectuals continue to jabber nonsense until, hoodwinked by the demagogue who despises them, they and the whole of society are led like Gadarene swine to perdition.

DENIS DUCLOS
Sokal Is No Socrates

Le Monde (Paris), 3 January 1997

Many of the attacks currently being led in the United States against not only "French intellectuals" (Jacques Lacan, Maurice Blanchot, Jacques Derrida), but also against such universal thinkers as Freud, would not themselves be classified as intellectual. They do not seek to understand, but rather to parody, to denigrate, to trick and to soil.

Their orchestration is above all the result of a commercial operation, or even of a psychological war. Their underlying philosophy is that of an anti-European chauvinism which would serve as a common denominator for zealots of a new sovereignty, of which we must accept above all to be vassals, including and especially in the realm of thought.

But where lies the thought of professor Alan Sokal (*Le Monde*, 20 December 1996)? It makes no sense to take his hoax seriously. The fact that a journal of social sciences let itself be tricked by errors in physics does not mean that social questions cease to merit their own radical autonomy. The fact that certain editors of ultra-specialized reviews (both in the sciences and in the humanities) understand nothing of the expertise of their neighbors does not mean that we should blame Lacan, who was a great thinker in natural sciences, introducer of Anglo-Saxon thought, and a tenacious debater with the best logicians.

That Lacan is less interesting to read than Bertrand Russell is not certain; the former discusses the latter and recalls, for example, how he instilled doubt in Frege as to the logical possibility of unifying the signifier and the signified, the thinking and the thought, culture and nature.

This old scientistic dream has not yet been extinguished, even if today it is in crisis for not having been able to save us from existential anguish, much to the detriment of Alan Sokal, among others. This does not prohibit us, of course, from reading Russell directly, astonishingly more open than our *pistoleros of intellectual correctness*.

What strikes us more than anything else in these vast operations of di-rected devaluation is their cynicism, that is to say their naïve belief in the infantile, all-powerful effect of the world. Their aggressive agents, hired or genuine, seem to have decided that we can speculate on the decline of thought, as on money or the art market. They are wrong; reflection interests only those who consecrate themselves to it from the inside, and their passion is unconditional, inelastic.

That others hang around and mimic that which they do not understand is completely insignificant. That they organize these sorts of symbolic auto-dafés to liberate American youth from pernicious influences is as stupid as the order, given way back when, to Socrates to drink the hemlock in order to stop making others think.

If we were looking for a means to spread the disturbing questions raised by Socrates everywhere, what better way than to kill him at the height of his reputation as a good thinker. In the end, it is just as well; let us leave all the fuss about Mr. Sokal to the visitors at an amusement park, and let us return to the questions posed to humanity by Freud or by Lacan (may his followers, by the way, start to publish a little more quickly).

BRUNO LATOUR

Is There Science after the Cold War?

Le Monde (Paris), 18 January 1997

In attempting to distinguish the "true importance of the Sokal affair," Jean Briemont (*Le Monde*, 14 January) reduces by far too much its range. He presents it as an elementary-school hullabaloo, the supervisors of section C expressing to the principal their indignation about the tricks played on them by the pesky honors students of section A.

The affair seems to me to be much more interesting than a simple question of academic policing. A very small number of theoretical physicists, deprived of their hefty Cold War budgets, are seeking a new menace, against which they will heroically offer the rampart of their intellect. It is no longer the war against the Soviets, but rather the war against the "postmodern" intellectuals from abroad.

France, in their eyes, has become another Colombia, a country of dealers who produce hard drugs—Derridium and Lacanium—which American academics cannot resist any more than crack. Turned away from their healthy and joyous campus life, forgetting even to take their daily dose of analytic philosophy (clear as water), they become debilitated in a sea of relativism!

Of this parodical form of the Enlightenment philosophers, a mix of Voltaire and McCarthy, we should say nothing. Yes, but we are talking about a farce, and like all farces, this one gets away from its author.

What, in effect, does our friend Sokal's joke prove? Let us suppose that an established socialist gets an article accepted in the National Front's journal, where he carries on about the scientific proofs of inequality amongst the races, and that he admits afterward, in a leftist journal, that he does not believe a word of what he wrote. We would not be amused. We have all learned from Michel Foucault that a text can get away from its author. Once the author has disappeared, the monstrosities are still there. Sokal has nothing interesting to say about his own article, which must, in turn, be evaluated for itself. The fireworks burn for a long time.

What can we say then about this article, published in a non-peer-reviewed journal? That it is typical of the postmodern gibberish that makes its reader yawn even before beginning to read. So Sokal wants to rid us of this literature? Excellent! All researchers will applaud enthusiastically. May someone rid us, in effect, of all these obliging journals, these repetitive articles, these cliques and these clans. May there remain only articles which are bold, precise, risqué, well written, innovative! And yet this magnificent program, alas, will not be able to distinguish the sciences, and the humanities, the moderns and the postmoderns, as every thinker knows very well. We would have to apply it everywhere, to all knowledgeable literature, in economics as in chemistry, in theoretical physics as in comparative literature. May good research chase away the bad. Bravo!

Why then was this boring article accepted by an obliging journal? Because, quite simply, it is a bad journal, of which, alas, there are so many, in all disciplines. "Science," said Roger Guillemin, Nobel Prize winner in medicine in 1977, "is not a self-cleaning oven."

But above all, and what is much more serious, the editors of this journal were at once impressed by Sokal's smart title, and condescending toward him. "Imagine that! A physicist who has read Lacan and who cites Virilio; it must be expected that he will say a fair amount of silly things, poor guy!" This was the fatal error. The time for condescension, as for inferiority complexes, is past. We are no longer in high school. The disciplines are too intermingled, too uncertain for us not to treat one another as equals.

If the journal is just as bad as the article, one may ask, why make such a big deal out of the whole affair? Here is where the story becomes interesting. We are witnessing the last acrobatics of Cold War science, mobilized against religion, against the Reds, against the irrationality of the masses.

Civilization as a whole, as we can see with the whole "mad cow" affair, is in the process of swerving from a culture of Science with a capital S, toward a culture of research. Instead of an autonomous and detached science, whose absolute knowledge would allow it to extinguish the fire of political passions and of subjectivity, we are entering into a new epoch; political controversies are added to scientific controversies. Instead of defining a science by its detachment, we define it by its attachments. Instead of recognizing a science by the absolute exactitude of its knowledge, we recognize it by the quality of the collective experience it builds with others, the civil averages that it trails in its wake.

Obviously, this change leaves some researchers in the lurch: those who still believe in a science of secrecy, who would willingly stand as the impasse between the public life and political life of research. It is up to them to recycle themselves, and not necessarily up to others to go back to marching in formation. After all, relativism is an asset, not a weakness. It is the ability to change one's point of view, to establish relations between incommensurable worlds. This virtue has only one opposite: absolutism.

And yet, one may object, this affair would not have taken on such proportions had the jokesters not been from the Left. They have even been called feminists and radicals (in the English sense). What? It suffices to be from the Left for us to be sure of someone's intentions? The socialism of the socialists would suffice to purify their intentions and their actions? It is true that the Left is in a sense linked to a certain idea of science, this beautiful idea of emancipation and of progress that was useful for so long. But it is also linked to the idea, less and less attractive, of information which would, simply because it is true, be spared all the risks of political life, that is to say all the risks or the progressive shaping of a collective will to resist destiny.

If researchers should make an effort to move (after everyone else) from a culture of science to a culture of research, the Left should also make more of an effort to rediscover a taste for the communal exploration of the world which surrounds it. The two concepts are too closely tied to not crumble at the same time. In any case, we could no longer look to an old notion of the Left to save a more and more outdated concept of science.

One last point to conclude. How does sociology or social history of the sciences come to play in this big mess? For, at last, here is a discipline which finally proposes a realistic vision of scientific activity. It focuses on the researchers, the instruments, the laboratories, the practices, the concepts. It is interested in the innumerable ties between the objects of the sciences and those of culture and history. It understands, in a new way and from a new angle, the texts produced by the great scientists. It is learning to admire knowledgeable intelligence in a new way. It explores the astonishing ties woven between the cosmos and public life. How could we see any problems to defeat in these researchers who are attentive to the world of research, to its history, to its crises? We must get used to these other realities of life; facts are not born out of thin air!

Let's be serious. The sciences are too fragile to deprive themselves of the rare allies that are to be found in the domains of the humanities and the social sciences. All of us, researchers in exact and less exact sciences, politicians and users, we would do well to possess the most realistic vision possible of what the sciences can and cannot do. We are all in the same boat, afloat in the same controversies. The Cold War is over. Let's try not to parody another.

ALAN SOKAL
Why I Wrote My Parody
Le Monde (Paris), 31 January 1997

The debate over objectivity and relativism, science and postmodernism, which for the past eight months has been rocking American academic circles—particularly those of the political left—has apparently now arrived in France. And with what a bang! Following Denis Duclos (*Le Monde*, 3 January), we now have the eminent sociologist Bruno Latour offering his interpretation of the so-called "Sokal affair" (18 January). Alas, his article is both too audacious and too modest.

Latour is too audacious when he claims, without offering the slightest evidence, that "a very small number of theoretical physicists, deprived of their fat Cold War budgets, are searching for a new threat" by attacking postmodern intellectuals. Ah, would that things were so simple! But how then does one explain the numerous sociologists, historians, literary critics and philosophers who have joined in the critique of postmodern relativism? I don't pretend to guess other people's motivations, but I am more than happy to explain my own: I wrote my parody not to defend science against the supposed barbarian hordes of sociology, but to defend the American academic left against irrationalist tendencies which, though fashionable, are nevertheless suicidal.

Even more audaciously, Latour accuses me of leading a crusade against France, portrayed as "another Colombia, a country of dealers who produce hard drugs—derridium, lacanium—that American graduate students are unable to resist any more than they resist crack." It's a beautiful image, but what is the reality? Far from the nationalism conjured up by Latour, I am in fact a convinced internationalist (it's not by accident that I taught mathematics in Sandinista Nicaragua). What matters is never the origin of an idea, but its content; intellectual laziness and posturing deserve to be criticized, wherever they come from. To be sure, the postmodernist/poststructuralist gibberish that is now hegemonic in some sectors of the American academy is in part of French origin; but my compatriots have long ago given it a home-grown flavor that faithfully reflects our own national obsessions. The targets of my parody are thus eminent French and American intellectuals, without discrimination on the basis of national origin.

Latour is, by contrast, too modest when he tries to minimize the lessons of the "affair" by claiming that *Social Text* is "quite simply a bad journal." First of all, that's not true: *Social Text*'s latest issue, devoted to the crisis of academic labor, is well written and extremely interesting. But above all this reasoning evades the real scandal, which lies not in the mere fact that my article was published, but in its content. And here's the secret that makes the article so amusing, and which Latour would prefer to hide: the most hilarious parts of my article were not written by me! Rather, they are direct quotes from the Masters (whom I flatter with shameless praise). And among these Masters one indeed finds Derrida and Lacan, Aronowitz and Haraway—but one also finds our overly modest friend . . . Bruno Latour.

It must thus have taken Professor Latour a goodly dose of chutzpah to proclaim: "It's a clever joke, an astute intervention. It gives a good thrashing to people who deserve it. [But not to] researchers who, like me, work in Science Studies" and "have scientific training" (*Libération*, 3 December 1996). I won't bore the readers of *Le Monde* by making explicit the "scientific training" exhibited by Latour in his essay on Einstein's theory of relativity—a theory that he interprets as "a contribution to the sociology of delegation" (*Social Studies of Science* 18 [1988]: 3–44). The details will appear in a book that Jean Bricmont and I are currently writing, on "les impostures scientifiques des philosophes (post-)modernes" [The (post-)modern philosophers' fraudulent science]. Suffice it to say that some colleagues have suspected Latour's article to be, like mine, a parody.

In the remainder of his *Le Monde* article, Latour purports to address issues of the sociology of science, but his exposition is confused: he mixes up ontology and epistemology, and he attacks positions that no one would defend. "Instead of recognizing a science in the absolute exactitude of its knowledge, one recognizes it in the quality of collective experience that it sets up"—but who nowadays would claim that science provides "absolute exactitudes"? Newtonian mechanics describes the motions of the planets (and many other things) to an extraordinary precision—and this is an objective fact about the world—but Newtonian mechanics is nevertheless wrong. Quantum mechanics and general relativity are closer approximations to the truth—and this too is an objective fact—but these theories too, being mutually incompatible, will have to be superseded by an as-yet-nonexistent theory of quantum gravity. Every scientist knows perfectly well that our knowledge is always partial and subject to revision—which does not make it any less objective. In the same way, Latour reduces relativism to a banal "ability to change one's point of view," as if this were not a long-standing characteristic par excellence of the scientific attitude.

But Latour's main tactic, in presenting his vision of the sociology of science, is to empty it of all its content by retreating into platitudes that no one would question. The social history of science "proposes a realistic view of scientific activity" and "studies with excitement the innumerable links between the objects of science and those of culture"—who could fail to applaud? But where is the much-vaunted rupture with the traditional sociology of science à la Merton? This tactic hides everything that is radical, original and false in the "new" sociology of science: notably, its claim that one can (and should) explain the history of science without taking into account the truth or falsity of the scientific theories in question. Which means, if one is honest, that one must explain the acceptance of Newton's or Darwin's theories without ever invoking the empirical evidence supporting them. To pass from this attitude to the idea that there is no such thing as empirical evidence, or that such evidence is in any case unimportant, is a step that is too often taken (by Feyerabend, for example) and that leads straight to irrationalism.

To better appreciate the ambiguities in Latour's theses, let us reread the Third Rule of Method from his book *Science in Action*: "Since the settlement of a controversy is the cause of Nature's representation, not the consequence, we can never use the outcome—Nature—to explain how and why a controversy has been settled." We obviously have here a profound confusion between "Nature's representation" and "Nature," that is, between our theories about the world and the world itself. Depending on how one resolves the ambiguity (using twice "Nature's representation" or "Nature"), one can obtain the truism that our scientific theories are the result of a social process (as the so-called traditional sociology of science had demonstrated perfectly well); or the radically idealist claim that the external world is created by scientists' negotiations; or again the truism that the outcome of a scientific controversy cannot be explained solely by the state of the world; or else the radically constructivist claim that the state of the world can play no role when one explains how and why a controversy has been settled.

However, the problems of the philosophy of science, and of the human sciences quite generally, are too important to be treated with such sloppiness. On the contrary, they require a great intellectual rigor. The "hard" and "soft" sciences are indeed in the same boat. Flirting with relativism and irrationalism won't lead us anywhere.

5

Longer Essays

ELLEN WILLIS

My Sokaled Life; Or, Revenge of the Nerds

Village Voice, 25 June 1996

It felt extremely odd to pick up *The New York Times* on a recent Saturday morning and see a picture of *Social Text* [*ST*] on page one—as if a relative's domestic scandal had popped up in the headlines. To be sure, the story was a juicy one. A physicist dupes a prestigious cultural-studies journal, passing off as a serious article a parody of high-theoryspeak that questions the reality of the external world. He gets it published in the journal's special issue on the "Science Wars" between critics and defenders of scientific culture, then exposes the hoax in academia's gadfly review, *Lingua Franca*. But front-page news, even on Saturday?

I would in any case have taken more than a passing interest in the incident, since I've written for *Social Text*, the editor of the "Science Wars" issue is an NYU colleague and friend, and the man I live with is a founder of the journal (though he's no longer a working editor, I feel constrained to add in the no doubt futile hope of deflecting further prurient inquiries on the subject). But this startling bit of publicity set my cultural antennae to twitching fiercely.

The following week the *Times* ran a long op-ed by Stanley Fish, the executive director of *ST*'s publisher, Duke University Press, defending the journal with a dubious analogy between science and baseball and making the humorless suggestion that Alan Sokal, the author of the parody, had threatened the foundations of academic trust. (Perhaps Fish would have had Abbie Hoffman charged with littering for throwing dollar bills on the floor of the New York Stock Exchange.) Then a Week in Review piece by Edward Rothstein, playing a crass Samuel Johnson to *ST*'s Bishop Berkeley, approvingly cites Sokal's inviting "anybody who feels that physical laws are mere social constructs to defy them by leaping from his 21st-story window." Roger Kimball, who himself had been totally fooled by Sokal's parody and blasted it at length in an anti–*Social Text* polemic in *The New Criterion*, didn't miss a beat; he hoped in *The Wall Street Journal* that "the controversy . . . may finally convince college deans and presidents, parents and alumni, legislators and trustees, to take a hard look at the politicized nonsense they have been conned into subsidizing."

Leftist commentators expressed concern that their own politics had been unfairly tainted by the antics of pomo pretenders; they noted that Sokal is a professed leftist and feminist who taught math in Sandinista Nicaragua (as Sokal himself had made a point of mentioning in his *Lingua Franca* apologia). In the words of West Coast lefty Barbara Epstein (quoted in *In These Times*, which identified her as "a Sokal collaborator"), "The project is not really so much to defend science, it's to defend the left . . . from the faux-left." Feminist historian Ruth Rosen took up this theme in the *Los Angeles Times*, attacking the "hypocrisy" of "so-called cultural revolutionaries. They claim to be democratizing thought, but they purposely write in tongues for an initiated elite. . . . They focus obsessively on the linguistic and social construction of human consciousness, not on the hard reality of people's lives" [pt. 3, "A Physics Prof Drops a Bomb on the Faux Left"]. (Rosen also attested to having helped Sokal with his spoof.) In *The Nation*, Katha Pollitt, expressing similar sentiments, modestly referred to Sokal's teaching stint as "more than I ever did" for the left [pt. 3, "Pomolotov Cocktail"]. Meanwhile, with appropriate postmodern irony, copies of *Social Text* were disappearing from the racks at an unprecedented rate.

Like all effective media events, the Sokal hoax concentrates in one resonant symbol a stew of public anxieties, in this case about higher education. With their campaigns against "political correctness," multicultural contamination of the literary canon, revisionist views of Columbus, and MLA papers about masturbation in Emily Dickinson's poetry, conservatives have done a good job of fomenting hostility toward the professoriat. As they (accurately) see it, the university is an irritating obstacle to the cultural counterrevolution. Protected by tenure, too many academics remain stubbornly liberal and attached to the ideal (if not always the reality) of intellectual independence. Their sense of entitlement to relatively autonomous and human working conditions is an offense to the prevailing corporate regime of tight control from the top, longer and longer hours, slash-and-burn layoffs. And so, even as the right's rhetoric invokes the noble heritage of the liberal arts and sciences against "politicized nonesense," its professor-bashing agenda incites and exploits the anti-intellectual currents endemic to American culture.

Kimball's call for a "hard look" is disingenuous: the attack on the perquisites of the academy is already far advanced. State governments are cutting higher-education budgets, private as well as public universities have been hit by reduced federal support for student aid, programs are being consolidated and eliminated in the name of "efficiency." As legislators and administrators grouse about insufficiently onerous faculty workloads and question the value of tenure, the issue is fast becoming moot. Over the long term, university employment patterns are following the national trend; tenure-track appointments are dwindling, while the ranks of poorly paid, temporary, part-time adjunct professors steadily expand.

Never mind. We can now look forward to months of having the Sokal affair trotted out as definitive proof that radical criticism of science, and indeed the entire enterprise of cultural studies, boils down to mindless, fraudulent gibberish. This is caricature as broad as Sokal's article, if considerably less witty. Those who actually read *Social Text*'s "Science Wars" issue will find it mostly devoted to analyzing—in English, not poststructuralese—how the questions scientists ask, the research they choose to pursue, the ways they collect and interpret their data, and the technological applications of their work both reflect and shape certain social and political ends. Oddly, a couple of the more withering post-Sokal commentaries dismiss such analyses as "commonplaces" (Rothstein) and "banalities" (George Will, in the *Washington Post*). If the central assumptions of *ST*'s articles are as commonplace and banal as all that, what's the fight about?

As for the champions of the "true left" (Sokal included), I sense in their glee at *ST*'s blunder a familiar uneasiness with the idea that thinking and writing, especially about culture, are legitimate and necessary aspects of politics: real leftists aren't effete intellectuals, they soldier for the people in Nicaragua. Even Pollitt, who knows better, falls into this self-deprecating trap, though in truth—if it's a democratic left you're interested in—any random paragraph of her numerous columns attacking family values has done more to advance the cause than all the teachers in Nicaragua, Cuba, and name-your-revolutionary-dictatorship combined.

This isn't to suggest that the academic left in general, and *Social Text* in particular, bear no responsibility for their troubles. The anti-p.c. campaign has been motivated less by concern for free speech than by the lust to discredit criticism of racist and sexist power relations, but it hits a cultural nerve because an obnoxious strain of repressive left-wing orthodoxy does in fact exist. In similar fashion, conservative attacks on postmodernism and poststructuralism aim to discredit all criticism of conventional academic disciplines and received ideas about what counts as truth and beauty. Yet the ridicule would have far less effect if it didn't find so many deserving targets: adherents of identity politics for whom the worth or interest of an idea depends entirely on its source rather than its content; dogmatic social constructionists who, while not literally denying the existence of the physical or biological world, deny it any active role in shaping human culture; pop-culture critics who smother the vitality of their subject in ponderous theoretical abstractions and barbarous prose.

ST's editors were fooled in part because, ironically, they were excessively respectful of Sokal's standpoint as a physicist; in part because, whatever their own views, they belong to an intellectual community in which certain linguistic tics and brands of glib relativism are such a taken-for-granted part of the conversation that they are barely noticed, let alone criticized. Indeed, the "Science Wars" package contains one entirely serious example of social constructionism run amok—feminist biologist Ruth Hubbard's claim that "the Western assumption" that there are two sexes is belied by the estimated "1 or 2 per cent of children born with mixed or ambiguous sex characteristics" and needs to be rethought.

Language—specifically, the professional patois that so many academic cultural leftists have assembled from various strands of French theory—is not an incidental part of this debate; it's a central issue, and a tricky one. While other forms of jargon—like the functionalist pig Latin favored by mainstream sociologists and educational bureaucrats—attract their share of sneering, pomo lingo inspires an uncommonly intense hatred, in large part because its practitioners have tended to present it as the key to higher political consciousness. Some argue that distaste for its obscurity is akin to a philistine rejection of any art form other than social realism, or that clarity and coherence are inherently conservative because only by disrupting the smooth flow of language can you subvert the cultural assumptions that govern it.

I don't have much patience with these self-flattering contentions. Yes, philosophers, scientists, and artists may need to invent new languages to express new ideas and perceptions. But the legions of academics who write in Derridean, Foucaultian, and related dialects are merely appropriating other people's language. In the process they all too often reduce it to cliché and use it as shorthand (or a substitute) for ideas that could be articulated perfectly well in ordinary English—a supple and inventive language quite capable of subverting itself. It's hard to write well, in any language. Professors are not generally required to do this or rewarded for doing it, so most don't. When I was an editor at *VLS* [*Voice Literary Supplement*] in the mid '80s, much of my work involved prodding academics to translate their writing, my main expedient being simply to ask the writer, "What do you mean by this?" Most writers were able to say what they meant; when they weren't, it was because their hermetic verbiage had been covering up muddled thought.

Still, a lot of the complaining about language gives off whiffs of bad faith. The antipathy toward cultural studies is really about its challenge to cultural authority—its democratic impulse; its irreverence toward high cultural canons of truth and transcendence; its critique of modernism; its insistence on the aesthetic and human value of mass art; its blurring of boundaries between the art object and the world outside the frame.

These ideas and attitudes were anathema to cultural conservatives of both the right and the left long before they were associated with poststructuralism. They first gained public currency in the '60s, when they were put forward (in the U.S. at least) not by academics but by journalists. By far their most influential exponent was Tom Wolfe, a passionate devotee of realism as literary technique and reportorial stance. Wolfe was also a political conservative (unlike poor Leonard Bernstein, pomo leftists have so far been spared his attention). But even those of us who linked the emerging cultural explosion with political radicalism, and covered it all as participant-observers, were pretty much untrammeled by theory, French or otherwise. If anything, we were antiacademic (though we did have intense discussions about what would now be called the social construction of aesthetics; I remember arguing with Bob Christgau that the New York skyline certainly was more intrinsically beautiful then the vista of L.A.'s freeways). In any case, our livelihood depended on writing clearly. This did not deter most literary intellectuals from pronouncing us barbarians. The pomo connection merely gives them a chance to argue that the barbarians can't write.

But "true left" populist indignation at "exclusive" language also has its pitfalls. For one thing, if genuine democratic commitment is equated with speaking to a mass audience, few leftist intellectuals of any stripe can qualify. Publications like the *Voice, The Nation, Lingua Franca, In These Times*—the *L.A. Times*, for that matter—are aimed at an educated middle-class elite. In a society where the real mass medium is television, writing inherently limits one's audience, and writing serious social commentary, let alone social theory, limits it even further.

This is partly a question of access, but it also has to do with language that reflects the vocabulary, store of knowledge, and frame of reference of a relatively privileged minority. While in principle it may be possible to leap these barriers, in practice it's extremely difficult. Which means the underlying logic of intellectual populism is that cultural analysis is a waste of time, that the construction of consciousness has nothing to do with "hard reality." Capitalism is screwing people! What goes up must come down! What more do we need to know? Compared to this mentality, linguistic posturing is a minor nuisance. The most dangerous weakness of the American left is its pervasive substitution of moral indignation for ideas.

The other problem with the populist argument is that it takes no account of the messy, contradictory ways our intellectual culture actually works.

Rarefied academic writing can nonetheless convey useful ideas about democratizing knowledge, just as a man who's a pig in his personal life can have useful ideas about women's rights. Myself, I'll take useful ideas wherever I can find them, even if it means wading through passages that, if I were the writer's editor, would never have seen print. And ideas that matter, for better or worse, have a way of spreading, as they get picked up, translated, and recycled for different audiences up and down the media food chain.

Cultural criticism written by academics influences writers for journals of opinion, who in turn feed the heads of *New York Times* writers and commentators on PBS; eventually every aspect of the culture war finds its way into *USA Today*, "Roseanne," "ER," and the Movie of the Week. The work of academic theorists has also been known to influence political activists (Herbert Marcuse, who wasn't called the father of the new left for nothing, wasn't exactly an elegant English stylist). At the same time, academics are subject to the influence of popular media and social movements. There really is no ivory tower anymore. Could there be better proof of this than the Sokal flap itself?

MICHAEL BÉRUBÉ AND ALAN SOKAL

The Sokal Hoax

University of Chicago Free Press, August 1996

Earlier this summer, Alan Sokal revealed in *Lingua Franca* that his essay in the current "Science Wars" issues of the trendy journal *Social Text* was a parody of postmodern thought. The widely debated hoax led to this exchange between Sokal and Michael Bérubé on a small email list, printed here for the first time. Bérubé teaches English at the University of Illinois at Urbana-Champaign

Michael Bérubé has a question

Date: Sun, 2 June 1996 23:49:25 -0500
From: Michael Bérubé
To: Alan Sokal
Subject: Re: *Social Text*

OK, I've now had a number of messages about you and your *Social Text* [ST] scam forwarded to me, and I've had a number of exchanges with Norman Levitt himself, who's been inexplicably more civil in writing to me than in writing anything to anybody else in the world, it seems. But perhaps that's because I haven't yet done anything to piss off Mr. Levitt personally—and his responses do tend to focus obsessively on personal distastes (not liking Andrew Ross's demeanor, Kate Hayles's analogies, George Levine's ambivalences, etc.). Anyway, I wanted to ask you a few questions myself, and since this conversation seems to be widening across the Internet, I've copied it to the same people Levitt copied it to. You yourself, Professor Sokal, do seem interested in having a serious exchange about the intellectual integrity and purpose of science studies—and if that's so, then you may want to think twice about having your cause trumpeted by folks like Levitt and Gross, who seem to me to have that characteristic academic habit of being so obstreperous and self-righteous (only when confronting people they disagree with and dislike, of course) that they wind up sounding wrong even when they're right—to all but the already-converted. I admit that we have plenty of such people in the humanities and social sciences; many of my dearest colleagues are often obstreperous and self-righteous (though only when confronting people they disagree with and dislike). But when the issue is the restoration of reason to academic disciplines awash in superstition, illiteracy, and theoretical faddishness (as L & G claim), perhaps a higher standard of intellectual exchange is warranted.

Enough preamble. Here are my questions.

First, a tip of the hat. Whatever your motives and means, you did indeed manage to hoodwink a bunch of people I respect, and you did demonstrate, to whatever end, that it's worth asking what's going on in "science studies" if a journal like *Social Text* would publish your essay. I think the *ST* editors are quite right to reply that they're not a refereed journal and are not beholden to the standard of peer review by which such journals are supposed to operate, but then again, I also think your narrower point holds: the *ST* editors could easily have sent the essay to a physicist—not for "peer review," but simply to ask whether the piece was the work of a crank. In fact, I think it's pretty much beyond argument that *ST should* have gotten a quick read from a physicist (or at least someone literate in "quantum relativity," ahem), not only because this would have provided *ST* with a little expert testimony the journal needed in a case like this, but also because, politically speaking, had the journal done so the shoe would have been on the other foot: Andrew, Stanley et al. could have gone to *Lingua Franca* with the thing and said, "look what one of those Levitt-Gross-besotted science guys tried to do—and see how it calls into question all those science guys who are trying to cast aspersions on science studies without understanding what it is we do." With my eagle-eye hindsight, I can see that because *ST* didn't do such a thing, the ball's clearly in their court. And, of course, as a fellow self-professed leftist and feminist, I wish they *had* done such a thing.

But now to those questions. As I said, your narrower point is valid: *ST* should clearly have sent the essay to someone outside their own area(s) of expertise, so you've shown, at minimum, that the *ST* editorial collective was willing to publish an essay outside their area(s) of expertise. But does this show that all of science studies, by association, is illegitimate, being conducted by scientific illiterates who don't know their Schwarzchild radius from the Lorenz transformation? Norm Levitt says yes; you, so far, have said no. You claim you have every kind of respect for science studies well done, and every kind of contempt for science studies badly done. On that count, we're at one. What exactly, then, do you think you have proven by having your essay published?

Let me complicate that question slightly. Do you agree that your essay was accepted in part because you are a physicist? Again, I'm not saying that *ST* should have published it on those grounds; what I'm saying is this. It's entirely plausible that the *ST* collective might have (collectively) said, "We don't know about this. It could be something brilliant, or a farrago of nonsense. But jeez, it's from a physicist, so let's give the guy the benefit of the doubt. Maybe there's something to it." According to Andrew Ross's press release, you and Andrew had had more than one exchange about the essay before publication. Is this true? If so, you should understand that it significantly vitiates your claim that *ST* took your essay blind, in an act of sheer disciplinary arrogance and illiteracy (or innumeracy). Personally, I know that if I'd had a number of contacts with an author who assured me that he eagerly sought publication of his work, I would at least assume that the author's work was in earnest. That doesn't mean *ST* shouldn't have had the thing vetted by a scientist—but it *does* mean, paradoxically, that you purchased your authority to speak partly by *being* a scientist. The folks at *ST* assumed, in good faith, that you knew what you were talking about even when you were deliberately pulling a fast one. If I were you, I'd feel pretty sheepish about that. But if I were me, I'd say that this aspect of the hoax speaks volumes about the cultural authority of scientists: precisely the thing you think is challenged by "science studies" may be the thing that got you published in the first place.

Next question. Do you really think your hoax calls into question the status of evidence in nonscientific fields? It's worth noting here that the stakes are a good deal higher on this question than on the question of whether *ST* should or shouldn't have sought an external reader. You realize, of course, as a self-professed leftist and feminist, that your hoax is indeed being used as "evidence" (interestingly enough) that contemporary leftist/feminist work in the humanities and social sciences is a "freak show" (to quote Roger Kimball, a fellow combatant in the culture wars and one of the recipients of this here missive). And if it is true, as the papers have claimed, that you regard your hoax as evidence that the humanities don't give a shit about evidence, then I have a proposition or two for you:

The problem of the twentieth century is the problem of the color line; the history of all previously existing society is the history of class struggle; gender is the basis of all other oppressions; and last but not least, one of the vicissitudes an instinctual impulse may undergo is to meet with resistances the aim of which is to make the impulse inoperative; under certain conditions—the impulse then passes into the state of *repression*.

My question is this: are any of these things *true*?

If so, where is the "evidence" for them? The last bit's from Freud, of course, and the status of evidence in psychoanalysis remains a topic of some dispute, as I understand. But the first three are pretty bald declarations as well, and as far as I'm concerned, none of them are "true" in the sense that Andrew Wiles's proof of Fermat's Last Theorem is true. But they *are* invitations to see the world in a new way: they are manifesto-like declarations meant to spin your head around and call your attention to a realm of human deliberation overlooked by the dominant realms of human deliberation. Like the world's great poetry, they take the tops of our heads off; they offer imaginary gardens with real toads. And in the humanities, to our shame, we give these kinds of statements a great deal of leeway. We're not that concerned with whether they're true. We're more concerned with whether they have interesting, productive, illuminating, destructive, or earth-shattering results, and we'll gauge those results by the evidence of the *effects* of those claims rather than by their pre-existing evidentiary basis. (Marx was quite wrong to read every social conflict as an expression of class warfare, after all, and yet it still might make sense to read the debate over CEO compensation or the capital gains tax in this light.)

Last question. You say you believe in the fact/value distinction, and so do I—with this caveat: I suggest that the basis of the distinction is about as approachable as a Schwarzchild radius. Let me put the question this way: I agree with John Searle that there's a realm of "social reality," which we can plausibly talk about as "constructed," and a realm of "brute fact" in which our "constructions" may affect our understanding of things but not the existence of the things themselves (let's take Neptune here and not something biological like fruit flies, who demonstrably *are* affected by our understanding of them). Obviously, the fact/value distinction derives from (and perhaps even corresponds to) Searle's distinction between brute fact and social reality: facts for the former and values for the latter. In which case my question to you, as a fellow human, is this: is the distinction between "brute fact" and "social reality" *itself* a brute fact or a social reality? Is the distinction drawn cleanly by nature, demarcating the facts from the values, nonhuman matter from human affairs, or has the distinction itself been drawn differently in different human times and places?

This is not a trick question: you can still believe in "brute fact" (including the existence of Neptune and the inadvisability of jumping out your 21st-story window) while admitting that the fact/value distinction is fungible. But then if you admit that the fact/value distinction is fungible, then you're also admitting that our (human) understanding of nonhuman phenomena *is* dependent, in a strong sense, on the likelihood that the distinction between brute fact and social reality is itself a social reality rather than a brute fact.

Does this strike you as a reasonable proposition, or as just hairsplitting twaddle? I await your answer eagerly, though I know you're a busy man these days.

Yours sincerely, Michael Bérubé

Alan Sokal responds

Date: Mon, 3 Jun 1996 20:54:41 -0400
From: Alan Sokal
To: Michael Bérubé
Subject: response to your questions about the *Social Text* affair

Dear Prof. Bérubé, Many thanks for your letter. You're right that I'm a little overwhelmed these days: in addition to receiving about 50 e-mails per day concerning the *Social Text* affair, I just got back from a conference in Germany concerning REAL physics (the problem of "asymptotic freedom" in elementary-particle physics). But let me try to answer your questions at least briefly. First, I want to say that I don't endorse the tone of Norm Levitt's comments on Fuller's piece. I'm all in favor of bluntness, but there's nothing to be gained by rudeness. Regarding *Social Text* not being "peer reviewed," I endorse Katha Pollitt's comment (in *The Nation*, June 10): maybe it should be. Imagine the reverse situation: I, who used to serve on the editorial board of the *Journal of Statistical Physics*, receive an article for that journal which analyzes Boltzmann's theories on irreversibility in statistical mechanics and the "heat death of the universe," and relates these theories to the cultural environment of fin-de-siècle Vienna. What would I do? Well, first, I'd send the article to a physicist specializing in non-equilibrium statistical mechanics, for comments on the underlying physics. But I would *ALSO* send the article simultaneously to a historian (or better yet, historian of science) expert on the cultural environment of fin-de-siècle Vienna, for comments on this aspect of the article. And I would be derelict in my intellectual duty if I did not do this. Now, perhaps *Social Text*'s intellectual standards are lower than those of the *Journal of Statistical Physics*; but, if so, I don't see why the editors should be proud of this fact. Nor does it seem to me intrinsic in the nature of the social sciences and humanities that the intellectual standards should be lower. (I am *not* an "arrogant scientist" in this regard.)

I assume your first question is rhetorical, because the obvious answer is: of course not. The acceptance of my article by *Social Text* can show, at most, something about the intellectual standards at *one* trendy cultural-studies journal. Much more interesting than the scandal provoked by my article's *acceptance* is, I think, the scandal that ought to be provoked by its *content*. (Unfortunately, there hasn't been much discussion of the article's content, either in the press or in the Internet discussions; perhaps that's because it's not easy to get hold of a copy.) My essay, aside from being (if I may quote Katha Pollitt's flattery) "a hilarious compilation of pomo gibberish," is also an annotated bibliography of charlatanism and nonsense by dozens of prominent French and American intellectuals. This goes well beyond the narrow category of "postmodernism," and includes some of the most fashionable thinkers in "science studies," literary criticism, and cultural studies. The organizing principle of my article is to quote (or in some cases cite without quotation, in which case you'll have to go to the library and look up the original) the silliest things about mathematics and physics (and the philosophy of mathematics and physics) said by the most prominent academics in the various overlapping fields that I am parodying—and then to praise them. (Don't forget to read the endnotes! Some of the best stuff is in there.) Does this show that "ALL of science studies is illegitimate"? Again, the answer is: of course not. The sins can be attributed only to the authors quoted, or to others purveying similar ideas. But unfortunately the authors quoted are among the most prominent in the field. For example, nearly all of the most prominent French poststructuralists (Deleuze, Guattari, Derrida, Lacan, Lyotard, Serres, Irigaray, Virilio) are exhibited in my article spewing forth utter nonsense about mathematics and physics (all the while pretending to be knowledgeable). But perhaps no one in science studies takes these people seriously, anyway. OK—then take a look at what Bruno Latour says about relativity; what Sandra Harding says about mathematical conceptions of infinity; what David Bloor and Steve Woolgar say about logic and mathematics; and what Stanley Aronowitz says about quantum mechanics. Steve Fuller (in his otherwise reasonable response to Norm Levitt, this morning) says that "they pass a minimal threshold of competence in what they do." Really?

Yes—my guess (and it's only a guess, since I'm not privy to the internal discussions of the *ST* editors) is that they accepted it, even though they couldn't make head or tail of it, because it came from a leftist physicist and attacked Gross + Levitt. Acting not as intellectuals seeking the truth, but as self-appointed generals in the "Science Wars," they apparently leapt at the chance to get a "real" working scientist on their "side." Of course, I think that the military metaphor is a serious mistake. Ross and Aronowitz are not my enemies; nor should Gross + Levitt be the left's enemies. I agree with your point that the hoax speaks volumes about the cultural authority of scientists, which is accepted (when it suits their political and polemical goals) even by those who claim to be most skeptical of it. I myself pointed out this irony in my *Lingua Franca* article: Or are they more deferent to the so-called "cultural authority of technoscience" than they would care to admit?

Quite a bit of the chronology in the *Social Text* editors' response is at variance with the documentary record (e-mail and regular mail between Ross and myself, which I've saved). But I don't want to beat a dead horse, because as I said I think the more important scandal is to be found in the *content* of my article. Briefly: Ross and I had quite a few exchanges by e-mail; I repeatedly requested substantive comments, criticisms and suggestions from the reviewers concerning both the scientific parts (using the excuse of "is my exposition understandable to non-scientists?", in order to give the reviewers a face-saving way to make criticisms of things they don't understand) and the political parts. I got *no* substantive comments whatsoever. The only changes they requested were stylistic, viz., reducing the length by half (to fit the short-piece norm of the "Science Wars" issue) by deleting most of the footnotes. But they didn't have *any* comment on the *substance* of the text or footnotes.

Of course I don't think any such thing about "the humanities" as a whole! Which newspapers said that?? If they did, I should protest the misquotation.

I don't follow. I confess that I haven't read Searle's book, but I assume "social reality" refers to humans' beliefs about various things. These beliefs are the proper subject of empirical statements, and thus constitute facts (of sociology) in their own right. What does this have to do with the fact/value distinction ("is" versus "ought")? OK, I hope that answers your questions (except for the last one, which I didn't understand).

Best wishes, Alan Sokal

Michael Bérubé replies

Date: Tue, 4 Jun 1996 01:12:39 -0500
From: Michael Bérubé
To: Alan Sokal
Subject: Re: response to your questions about the *Social Text* affair

Dear Prof. Sokal, Many thanks for the alacrity—and, more important, the substance—of your reply. I get overloaded when I have more than 5 e-mails waiting for me, so I do appreciate what it means that you responded to my e-missive so quickly and thoughtfully.

Point granted. Really, my only caveat with regard to your method (that is, in submitting a parody rather than a "serious" questioning of the sociology of science) is that it brought up a host of red-herring issues—just the kind that are likely to be garbled up in translation to the papers. E.g., I share your disappointment with the Janny Scott article in the *Times*, partly because I'm familiar with her work and know full well she can do better than to feign alarm that bizarre words like "epistemology" appeared in your essay. (BTW, the miscue about "evidence in the humanities" was actually the work of the otherwise-solid *Chronicle of Higher Ed*, in which you appear in the "Hot Type" section as the scourge of evidence-less humanists.)

Exactly my point (and I read your essay, notes and all, even though I did so armed with the knowledge that it was a joke—thanks to Norman Levitt, who sent me advance notice). I realize that you tried to bring up this issue in your *LF* essay. But this is precisely the kind of thing that gets buried when the hoax becomes national news. No one at the *Washington Post* cares about the citations you puncture by citing them approvingly; that's a great parodic tactic, no doubt, but it just doesn't play in Peoria—or at the *Post*. What they care about is that you "demonstrated" that we incomprehensible intellectuals are charlatans and mountebanks. But by the Janny Scott "epistemology" standard of intelligibility, I could send Kenneth Ribet's and Brian Hayes' wonderful spring 1994 *American Scientist* essay, explaining Wiles and Fermat to interested laypersons, to the *Post* or the *Times*, and then let them have a field day with that, too.

Part of the moral of this, for me, is how much we're willing to overlook when we come across something that seems to prove us right. That's true not only of *ST*'s reading of your essay but of Levitt's reading of your hoax: for Levitt, the episode bears out everything he says in *Higher Superstition*—but only if you allow for logical missteps like false inference, guilt by association, and the genetic fallacy. Your conclusion is that the hoax shows that something's wrong with *ST*'s editorial procedure; perhaps even some *ST* editors might agree. Levitt's conclusion is that the hoax shows that the humanities are run by charlatans and mountebanks, and that involved false inference, guilt by association, and—you get the idea. But Levitt's willing to overlook a few logical missteps because your hoax seems so dramatically to prove him right, just as the *ST* editors were willing to overlook a whole mess of laughers because, as you say, your essay seemed to enlist a real-live working scientist on their "side." So in the end, to quote my friend Richard Powers, the *Social Text* affair winds up looking like the humanist's version of cold fusion.

There's still too much empiricism for me, frankly. The statement "the history of all hitherto existing society is the history of class struggles" is simply not the same kind of statement as "something is perturbing the orbit of Uranus." The latter statement can be checked—even when it's about something as arcane as the perihelion advance of Mercury (to take an example from 20th century theories of gravity instead of nineteenth century searches for "missing" planets).

What I meant was this: Searle's brute fact/social reality distinction is one of the more sophisticated versions of the fact/value distinction in our time. What Searle's doing is trying to give an account of how it is that twenty-dollar bills are "really" twenty-dollar bills in a social-realist sense), whereas Neptune exists and perturbs Uranus' orbit despite what you and I say about it (and is thus objectively there in a scientific sense). The difference, of course, is that Neptune is Neptune regardless of human social deliberation, whereas money is money only because of human social deliberation. Obvious enough. Here's the next thing: the "strict constructionists," insofar as they're postmodernist or poststructuralist versions of nineteenth-century idealists and eighteenth-century skeptics, would have it that Neptune "exists," in a sense, only insofar as it is "socially constructed" as Neptune. Before 1846, in other words, it may have been there—sure seems that way—but no human knew about it, so for humans it didn't exist. Here, you'd be right to object that the "strict social constructionist" is working with an impoverished (or deliberately parochial) sense of what it means to exist.

Let's say we agree that there's a distinction between facts and values, is and ought, and that it's hard to derive the one from the other. Which, then, has "priority" over the other, and what might "priority" mean? If we say that values determine facts—or, more precisely, that "social realities" like twenty-dollar bills are the basis from which we understand things like Neptune—we sound like we're courting lunacy: I think here of the Monty Python skit of the housing project built by a magician, consisting of buildings that stay up only because their tenants believe in them. Obviously, then, physical facts like Neptune and buildings don't depend on human belief for their existence, even though the latter certainly depend on human beliefs for their construction (in a literal sense). So there must be a strong, perhaps unassailable, sense in which physical facts precede human deliberation about facts.

STEVEN WEINBERG

Sokal's Hoax, and Selected Responses

New York Review of Books, 8 August 1996

Like many other scientists, I was amused by news of the prank played by the NYU mathematical physicist Alan Sokal. Late in 1994 he submitted a sham article to the cultural studies journal *Social Text*, in which he reviewed some current topics in physics and mathematics, and with tongue in cheek drew various cultural, philosophical and political morals that he felt would appeal to fashionable academic commentators on science who question the claims of science to objectivity.

The editors of *Social Text* did not detect that Sokal's article was a hoax, and they published it in the journal's Spring/Summer 1996 issue.[1] The hoax was revealed by Sokal in an article for another journal, *Lingua Franca*;[2] in which he explained that his *Social Text* article had been "liberally salted with nonsense," and in his opinion was accepted only because "(a) it sounded good and (b) it flattered the editors' ideological preconceptions." Newspapers and newsmagazines throughout the U.S. and Britain carried the story. Sokal's hoax may join the small company of legendary academic hoaxes, along with the pseudo-fossils of Piltdown man planted by Charles Dawson and the pseudo-Celtic epic *Ossian* written by James Macpherson. The difference is that Sokal's hoax served a public purpose, to attract attention to what Sokal saw as a decline of standards of rigor in the academic community, and for that reason it was unmasked immediately by the author himself.

The targets of Sokal's satire occupy a broad intellectual range. There are those "postmoderns" in the humanities who like to surf through avant-garde fields like quantum mechanics or chaos theory to dress up their own arguments about the fragmentary and random nature of experience. There are those sociologists, historians, and philosophers who see the laws of nature as social constructions. There are cultural critics who find the taint of sexism, racism, colonialism, militarism, or capitalism not only in the practice of scientific research but even in its conclusions. Sokal did not satirize creationists or other religious enthusiasts who in many parts of the world are the most dangerous adversaries of science,[3] but his targets were spread widely enough, and he was attacked or praised from all sides.

Entertaining as this episode was, from press reports I could not immediately judge what it proved. Suppose that, with tongue in cheek, an economist working for a labor union submitted an article to the *National Review*, giving what the author thought were false economic arguments against an increase in the statutory minimum wage. What would it prove if the article were accepted for publication? The economic arguments might still be cogent, even though the author did not believe in them.

I thought at first that Sokal's article in *Social Text* was intended to be an imitation of academic babble, which any editor should have recognized as such. But in reading the article I found that this is not the case. The article expresses views that I find surreal, but with a few exceptions Sokal at least makes it pretty clear what these views are. The article's title, "Transgressing the Boundaries: Toward a Transformative Hermeneutics of Quantum Gravity," is more obscure than almost anything in his text. (A physicist friend of mine once said that in facing death, he drew some consolation from the reflection that he would never again have to look up the word "hermeneutics" in the dictionary.) I got the impression that Sokal finds it difficult to write unclearly.

Where the article does degenerate into babble, it is not in what Sokal himself has written, but in the writings of the genuine postmodern cultural critics quoted by Sokal. Here, for instance, is a quote that Sokal takes from the oracle of deconstructionism, Jacques Derrida:

> The Einsteinian constant is not a constant, is not a center. It is the very concept of variability—it is, finally, the concept of the game. In other words, it is not the concept of *something*—of a center starting from which an observer could master the field—but the very concept of the game. [Pt. 1, sec. 2]

I have no idea what this is intended to mean.

I suppose that it might be argued that articles in physics journals are also incomprehensible to the uninitiated. But physicists are forced to use a technical language, the language of mathematics. Within this limitation, we try to be clear, and when we fail we do not expect our readers to confuse obscurity with profundity. It never was true that only a dozen people could understand Einstein's papers on general relativity, but if it had been true, it would have been a failure of Einstein's, not a mark of his brilliance. The papers of Edward Witten of the Institute for Advanced Study at Princeton, which are today consistently among the most significant in the promising field of string theory, are notably easier for a physicist to read than most other work in string theory. In contrast, Derrida and other postmoderns do not seem to be saying anything that requires a special technical language, and they do not seem to be trying very hard to be clear. But those who admire such writings presumably would not have been embarrassed by Sokal's quotations from them.

Part of Sokal's hoax was in his description of developments in physics. Much of his account was quite accurate, but it was heavily adulterated with howlers, most of which would have been detected by any undergraduate physics major. One of his running jokes had to do with the word "linear." This word has a precise mathematical meaning, arising from the fact that certain mathematical relationships are represented graphically by a straight line.[4] But for some postmodern intellectuals, "linear" has come to mean unimaginative and old-fashioned, while "nonlinear" is understood to be somehow perceptive and avant-garde. In arguing for the cultural importance of the quantum theory of gravitation, Sokal refers to the gravitational field in this theory as "a noncommuting (and hence nonlinear) operator." Here "hence" is ridiculous; "noncommuting"[5] does not imply "nonlinear," and in fact quantum mechanics deals with things that are both noncommuting and linear.

Sokal also writes that "Einstein's equations [in the general theory of relativity] are highly nonlinear, which is why traditionally trained mathematicians find them so difficult to solve." The joke is in the words "traditionally trained;" Einstein's equations are nonlinear, and this does make them hard to solve, but they are hard for anyone to solve, especially someone who is not traditionally trained. Continuing with general relativity, Sokal correctly remarks that its description of curved space-time allows arbitrary changes in the space-time coordinates that we use to describe nature. But then he solemnly pronounces that "the π of Euclid and the G of Newton, formerly thought to be constant and universal, are now perceived in their ineluctable historicity" [pt. 1, sec. 2]. This is absurd—the meaning of a mathematically defined quantity like pi cannot be affected by discoveries in physics, and in any case both pi and G continue to appear as universal constants in the equations of general relativity.

In a different vein, Sokal pretends to give serious consideration to a crackpot fantasy known as the "morphogenetic field." He refers to complex number theory as a "new and still quite speculative branch of mathematical physics," while in fact it is nineteenth century mathematics and has been as well established as anything ever is. He even complains (echoing the sociologist Stanley Aronowitz) that all of the graduate students in solid-state physics will be able to get jobs in that field, which will be news to many of them.

Sokal's revelation of his intentional howlers drew the angry response that he had abused the trust of the editors of *Social Text* in his credentials as a physicist, a complaint made by both sociologist Steve Fuller and English professor Stanley Fish.[6] (Fish is the executive director of Duke University Press, which publishes *Social Text*, and is reputed to be the model for Morris Zapp, the master of the academia game in David Lodge's comic novels.) The editors of *Social Text* also offered the excuse that it is not a refereed journal, but a journal of opinion.[7] Maybe under these circumstances Sokal was naughty in letting the editors rely on his sincerity, but the article would not have been very different if Sokal's account of physics and mathematics had been entirely accurate. What is more revealing is the variety of physics and mathematics bloopers in remarks of others that Sokal slyly quotes with mock approval. Here is the philosopher Bruno Latour on special relativity:

> How can one decide whether an observation made in a train about the behavior of a falling stone can be made to coincide with the observation of the same falling stone from the embankment? If there are only one, or even *two*, frames of reference, no solution can be found . . . Einstein's solution is to consider *three* actors . . .

This is wrong; in relativity theory there is no difficulty in comparing the results of two, three, or any number of observers. In other quotations cited by Sokal, Stanley Aronowitz misuses the term "unified field theory;" feminist theorist Luce Irigaray deplores mathematicians' neglect of spaces with boundaries, though there is a huge literature on the subject. The English professor Robert Markley calls quantum theory nonlinear, though it is the only known example of a precisely linear theory. And both philosopher Michael Serres (a member of the Académie Française) and arch-postmodernist Jean-François Lyotard grossly misrepresent the view of time in modern physics. Such errors suggest a problem not just in the editing practices of *Social Text*, but in the standards of a larger intellectual community.

It seems to me though that Sokal's hoax is most effective in the way that it draws cultural or philosophical or political conclusions from developments in physics and mathematics. Again and again Sokal jumps from correct science to absurd implications, without the benefit of any intermediate reasoning. With a straight face, he leaps from Bohr's observation that in quantum mechanics "a complete elucidation of one and the same object may require diverse points of view which defy a unique description" to the conclusion that "postmodern science" refutes "the authoritarianism and elitism inherent in traditional science." He blithely points to catastrophe theory and chaos theory as the sort of mathematics that can lead to social and economic liberation. Sokal shows that people really do talk in this way by quoting work of others in the same vein, including applications of mathematical topology to psychiatry by Jacques Lacan and to film criticism by Jacques-Alain Miller.

I find it disturbing that the editors of *Social Text* thought it plausible that a sane working physicist would take the positions satirized in Sokal's article. In their defense of the decision to publish it, the editors explain that they had judged that it was "the earnest attempt of a professional scientist to seek some sort of affirmation from postmodern philosophy for developments in his field."[8] In an introduction to the issue of *Social Text* in which Sokal's article appears, one of the editors mentions that "many famous scientists, especially physicists, have been mystics."[9] There may be some working physicists who are mystics, though I have never met any, and I can't imagine any serious physicist who holds views as bizarre as those that Sokal satirized. The gulf of misunderstanding between scientists and other intellectuals seems to be at least as wide as when C. P. Snow worried about it three decades ago.

After Sokal exposed his hoax, one of the editors of *Social Text* even speculated that "Sokal's parody was nothing of the sort, and that his admission represented a change of heart, or a folding of his intellectual resolve."[10] I am reminded of the case of the American spiritualist Margaret Fox. When she confessed in 1888 that her career of séances and spirit rappings had all been a hoax, other spiritualists claimed that it was her confession that was dishonest.

Those who seek extrascientific messages in what they think they understand about modern physics are digging dry wells. In my view, with two large exceptions, the results of research in physics (as opposed, say, to psychology) have no legitimate implications whatever for culture or politics or philosophy. (I am not talking here about the technological applications of physics, which of course do have a huge effect on our culture, or about its use as metaphor, but about the direct logical implications of purely scientific discoveries themselves.) The discoveries of physics may become relevant to philosophy and culture when we learn the origin of the universe or the final laws of nature, but not for the present.

The first of my exceptions to this statement is jurisdictional: discoveries in science sometimes reveal that topics like matter, space, and time, which had been thought to be proper subjects for philosophical argument, actually belong in the province of ordinary science. The other, more important, exception to my statement is the profound cultural effect of the discovery, going back to the work of Newton, that nature is strictly governed by impersonal mathematical laws. Of course, it still remains for us to get the laws right, and to understand their range of validity; but as far as culture or philosophy is concerned the difference between Newton's and Einstein's theories of gravitation or between classical and quantum mechanics is immaterial.

There is a good deal of confusion about this, because quantum mechanics can seem rather eerie if described in ordinary language. Electrons in atoms do not have definite positions or velocities until these properties are measured, and the measurement of an electron's velocity wipes out all knowledge of its position. This eeriness has led Andrew Ross, one of the editors of *Social Text,* to remark elsewhere that "quantitative rationality—the normative description of scientific materialism—can no longer account for the behavior of matter at the level of quantum reality."[11] This is simply wrong. By rational processes today we obtain a complete quantitative description of atoms in terms of what is called the wave function of the atom.[12] Once one has calculated the wave function, it can be used to answer any question about the energy of the atom or its interaction with light. We have replaced the precise Newtonian language of particle trajectories with the precise quantum language of wave functions, but as far as quantitative rationality is concerned, there is no difference between quantum mechanics and Newtonian mechanics.

I have to admit at this point that physicists share responsibility for the widespread confusion about such matters. Sokal quotes some dreadful examples of Werner Heisenberg's philosophical wanderings, as for instance: "Science no longer confronts nature as an objective observer, but sees itself as an actor in this interplay between man [*sic*] and nature." (Heisenberg was one of the great physicists of the twentieth century, but he could not always be counted on to think carefully, as shown by his technical mistakes in the German nuclear weapons program.[13]) More recently scientists like Ilya Prigogine[14] have claimed a deep philosophical significance for work on nonlinear dynamics,[15] a subject that is interesting enough without the hype.

So much for the cultural implications of discoveries in science. What of the implications for science of its cultural and social context? Here scientists like Sokal find themselves in opposition to many sociologists, historians, and philosophers as well as postmodern literary theorists. In this debate, the two sides often seem to be talking past each other. For instance, the sociologists and historians sometimes write as if scientists had not learned anything about the scientific method since the days of Francis Bacon, while of course we know very well how complicated the relation is between theory and experiment, and how much the work of science depends on an appropriate social and economic setting. On the other hand, scientists sometimes accuse others of taking a completely relativist view, of not believing in objective reality. With dead seriousness, Sokal's hoax cites "revisionist studies in the history and philosophy of science" as casting doubt on the post-Enlightenment dogma that "there exists an external world, whose properties are independent of any individual human being and indeed of humanity as a whole" [pt. 1, intro.]. The trouble with the satire of this particular message is that most of Sokal's targets deny that they have any doubt about the existence of an external world. Their belief in objective reality was reaffirmed in response to Sokal's hoax both in a letter to *The New York Times* by the editors of *Social Text*[16] and in the Op-Ed article by Stanley Fish [pt. 3, "Professor Sokal's Bad Joke"].

I don't mean to say that this part of Sokal's satire was unjustified. His targets often take positions that seem to me (and I gather to Sokal) to make no sense if there is an objective reality. To put it simply, if scientists are talking about something real, then what they say is either true or false. If it is true, then how can it depend on the social environment of the scientist? If it is false, how can it help to liberate us? The choice of scientific question and the method of approach may depend on all sorts of extrascientific influences, but the correct answer when we find it is what it is because that is the way the world is. Nevertheless, it does no good to satirize views that your opponent denies holding.

I have run into the same sort of stumbling block myself. In an early draft of my book *Dreams of a Final Theory*,[17] I criticized the feminist philosopher of science, Sandra Harding (a contributor to *Social Text*), for taking a relativist position that denied the objective character of physical laws. In evidence I quoted her as calling modern science (and especially physics) "not only sexist but also racist, classist, and culturally coercive," and arguing that "physics and chemistry, mathematics and logic, bear the fingerprints of their distinctive cultural creators no less than do anthropology and history."[18] It seemed to me that this statement could make sense only to a relativist. What is the good of claiming that the conclusions of scientific research should be friendlier to multicultural or feminist concerns if these conclusions are to be an accurate account of objective reality? I sent a draft of this section to Harding, who pointed out to me various places in her writing where she had explicitly denied taking a relativist position. I took the easy way out; I dropped the accusation of relativism, and left it to the reader to judge the implications of her remarks.

Perhaps it would clarify what is at issue if we were to talk not about whether nature is real but about the more controversial question, whether scientific knowledge in general and the laws of physics in particular are real.

When I was an undergraduate at Cornell I heard a lecture by a professor of philosophy (probably Max Black) who explained that whenever anyone asked him whether something was real, he always gave the same answer. The answer was "Yes." The tooth fairy is real, the laws of physics are real, the rules of baseball are real, and the rocks in the fields are real. But they are real in different ways. What I mean when I say that the laws of physics are real is that they are real in pretty much the same sense (whatever that is) as the rocks in the fields, and not in the same sense (as implied by Fish[19]) as the rules of baseball. We did not create the laws of physics or the rocks in the field, and we sometimes unhappily find that we have been wrong about them, as when we stub our toe on an unnoticed rock, or when we find we have made a mistake (as most physicists have) about some physical law. But the languages in which we describe rocks or in which we state physical laws are certainly created socially, so I am making an implicit assumption (which in everyday life we all make about rocks) that our statements about the laws of physics are in a one-to-one correspondence with aspects of objective reality. To put it another way, if we ever discover intelligent creatures on some distant planet and translate their scientific works, we will find that we and they have discovered the same laws.

There is another complication here, which is that none of the laws of physics known today (with the possible exception of the general principles of quantum mechanics) are exactly and universally valid. Nevertheless, many of them have settled down to a final form, valid in certain known circumstances. The equations of electricity and magnetism that are today known as Maxwell's equations are not the equations originally written down by Maxwell; they are equations that physicists settled on after decades of subsequent work by other physicists, notably the English scientist Oliver Heaviside. They are understood today to be an approximation that is valid in a limited context (that of weak, slowly-varying electric and magnetic fields), but in this form and in this limited context they have survived for a century and may be expected to survive indefinitely. This is the sort of law of physics that I think corresponds to something as real as anything else we know. On this point, scientists like Sokal and myself are apparently in clear disagreement with some of those whom Sokal satirizes. The objective nature of scientific knowledge has been denied by Andrew Ross[20] and Bruno Latour[21] and (as I understand them) by the influential philosophers Richard Rorty and the late Thomas Kuhn,[22] but it is taken for granted by most natural scientists.

I have come to think that the laws of physics are real because my experience with the laws of physics does not seem to me to be very different in any fundamental way from my experience with rocks. For those who have not lived with the laws of physics, I can offer the obvious argument that the laws of physics as we know them work, and there is no other known way of looking at nature that works in anything like the same sense. Sarah Franklin (in an article in the same issue of *Social Text* as Sokal's hoax) challenges an argument of Richard Dawkins that in relying on the working of airplanes we show our acceptance of the working of the laws of nature, remarking that some airlines show prayer films during takeoff to invoke the aid of Allah to remain safely airborne.[23] Does Franklin think that Dawkin's argument does not apply to her? If so, would she be willing to give up the use of the laws of physics in designing aircraft, and rely on prayers instead?

There is also the related argument that although we have not yet had a chance to compare notes with creatures on a distant planet, we can see that on Earth the laws of physics are understood in the same way by scientists of every nation, race, and—yes—gender. Some of the commentators on science quoted by Sokal hope that the participation of women or victims of imperialism will change the character of science; but as far as I can see, women and Third-World physicists work in just the same way as Western white male physicists do. It might be argued that this is just a sign of the power of entrenched scientific authority or the pervasive influence of Western society, but these explanations seem unconvincing to me. Although natural science is intellectually hegemonic, in the sense that we have a clear idea of what it means for a theory to be true or false, its operations are not socially hegemonic—authority counts for very little.

From time to time distinguished physicists who are past their best years, like Heisenberg in Germany in the 1950s or De Broglie in France, have tried to force physics in the direction of their own ideas; but where such mandarins succeed at all, it is only in one country, and only for a limited time. The direction of physics today is overwhelmingly set by young physicists, who are not yet weighed down with honors or authority, and whose influence—the excitement they stir up—derives from the objective progress that they are able to make. If our expression of the laws of nature is socially constructed, it is constructed in a society of scientists that evolves chiefly through grappling with nature's laws.

Some historians do not deny the reality of the laws of nature, but nevertheless refuse to take present scientific knowledge into account in describing the scientific work of the past.[24] This is partly to avoid anachronisms, like supposing that scientists of the past ought to have seen things in the way we do, and partly out of a preoccupation with maintaining the intellectual independence of historians.[25] The problem is that in ignoring present scientific knowledge, these historians give up clues to the past that cannot be obtained in any other way. In the late 1890s, J. J. Thomson carried out a celebrated series of measurements of the ratio of the electron's mass and charge, and though the values he found were spread over a wide range, he persistently emphasized measurements that gave results at the high end of the range. The historical record alone would not allow us to decide whether this was because these results tended to confirm his first measurement, or because these were actually more careful measurements. Why not use the clue that the second alternative is unlikely because the large value that was favored by Thomson is almost twice what we know today as the correct value?

A historian of science who ignores our present scientific knowledge seems to me like a historian of US military intelligence in the Civil War who tells the story of McClellan's hesitations in the Virginia peninsula in the face of what McClellan thought were overwhelming Confederate forces without taking into account our present knowledge that McClellan was wrong. Even the choice of topics that attract the interest of historians has to be affected by what we now know were the paths that led to success. What Herbert Butterfield called the Whig interpretation of history is legitimate in the history of science in a way that it is not in the history of politics or culture, because science is cumulative, and permits definite judgments of success or failure.

Sokal was not the first to address these issues,[26] but he has done a great service in raising them so dramatically. They are not entirely academic issues, in any sense of the word "academic." If we think that scientific laws are flexible enough to be effected by the social setting of their discovery, then some may be tempted to press scientists to discover laws that are more proletarian or feminine or American or religious or Aryan or whatever else it is they want. This is a dangerous path, and more is at stake in the controversy over it than just the health of science. As I mentioned earlier, our civilization has been powerfully affected by the discovery that nature is strictly governed by impersonal laws. As an example I like to quote the remark of Hugh Trevor-Roper, that one of the early effects of this discovery was to reduce the enthusiasm for burning witches. We will need to confirm and strengthen the vision of a rationally understandable world if we are to protect ourselves from the irrational tendencies that still beset humanity.

Notes

1   Alan D. Sokal, "Transgressing the Boundaries: Toward a Transformative Hermeneutics of Quantum Gravity," *Social Text* (Spring/Summer 1996), pp. 217–252 (1996). [Pt. 1]

2   Alan D. Sokal, "A Physicist Experiments with Cultural Studies," *Lingua Franca* (May/June 1996), pp. 62–64. [Pt. 2, "Revelation"]

3   In an afterword, "Transgressing the Boundaries," submitted to *Social Text*, Sokal explained that his goal was not so much to defend science as to defend the left from postmodernists, social constructivists, and other trendy leftists.

4   For instance, there is a linear relation between the number of calories in a cake and the amounts of each of the various ingredients: the graph of calories verses ounces of any one ingredient, holding the amounts of all the other ingredients fixed, is a straight line. In contrast, the relation between the diameter of a cake (of fixed height) and the amounts of its ingredients is not linear.

5   Operations are said to be noncommuting if the result when you perform several of them depends on the order in which they are performed. For instance, rotating your body by, say, thirty degrees around the vertical axis and then rotating it by thirty degrees around the north-south direction leaves you in a different position than these operations would if they were carried out in the opposite order. Try it and see.

6   Steve Fuller, letter to *The New York Times*, May 23, 1996, p. 28, and Stanley Fish, "Professor Sokal's Bad Joke," Op-Ed article in *The New York Times*, May 21, 1996, p. 23.

7   Bruce Robbins and Andrew Ross, "Mystery Science Theater," *Lingua Franca* (July/August 1996). [Pt. 2, "Response"]

8   Robbins and Ross, "Mystery Science Theater."

9   Andrew Ross, "Introduction," *Social Text* (Spring/Summer 1996), pp. 1–13.

10 Quoted by Robbins and Ross in "Mystery Science Theater."

11 Andrew Ross, *Strange Weather* (Verso, London, 1991), p. 42.

12 In general, the wave function of any system is a list of numbers, one number for every possible configuration of the system. For a single electron in an atom, the list includes a different number for each possible position of the electron. The values of these numbers give a complete description of the state of the system at any moment. One complication is that the possible configurations of any system can be described in different ways; for instance, an electron could be described in terms of its possible velocities, rather than its possible positions (but not by both at the same time). There are well-understood rules for calculating the numbers making up the wave function in one description if we know what these numbers are in any other description. Another complication is that these numbers are complex, in the sense that they generally involve the quantity known as i, equal to the square root of minus one, as well as ordinary real numbers.

13 See Jeremy Bernstein, *Hitler's Uranium Club* (American Institute of Physics, 1995).

14 For quotes and comments, see Jean Bricmont, "Science of Chaos or Chaos in Science?" *Physicalia Magazine* 17 (1995), pp.159–208, reprinted in *The Flight from Science and Reason* (New York Academy of Sciences, 1996). A rejoinder and response are given by Ilya Prigogine and I. Antoniou, "Science of Chaos or Chaos in Science: A Rearguard Battle," *Physicalia Magazine* 17, pp. 213–218; Jean Bricmont, "The Last Word from the Rearguard," *Physicalia Magazine* 17, pp. 219–221.

15 Nonlinear dynamics deals with cases in which the rates of change of various quantities depend nonlinearly on these quantities. For instance, the rates of change of the pressures, temperatures, and velocities at various points in a fluid like the atmosphere depend nonlinearly on these pressures, temperatures, and velocities. It has been known for almost a century that the long-term behavior of such systems often exhibits chaos, an exquisite sensitivity to the initial condition of the system. (The classic example is the way that the flapping of a butterfly's wings can change the weather weeks later throughout the world.) For physicists, the current interest in nonlinear dynamical systems stems from the discovery of general features of chaotic behavior that can be precisely predicted.

16 Bruce Robbins and Andrew Ross, letter to *The New York Times*, May 23, 1996, p. 28.

17 Pantheon, 1993.

18 Sandra Harding, *The Science Question in Feminism*, (Cornell University Press, Ithaca, 1986), pp. 9, 250.

19 Fish, "Professor Sokal's Bad Joke."

20 Andrew Ross was quoted by *The New York Times* on May 18, 1996, to the effect that "scientific knowledge is affected by social and cultural conditions and is not a version of some universal truth that is the same in all times and places."

21 Bruno Latour, *Science in Action* (Harvard University Press, 1987).

22 For instance, see Thomas Kuhn, "The Road Since Structure," in *PSA 1990* (Philosophy of Science Association, 1991), and "The Trouble with the Historical Philosophy of Science," (1991 lecture published by the Department of the History of Science, Harvard University, 1992).

23 Sarah Franklin, "Making Transparencies—Seeing Through the Science Wars," *Social Text* (Spring/Summer 1996), pp. 141–155.

24 This point of view was expressed to me by the historian Harry Collins, then at the Science Studies Centre of the University of Bath.

25 In "Independence, Not Transcendence, for the Historian of Science," *ISIS* (March 1991), Paul Forman called for historians to exercise an independent judgment not just of how scientific progress is made, but even of what constitutes scientific progress.

26 See especially Gerald Holton, *Science and Anti-Science* (Harvard University Press, 1993), and Paul R. Gross and Norman Levitt, *Higher Superstition* (Johns Hopkins Press, 1994). The issue of *Social Text* in which Sokal's hoax appeared was intended as a response to Gross and Levitt's book, which also, according to Sokal, inspired his hoax.

Sokal's Hoax: An Exchange

New York Review of Books, 3 October 1996

To the Editors:

Alan Sokal's hoax is rapidly ceasing to be funny. An enterprise that originally had all the marks of a good joke is beginning to bring out the worst in respondents. This was obvious first in Sokal's own account in *Lingua Franca* of what he had done (very amusing) and why (tedious and self-righteous), and then in the firestorm of letters in *The New York Times* and various professional journals. But as teachers of a course on literature and science at Yale, we found Steven Weinberg's response to the hoax particularly troubling.

We do not, of course, wish to defend the shoddy scholarship of the *Social Text* editors, and we deplore the pan-culturalist views of those whom Weinberg attacks. But Weinberg has gone to the other extreme. If, in what follows, we concentrate on his views, it is because as a distinguished scientist, his intervention has the capacity to create mischief far beyond that of *Social Text*. Culture is too important to be left to *soi-disant* cultural critics, but it is also the case that Nobel prize-winning physicists should not go unchallenged when they pronounce on culture—or science.

Alan Sokal and other scientists like Weinberg who have declared him a hero share one important feature with the editors of *Social Text*: both sides wish to locate science in a particular relation to other aspects of culture. The *Social Text* tribe sees science as merely a subfunction of the covering category "culture," while Weinberg flatly states, "The discoveries of physics may become relevant to philosophy and culture when we learn the origin of the universe or the final laws of nature, but not for the present." The *Social Text* editors fail to grant science sufficient distinctiveness in their homogenizing zeal. And Weinberg errs in the other direction: he argues science has *no* connection to the rest of culture. Both sides are guilty of egregious overstatement and impatiently exclude a middle where the real complexities are to be found.

Social Text and Weinberg both get the relation of science and culture wrong, but they do so in different ways. The claims of the *Social Text* editors have been self-discredited, not only by their acceptance of the Sokal piece, but by subsequent attempts they have made in statements to the press and in a *Lingua Franca* article to explain away their simple lack of basic seriousness, not only as scholars, but as intellectuals. Of Weinberg's seriousness, however, there can be no doubt. For this reason his argument is ultimately the more dangerous of the two, not only because it has a certain superficial plausibility (especially when presented in such clear prose and with so many entertaining examples), but because it represents in highly reductive terms a view probably held by many other scientists.

Such believers hold that science is an undertaking fundamentally different from other human activities for a number of reasons, but primarily because of its relation to a reality that is ultimate in the sense that its truths cannot be reduced to any other form of explanation. Such truths are objective, impersonal laws (a phrase Weinberg repeats like a mantra). Insofar as it is universal and extrahistorical, science is qualitively distinct from the rest of culture: science *is* nature, and therefore the very opposite of culture.

The most striking feature of this argument is its radical dualism: on the one side are timeless laws and selfless truths; on the other, is the social world of culture, with its ineluctable contingency, its ramifying particularity, its dictates that change with time. But the poles of this opposition are not equally weighted. Despite Weinberg's claim that in natural science "authority counts very little," his remarks are clearly intended to be definitive: Weinberg clearly sees himself as giving voice to the impersonal laws of natural science. These two fundamental aspects of Weinberg's argument—its obsessive dualism and its assumption of overwhelming authority—are grounded in a mode of thought frequently encountered in traditional societies where the distinctive feature of the culture is the dualism that separates the world of the profane from the sacred.

It would be absurd to compare the erudite and cosmopolitan scientist to a member of, say, one of the tribes of central Australia described by Durkheim in *The Elementary Forms of Religious Life* were it not for the binarism that so compulsively attends the thinking of both: " . . . The real characteristic of religious phenomena is that they always suppose a bipartite division of the whole universe, known and knowable, into two classes which embrace all that exists, but which radically exclude each other."

What does Weinberg's dualism include—and exclude? The innermost sanctum of his temple (before which all else is, in the etymological sense of the word, *profane*) is occupied by particle physicists. His use of the covering term "science" is deceptive, for it excludes microbiology, genetics, and the new brain sciences, to name merely a few. "Science" boils down to the work being done by a relatively small number of men in theoretical and high-energy physics. Outside the temple would be found first of all the enemies of the truth Weinberg specifically attacks for their impurity—the *Social Text* editors, of course, but as well most other historians, sociologists, and philosophers of science: "Scientists like Sokal [among whom Weinberg clearly counts himself] find themselves in opposition to many sociologists, historians, and philosophers as well as postmodern literary theorists." But in another circle of darkness would be found even other scientists, heretics such as Heisenberg and de Broglie. This list of apostsates can be extended, by the same logic, to include the Newton who in his old age said, "I do not know what I may appear to the world; but to myself I seem to have been only like a boy playing on the seashore, and diverting myself now and then finding a smoother pebble or a prettier shell than ordinary, whilst the great ocean of truth lay all undiscovered before me."

Why, we may reasonably ask, has the mantle of purity Weinberg assumes in his attack on the editors of *Social Text* fallen precisely on the shoulders of particle physicists? Is it because defending pure science against philistine non-scientists gives particle physicists the opportunity to define science in their own image? The particle physicist stands ready in his role as pre-Kantian shaman to declare taboo all that which falls outside his narrow definitions. He defends pure science from the philistine laity by defining "science" in his own image. But it is not necessary to accept the mantras of particle physicists, with their reductionist view of science, to reject the foolishness of *Social Text*.

Since at least the pre-Socratics the greatest minds have striven to understand the relation of the incommensurable to our situatedness at a particular moment in a specific time. Since at least the Enlightenment this problem has been articulated in questions about how we relate physical sensation to processes of the understanding. All the gains we have made in this inclusive endeavor that has given new power not only to the natural sciences, but to other aspects of culture such as poetry and art as well, are now endangered by new polarizations in the science wars that rage about us. If we are to preserve a more holistic view of nature and our own place in it, we must resist not only those extremists who exclude formal knowledge in the name of a homgenizing concept of culture, but those as well who make equally privative claims for an immaculate conception of science. Or as Lionel

Trilling deduced from the Leavis-Snow controversy, what gets lost in such conflicts between extremists is that quality of mind which creates the culture they claim to protect.

Michael Holquist
Professor of Comparative Literature
Yale University
New Haven, Connecticut

Robert Shulman
Sterling Professor of Molecular Biophysics and Biochemistry
Yale University
New Haven, Connecticut

To the Editors:

With all the broad discussion of the Sokal affair, not enough has been made of the way the counter-attackers against "postmodernism" and science studies get irrational and unscientific in the name of science and with the voice of common sense. Since part of the project of the writers Sokal mocks and Steven Weinberg criticizes is to force awareness of the metaphysical assumptions embedded in the language of common sense, they will often, even when sensible, sound obscure and irrational. I hope nobody wants to defend the awful jargon of much current theory and criticism. But Weinberg's demonstration of Derrida's vacuity on the basis of his failure to make sense of a passage selected by Sokal for mockery has no more weight than would a similar comment on science from a distinguished literary critic. Like Derrida or not, his linguistic project can't be dismissed with a commonsensical "I don't understand it."

Moreover, whereas every writer knows that all written words escape authorial control, Weinberg claims that the conclusions of physics can have no cultural implications. This is an extraordinary, a profoundly irrational claim. "Those who seek extrascientific messages in what they think they understand about modern physics," says Weinberg, "are digging dry wells." This is special pleading with a vengeance and Weinberg even provides two counterexamples.

How special the pleading is can be suggested by making an example of material from Sokal's parody. Sokal, Weinberg, chortles, "leaps from Bohr's observation that in quantum mechanics 'a complete elucidation of one and the same object may require diverse points of view which defy a unique description' to the conclusion that 'postmodern science' refutes 'the authoritarianism and elitism inherent in traditional science.'" Weinberg laughs at the obvious absurdity of the conclusion, and then concludes that ANY cultural inference from Bohr's argument is illegitimate. Sure, Sokal probably had some real targets among cultural critics; but that an absurd inference is drawn doesn't for a moment preclude the possibility that there are other more reasonable ones. It is difficult *not* to see Bohr's argument as loaded with telling cultural implications. If Weinberg is right that such ideas apply always and everywhere, Bohr's observation ought to change the way lay people look at the world. Denying such possibility sounds more irrational, ideological, and misguided than anything *Social Text* did when it gave Sokal too much trust. It was not after all *Social Text* that drew the absurd conclusion about authoritarianism and elitism; it was Sokal, trying to ventriloquize work he didn't fully understand.

The new counter-aggression of scientists hostile to "postmodernism" is surely the consequence of an economic pinch hurting them as well as humanists and social scientists. On all sides intellectual activity—not for profit or salvation—is under pressure. Both sides have got far too defensive and should be taking the awkward moment as an occasion for recognizing common interests and arguing their positions rationally. The most dangerous thing about Weinberg's kind of response is that it closes doors. He waves the banner of common sense, a banner that has been held higher, and waved more effectively by ideologues and demagogues, and in the vanguard of a war that inhibits science and crushes cultural critique.

George Levine
Center for the Critical Analysis of Contemporary Culture
Rutgers University
New Brunswick, New Jersey

To the Editors:

Steven Weinberg has used Alan Sokal's entertaining hoax (perpetrated against the editors of the formerly obscure journal *Social Text*) as an occasion for airing his own view on the nature of science, which he represents as those of "scientists" in contrast to "others" (historians, philosophers, and sociologists). He hopes thereby to "strengthen the vision of a rationally understandable world" so that we can "protect ourselves from the irrational tendencies that still beset humanity," for he is convinced that the "others" are promoting irrationality with their cultural relativism and attendant denial of objective reality. The difficulty with this representation is that all historians, philosophers, and sociologists that I know share Weinberg's hope for rational understanding and that none of them deny objective reality as Weinberg presents it. As a historian of physics I will remark on the relation between reality and relativism.

To evoke objective reality, Weinberg says that the laws of physics are as real as rocks and that we did not create them. Recognizing, however, that we have no access to any laws that we have not ourselves expressed, he retreats to the mundane formulation that our lawlike statements about aspects of the world correspond consistently to our experience of those aspects. Such laws he epitomizes by Maxwell's equations of electromagnetism, stressing that they are "an approximation that is valid in a limited context" or better, "valid in certain known circumstances." This validity criterion for realism—if it works it's real—would convert every empirically adequate simulation into reality and every anti-realist into a realist. If such validity constitutes objective reality, Weinberg will search in vain for any historian who has ever denied the objective reality of Maxwell's equations. (His citation among others of Thomas Kuhn—so recently deceased after a lifelong attempt to articulate the nature of objectivity and rationality in science, including rigorous graduate courses in the history of electromagnetism—is outrageous.)

The issue of cultural relativism is not validity; it concerns multiplicity: the multiplicity of valid positions that have been available at any time, the many ways in which those positions have been embedded in the cultures from which they emerged, and the diverse processes through which they have both crossed cultural boundaries and have changed fundamentally over time, with massive implications for both science and the rest of culture. These objective realities leave contentious historians in a somewhat relativistic position as compared with such absolutist claims as Weinberg's that "as far as the culture of philosophy is concerned the difference between Newton's and Einstein's theories of gravitation or between classical and quantum mechanics is immaterial." This strange notion denied the experience of virtually every physicist who lived through the changes from 1900 to 1930. Continuing, Weinberg repeats the standard Copenhagen interpretation of quantum mechanics—sometimes called observer-created reality—according to which "electrons in atoms do not have definite positions or velocities until these properties are measured." While Einstein, among others, regarded this interpretation as unacceptable subjectivism, Weinberg presents it as an objective reality of no great historical significance, without telling us that it involved a renunciation (Bohr's term) of the classical causal description in space and time of the trajectory of a particle and without telling us that it has once again become controversial with the revival of David Bohm's long-dismissed deterministic (and holistic) alternative. Is Weinberg's blatant falsification of history excusable in the interest of damning the literary critic Andrew Ross as "simply wrong" in his remarks about the cultural significance of quantum mechanics? Multiplying errors, unlike multiplying interpretations, does not lead to wisdom.

There is a deeper question. Is it justifiable to try to expunge all mystical physicists (whom Weinberg has "never met"), "creationists and other religious enthusiasts" from the historical processes that have contributed to the immense power of science to predict and control events in the material world? Consider Maxwell's equations. They emerged during the course of the nineteenth century from the work of some of the most deeply religious people who have ever contemplated a battery: Oersted, discoverer of electromagnetism and author of *The Soul in Nature*; Faraday, devout member of the Sandemanian sect who discovered electromagnetic induction and articulated field theory; William Thomson (Lord Kelvin) and Maxwell, who mathematized field theory while holding that mathematical physics could produce only idealized accounts, accessible to finite human minds, of limited aspects of God's infinite action in the world; and a whole bevy of more spiritualist physicists who saw the electromagnetic field as the carrier of their dreams of uniting religion and science. These are some of the objective realities that historians of physics must learn to understand, however much we may disdain their role in contemporary society, for they are crucial aspects of the work in physics of the people who made Maxwell's equations. Again, the issue is not the validity of field theory (nor of the long-competing theories of action at a distance using retarded potentials) but of culturally embedded meanings.

And it does no good to suppose that science is no longer like that. Wolfgang Pauli, certainly one of the best mathematical physicists of the twentieth century, interpreted the oft-cited mysticism of Johannes Kepler, concerning the harmonies of planetary motion, in terms of his own belief in Jungian archetypes, which promised to account for both mathematical forms and his own dreams during years of analysis in the 1930s under Jungian guidance. More radically, Pascual Jordan, another of the primary mathematical founders of quantum mechanics and quantum field theory, presented these theoretical accomplishments during the Thirties as a foundation not only for telepathy and clairvoyance but for Nazi politics as well. The only surprise is that (so far as I know) no physicist has yet presented the beautiful mathematical work of Edward Witten and others on string theory as the best-ever form of Platonic mysticism, since no direct empirical test seems conceivable at present.

In short, Weinberg presents us with an ideology of science, an ideology which radically separates science from culture, scientists from "others," and splits the personalities of rational and irrational components. However desirable this ideology may be in other respects, it will never do for comprehending the history of science. To preserve it, he has to indulge in the unsavory rhetorical ploy of dismissing other Nobelists, who have regarded their physics as having considerable philosophical and cultural significance, as aged oddballs appearing "from time to time" and "past their best." Thus Heisenberg's discussions of the subject-object problem become "philosophical wanderings" from someone who "could not always be counted on to think carefully." But scientists who have drawn on their philosophical, political, economic, and other beliefs for conceptual resources and motivation in pursuing their best scientific work permeate the history of physics. To remove them from quantum mechanics would be to wipe out the field: Planck, Bohr, de Broglie, Heisenberg, Pauli, Jordan, Schrödinger, Weizsäcker, to list only the obvious. So what is Weinberg up to? Is he not promoting a cultural agenda of his own in his attempt to rewrite history? Historical realities can be interpreted with validity in various ways, but like physical laws and rocks, they resist when kicked.

M. Norton Wise
Program in History of Science
Princeton University
Princeton, New Jersey

To the Editors:

Sokal's hoax and Weinberg's article explaining and amplifying its message effectively remove the smoke and mirrors from those social critics, philosophers, and historians of science who want to regard the human circumstances of a scientific discovery as more important than the discovery itself. As working physicists we know that the laws of nature we study are apprehended—tested and validated by independent experiments the same by women and men, and by people in every culture. The scientific revolution and continued discoveries give knowledge about the universe that can be comprehended and used by all. We commend Sokal and Weinberg for their defense of the scientific revolution.

Nina Byers
Professor of Physics
University of California at Los Angeles
Los Angeles, California

Claudio Pellegrini
Professor of Physics
University of California at Los Angeles
Los Angeles, California

Steven Weinberg replies

I am grateful to those who sent comments on my article "Sokal's Hoax," including those who, by disagreeing with me, have given me this chance to take another whack at the issues it raised.

Professors Holquist and Shulman have me dead to rights in calling my views dualist. I think that an essential element needed in the birth of modern science was the creation of a gap between the world of physical science and the world of human culture.[1] Endless trouble has been produced throughout history by the effort to draw moral or cultural lessons from discoveries of science. The physics and biology of Aristotle were largely based on a conception of naturalness, which was believed also to have moral and cultural implications, as for instance that some people are naturally slaves. After relativity theory became widely publicized in 1919, the Archbishop of Canterbury like many others conscientiously worried over the effect that relativity was going to have on theology, and had to be reassured by Einstein himself in 1921 that relativity had no implications for religion.[2] Professors Holquist and Shulman quote Durkheim for the proposition that a gap between ways of viewing reality such as that between science and culture is characteristic of religious phenomena, but I think that just the opposite is true; if you want to find astronomy all muddled with cultural or moral values, you would turn to Dante's *Paradiso* rather than Galileo's *Dialogo*. In trying to revive a "holistic view of nature," Professors Holquist and Shulman are seeking to fill a much-needed gap.

Quantum mechanics provides a good example of the need to maintain this separation between physics and other forms of culture. Quantum mechanics has been variously cited as giving support to mysticism, or free will, or the decline of quantitative rationality. Now, I would agree that anyone is entitled to draw any inspiration they can from quantum mechanics, or from anything else. This is what I meant when I wrote that I had nothing to say against the use of science as metaphor. But there is a difference between inspiration and implication, and in talking of the "telling cultural implications" of quantum mechanics, Professor Levine may be confusing the two. There is simply no way that any cultural consequences can be *implied* by quantum mechanics. It is true that quantum mechanics does "apply always and everywhere," but what applies is not a proverb about diverse points of view but a precise mathematical formalism, which among other things tells us that the difference between the predictions of quantum mechanics and pre-quantum classical mechanics, which is so important for the behavior of atoms, becomes negligible at the scale of human affairs.

I suggest the following thought experiment. Suppose that physicists were to announce the discovery that, beneath the apparently quantum mechanical appearance of atoms, there lies a more fundamental substructure of fields and particles that behave according to the rules of plain old classical mechanics. Would Professor Levine find it necessary to rethink his views about culture of philosophy? If so, why? If not, then in what sense can these views be said to be implied by quantum mechanics?

I was glad to see that Professor Wise, an expert on late-nineteenth-century physics, finds no error in what I had to say about the history of science. Unfortunately he does find a great many errors in things that I did not say. I never said there were no physicists in the early twentieth century who found cultural or philosophical implications in relativity or quantum mechanics, only that in my view these inferences were not valid. I never said that the apparent subjectivism of quantum mechanics was "of no great historical significance," only that I think we know better now. Just as anyone may get inspiration from scientific discoveries, scientists in their work may be inspired by virtually anything in their cultural background, but that does not make these cultural influences a permanent part of scientific theories. I never tried "to expunge all mystical physicists" as well as "creationists and other religious enthusiasts" from the history of science. I did say that I had never met a physicist who was a mystic, but my article had nothing to say about the frequency of other forms of religious belief among scientists, past or present.

On the subject of mystical physicists, it is interesting that when Professor Wise tries to find up-to-date examples, he can get no closer than two physicists whose major work was done more than sixty years ago. He expresses surprise that no physicist has yet presented string theory as a form of Platonic mysticism, but I think I can explain this. It is because we expect that string theory *will* be testable—if not directly, by observing the string vibrations, then indirectly, by calculating whether string theory correctly accounts for all of the currently mysterious features of the standard model of elementary particles and general relativity. If it were not for this expectation, string theory would not be worth bothering with.

I tried in my article to put my finger on precisely what divides me and many other scientists from cultural and historical relativists by saying that the issue is not the belief in the reality of the laws of nature. Professor Wise makes a good point that, in judging the reality of the laws of nature, the test is not just their validity, but also their lack of "multiplicity." Indeed, as I wrote in my article, one of the things about laws of nature like Maxwell's equations that convinces me of their objective reality is the absence of a multiplicity of valid laws governing the same phenomena, with different laws of nature of different cultures.

(To be precise, I don't mean that there is no other valid way of looking at the electric and magnetic phenomena that Maxwell's equations describe, because there are mathematically equivalent ways of rewriting Maxwell's theory, and the theory itself can be replaced with a deeper theory, quantum electrodynamics, from which it can be derived. What I mean is that there is no valid alternative way of looking at the phenomena described by Maxwell's equations that does not have Maxwell's equations as a mathematical consequence.)

Whatever cultural influences went into the discovery of Maxwell's equations and other laws of nature have been refined away, like slag from ore. Maxwell's equations are now understood in the same way by everyone with a valid comprehension of electricity and magnetism. The cultural backgrounds of the scientists who discovered such theories have thus become irrelevant to the lessons that we should draw from the theories. Professor Wise and some others may be upset by such distinctions because they see them as a threat to their own "agenda," which is to emphasize the connections between scientific discoveries and their cultural context; but that is just the way the world is.

On the other hand, the gap between science and other forms of culture may be narrow or absent for the sciences that specifically deal with human affairs. This is one of the reasons that in writing of this gap in my article, I wrote about physics, and explicitly excluded science like psychology from my remarks. I concentrated on physics also because that is what I know best. Professors Holquist and Shulman are mistaken in thinking that when talking of "science," I meant just physics, and excluded "microbiology, genetics, and the new brain sciences." I was pretty careful in my article to write of physics when I meant physics, and of science when I meant science. I can't see why Professor Shulman, a distinguished molecular biophysicist and biochemist, should be unhappy with my *not* offering opinions about the cultural implications of biology.

I should perhaps have made more clear in my article that I have no quarrel with most historians, philosophers, and sociologists of science. I am a fan of the history of science, and in my recent books I have acknowledged debts to writings of numerous historians, philosophers, and sociologists of science.[3] In contrast with Alan Sokal, who in perpetrating his hoax was mostly concerned about a breakdown of the alliance between science and the political left, my concern was more with the corruption of history and sociology by postmodern and constructivist ideologies. Contrary to what Professor Levine may think, my opposition to these views is not due to any worry about the effect they may have on the economic pinch hurting science. In years of lobbying for federal support of scientific programs, I never heard anything remotely postmodern or constructivist from a member of Congress.

Among philosophers of science, Thomas Kuhn deserves special mention. He was a friend of mine whose writings I often found illuminating, but over the years I was occasionally a critic of his views.[4] Even in his celebrated early *Structure of Scientific Revolutions*, Kuhn doubted that "changes of paradigm carry scientists and those who learn from them closer and closer to the truth." I corresponded with him after we met for the last time at a ceremony in Padua in 1992, and I found that his skepticism had become more radical. He sent me a copy of a 1991 lecture,[5] in which he had written that "it's hard to imagine . . . what the phrase 'closer to the truth' can mean"; and "I am not suggesting, let me emphasize, that there is a reality which science fails to get at. My point is rather that no sense can be made of the notion of reality as it has ordinarily functioned in philosophy of science." I don't think that it was "outrageous" for me to have said that, as I understood his views, Kuhn denied the objective nature of scientific knowledge.

Professor Levine and several others object to my criticism of Jacques Derrida, based as it seems to them on a single paragraph chosen by Sokal for mockery, which begins, "The Einsteinian constant is not a constant, is not a center. It is the very concept of variability—it is, finally, the concept of the game." When, in reading Sokal's *Social Text* article, I first encountered this paragraph, I was bothered not so much by the obscurity of Derrida's terms "center" and "game." I was willing to suppose that these were terms of art, defined elsewhere by Derrida. What bothered me was his phrase "the Einsteinian constant," which I had never met in my work as a physicist. True, there is something called Newton's constant which appears in Einstein's theory of gravitation, and I would not object if Derrida wanted to call it "the Einsteinian constant," but this constant is just a number (0.00000006673 in conventional units); I did not see how it could be the "center" of anything, much less the concept of a game.

So I turned for enlightenment to the talk by Derrida from which Sokal took this paragraph. In it, Derrida explains the word "center" as follows: "Nevertheless, . . . structure—or rather, the structurability of structure—although it has always been involved, has always been neutralized or re-duced, and this by a process of giving it a center or referring it to a point of presence, a fixed origin."[6] This was not much help.

Lest the reader think that I am quoting out of context or perhaps just being obtuse, I will point out that, in the discussion following Derrida's lecture, the first question was by Jean Hyppolite, professor at the CollÈge de France, who, after having sat through Derrida's talk, had to ask Derrida to explain what he meant by a "center." The paragraph quoted by Sokal was Derrida's answer. It was Hyppolite who introduced "the Einsteinian con-stant" into the discussion, but while poor Hyppolite was willing to admit that he did not understand what Derrida meant by a center, Derrida just started talking about the Einsteinian constant, without letting on that (as seems evident) he had no idea of what Hyppolite was talking about. It seems to me that Derrida in context is even worse than Derrida out of context.

Notes

1   On this, see Herbert Butterfield in *The Origins of Modern Science* (Free Press, 1957), especially Chapter 2.

2   Gerald Holton, *Einstein, History, and Other Passions* (Addison-Wesley, 1996), p. 129.

3   This includes contemporary historians of science like Laurie Brown, Stephen Brush, Gerald Holton, Arthur Miller, Abraham Pais, and Sam Schweber; sociologists of science like Robert Merton, Sharon Traweek, and Stephen Woolgar; and philosophers like Mario Bunge, George Gale, Ernest Nagel, Robert Nozick, Karl Popper, Hilary Putnam, and W.V. Quine. These references can be found in *Dreams of a Final Theory* (Pantheon, 1993), and *The Quantum Theory of Fields* (Cambridge University Press, 1995). There are many others whose works I have found illuminating, including the historian of science Peter Galison, the sociologist of science Harriet Zuckerman, and the philosophers Susan Haack and Bernard Williams.

4   See *Dreams of a Final Theory*, and "Night Thoughts of a Quantum Physicist," *Bulletin of the American Academy of Arts and Sciences*, Volume 69, No. 3 (December 1995), p. 51.

5   Thomas Kuhn, "The Trouble with the Historical Philosophy of Science," Rothschild Distinguished Lecture, November 19, 1991 (Department of the History of Science, Harvard College, 1992).

6   Jacques Derrida, "Structure, Sign, and Play in the Discourse of the Human Sciences" in *The Structuralist Controversy*, edited by R. Macksey and E. Donato (Johns Hopkins University Press, 1972), p. 247.

PAUL BOGHOSSIAN

What the Sokal Hoax Ought to Teach Us:
The Pernicious Consequences and Internal Contradictions
of "Postmodernist" Relativism, and selected responses

Times Literary Supplement, 13 December 1996

In the autumn of 1994, a New York University theoretical physicist, Alan Sokal, submitted an essay to *Social Text*, the leading journal in the field of cultural studies. Entitled "Transgressing the Boundaries: Toward a transformative hermeneutics of quantum gravity," it purported to be a scholarly article about the "postmodern" philosophical and political implications of twentieth-century physical theories. However, as the author himself later revealed in the journal *Lingua Franca*, his essay was merely a farrago of deliberate solecisms, howlers and *non-sequiturs*, stitched together so as to look good and to flatter the ideological preconceptions of the editors. After review by five members of *Social Text*'s editorial board, Sokal's parody was accepted for publication as a serious piece of scholarship. It appeared in April 1996, in a special double issue of the journal devoted to rebutting the charge that cultural-studies critiques of science tend to be riddled with incompetence.

Sokal's hoax is fast acquiring the status of a classic *succès de scandale*, with extensive press coverage in the United States and to a growing extent in Europe and Latin America. In the USA, over twenty public forums devoted to the topic either have taken place or are scheduled, including packed sessions at Princeton, Duke, the University of Michigan, and New York University. But what exactly should it be taken to show?

I believe it shows three important things. First, that dubiously coherent relativistic views about truth and evidence really have gained wide acceptance within the contemporary academy, just as it has often seemed. Second, that this has had precisely the sorts of pernicious consequences for standards of scholarship and intellectual responsibility that one would expect it to have. Finally, that neither of the preceding two claims need reflect a particular point of view, least of all a conservative one.

It's impossible to do justice to the egregiousness of Sokal's essay without quoting it more or less in its entirety; what follows is a tiny sampling. Sokal starts off by establishing his postmodernist credentials; he derides scientists for continuing to cling to the "dogma imposed by the long post-

Enlightenment hegemony over the Western intellectual outlook" [pt. 1, intro.]: that there exists an external world, whose properties are independent of human beings, and that human beings can obtain reliable, if imperfect and tentative knowledge of these properties "by hewing to the 'objective' procedures and epistemological strictures prescribed by the (so-called) scientific method" [pt. 1, intro.]. He asserts that this "dogma" has already been thoroughly undermined by the theories of general relativity and quantum mechanics, and that physical reality has been shown to be "at bottom a social and linguistic construct." In support of this, he adduces nothing more than a couple of pronouncements from physicists like Niels Bohr and Werner Heisenberg, pronouncements that have been shown to be dubious by sophisticated discussions in the philosophy of science over the past fifty years.

Sokal then picks up steam, moving to his central thesis that recent developments within quantum gravity—an emerging and still speculative physical theory—go much further, substantiating not only postmodern denials of the objectivity of truth, but also the beginnings of a kind of physics that would be truly "liberatory," of genuine service to progressive political causes. Here his "reasoning" becomes truly venturesome, as he contrives to generate political and cultural conclusions from the physics of the very, very small. His inferences are mediated by nothing more than a hazy patchwork of puns (especially on the words "linear" and "discontinuous"), strained analogies, bald assertions, and what can only be described as *non-sequiturs* of numbing grossness (to use a phrase that Peter Strawson applied to the far less deserving Immanuel Kant). For example, Sokal moves immediately from Bohr's observation that in quantum mechanics "a complete elucidation of one and the same object may require diverse points of view" to:

> In such a situation, how can a self-perpetuating secular priesthood of credentialed "scientists" purport to maintain a monopoly on the production of scientific knowledge? . . . The content and methodology of postmodern science thus provide powerful intellectual support for the progressive political project, understood in its broadest sense: the transgressing of boundaries, the breaking down of barriers, the radical democratization of all aspects of social, economic, political and cultural life. [Pt. 1, sec. 6]

He concludes by calling for the development of a correspondingly emancipated mathematics, one that, by not being based on standard (Zermelo-Fraenkel) set theory, would no longer constrain the progressive and postmodern ambitions of emerging physical science.

As if all this weren't enough, *en passant*, Sokal peppers his piece with as many smaller bits of transparent nonsense as could be made to fit on any given page. Some of these are of a purely mathematical or scientific nature—that the well-known geometrical constant pi is a variable, that complex number theory, which dates from the nineteenth century and is taught to schoolchildren, is a new and speculative branch of mathematical physics, that the crackpot New Age fantasy of a "morphogenetic field" constitutes a leading theory of quantum gravity. Others have to do with the alleged philosophical or political implications of basic science—that quantum field theory confirms Lacan's psychoanalytic speculations about the nature of the neurotic subject, that fuzzy logic is better suited to leftist political causes than classical logic, that Bell's theorem, a technical result in the foundations of quantum mechanics, supports a claimed linkage between quantum mechanics and "industrial discipline in the early bourgeois epoch." Throughout, Sokal quotes liberally and approvingly from the writings of leading postmodern theorists, including several editors of *Social Text*, passages that are often breathtaking in their combination of self-confidence and absurdity.

Commentators have made much of the scientific, mathematical and philosophical illiteracy that an acceptance of Sokal's ingeniously contrived gibberish would appear to betray. But talk about illiteracy elides an important distinction between two different explanations of what might have led the editors to decide to publish Sokal's piece. One is that, although they understood perfectly well what the various sentences of his article actually mean, they found them plausible, whereas he, along with practically everybody else, doesn't. This might brand them as kooky, but wouldn't impugn their motives. The other hypothesis is that they actually had very little idea what many of the sentences mean, and so were not in a position to evaluate them for plausibility in the first place. The plausibility, or even the intelligibility, of Sokal's arguments just didn't enter into their deliberations.

I think it's very clear, and very important, that it's the second hypothesis that's true. To see why consider, by way of example, the following passage from Sokal's essay:

> Just as liberal feminists are frequently content with a minimal agenda of legal and social equality for women and "pro-choice," so liberal (and even some socialist) mathematicians are often content to work within the hegemonic Zermelo-Fraenkel framework (which, reflecting its nineteenth-century origins, already incorporates the axiom of equality) supplemented only by the axiom of choice. But this framework is grossly insufficient for a liberatory mathematics, as was proven long ago by Cohen 1966. [Pt. 1, n.54]

It's very hard to believe that an editor who knows what the various ingredient terms actually mean would not have raised an eyebrow at this passage.

For the axiom of equality in set theory simply provides a definition of when it is that two sets are the same set, namely, when they have the same members; obviously, this has nothing to do with liberalism, or, indeed, with a political philosophy of any stripe. Similarly, the axiom of choice simply says that, given any collection of mutually exclusive sets, there is always a set consisting of exactly one member from each of those sets. Again, this clearly has nothing to do with the issue of choice in the abortion debate. But even if one were somehow able to see one's way clear—I can't—to explaining this first quoted sentence in terms of the postmodern love for puns and wordplay, what would explain the subsequent sentence? Paul Cohen's 1966 publication proves that the question whether or not there is a number between two other particular (transfinite cardinal) numbers isn't settled by the axioms of Zermelo-Fraenkel set theory. How could this conceivably count as a proof that Zermelo-Fraenkel set theory is inadequate for the purposes of a "liberatory mathematics," whatever precisely that is supposed to be? Wouldn't any editor who knew what Paul Cohen had actually proved in 1966 have required just a little more by way of explanation here, in order to make the connection just a bit more perspicuous?

Since one could cite dozens of similar passages—Sokal goes out of his way to leave tell-tale clues about his true intent—the conclusion is inescapable that the editors of *Social Text* didn't know what many of the sentences in Sokal's essay actually meant; and that they just didn't care. How could a group of scholars, editing what is supposed to be the leading journal in a given field, allow themselves such a sublime indifference to the content, truth and plausibility of a scholarly submission accepted for publication?

By way of explanation, co-editors Andrew Ross and Bruce Robbins have said that as "a non-refereed journal of political opinion and cultural analysis produced by an editorial collective . . . *Social Text* has always seen itself in the 'little magazine' tradition of the independent left as much as in the academic domain" [pt. 2, "Response"]. But it's hard to see this as an adequate explanation; presumably, even a journal of political opinion should care whether what it publishes is intelligible.

What Ross and Co. should have said, it seems to me, is that *Social Text* is a political magazine in a deeper and more radical sense: under appropriate circumstances, it is prepared to let agreement with its ideological orientation trump every other criterion for publication, including something as basic as sheer intelligibility. The prospect of being able to display in their pages a natural scientist—a physicist, no less—throwing the full weight of his authority behind their cause was compelling enough for them to overlook the fact that they didn't have much of a clue exactly what sort of support they were being offered. And this, it seems to me, is what's at the heart of the issue raised by Sokal's hoax: not the mere existence of incompetence within the academy, but rather that specific form of it that arises from allowing ideological criteria to displace standards of scholarship so completely that not even considerations of intelligibility are seen as relevant to an argument's acceptability. How, given the recent and sorry history of ideologically motivated conceptions of knowledge—Lysenkoism in Stalin's Soviet Union, for example, or Nazi critiques of "Jewish science"—could it again have become acceptable to behave in this way?

The complete historical answer is a long story, but there can be little doubt that one of its crucial components is the brushfire spread, within vast sectors of the humanities and social science, of the cluster of simple-minded relativistic views about truth and evidence that are commonly identified as "postmodernist." These views license, and indeed typically insist upon, the substitution of political criteria for the historically more familiar assessment in terms of truth, evidence and argument.

Most philosophers accept the claim that there is no such thing as a totally disinterested inquirer, one who approaches his or her topic utterly devoid of any prior assumptions, values or biases. Postmodernism goes well beyond this historicist observation, as feminist scholar Linda Nicholson explains (without necessarily endorsing):

> The traditional historicist claim that all inquiry is inevitably influenced by the values of the inquirer provides a very weak counter to the norm of objectivity. . . . [T]he more radical move in the postmodern turn was to claim that the very criteria demarcating the true and the false, as well as such related distinctions as science and myth or fact and superstition, were internal to the traditions of modernity and could not be legitimized outside of those traditions. Moreover, it was argued that the very development and use of such criteria, as well as their extension to ever wider domains, had to be described as representing the growth and development of "specific regimes of power." (From the introduction to her anthology, *Feminism and Postmodernism*)

As Nicholson sees it, historicism, however broadly understood, doesn't entail that there is no such thing as objective truth. To concede that no one ever believes something *solely* because it's true is not to deny that anything is objectively true. Furthermore, the concession that no inquirer or inquiry is fully bias-free doesn't entail that they can't be more or less damaging. To concede that the truth is never the only thing that someone is tracking isn't to deny that some people or methods are better than others at staying on its track.

Historicism leaves intact, then, both the claim that one's *aim* should be to arrive at conclusions that are objectively true and justified, independently of any particular perspective, and that science is the best idea that anyone has had about how to satisfy that aim. Postmodernism, in seeking to demote science from the privileged epistemic position it has come to occupy, and thereby to blur the distinction between it and "other ways of knowing"— myth and superstition, for example—needs to go much further than historicism, all the way to the denial that objective truth is a coherent aim that inquiry may have. Indeed, according to postmodernism, the very development and use of the rhetoric of objectivity, far from embodying a serious metaphysics and epistemology of truth and evidence, represents a mere play for power, a way of silencing these "other ways of knowing." It follows, given this standpoint, that the struggle against the rhetoric of objectivity isn't primarily an intellectual matter, but a political one: the rhetoric needs to be defeated, rather than just refuted. Against this backdrop, it becomes very easy to explain the behavior of the editors of *Social Text*.

Although it may be hard to understand how anyone could actually hold views as extreme as these, their ubiquity these days is a distressingly familiar fact. A front-page article in the *New York Times* of October 22, 1996, provided recent illustration. The article concerned the conflict between two views of where Native American populations originated—the scientific archaeological account, and the account offered by some Native American creation myths. According to the former, extensively confirmed view, humans first entered the Americas from Asia, crossing the Bering Strait over 10,000 years ago. By contrast, some Native American creation accounts hold that native peoples have lived in the Americas ever since their ancestors first emerged onto the surface of the earth from a subterranean world of spirits. The *Times* noted that many archaeologists, torn between their commitment to scientific method and their appreciation for native culture, "have been driven close to a postmodern relativism in which science is just one more belief system." Roger Anyon, a British archaeologist who has worked for the Zuni people, was quoted as saying: "Science is just one of many ways of knowing the world. . . . [The Zunis' world-view is] just as valid as the archaeological viewpoint of what history is about."

How are we to make sense of this? (Sokal himself mentioned this example at a recent public forum in New York and was taken to task by Andrew Ross for putting Native Americans "on trial." But this issue isn't about Native American views; it's about postmodernism.) The claim that the Zuni myth can be "just as valid" as the archeological theory can be read in one of three different ways, between which postmodern theorists tend not to distinguish sufficiently: as a claim about truth, as a claim about justification, or as a claim about purpose. As we shall see, however, none of these claims is even remotely plausible.

Interpreted as a claim about truth, the suggestion would be that the Zuni and archeological views are equally true. On the face of it, though, this is impossible, since they contradict each other. One says, or implies, that the first humans in the Americas came from Asia; the other says, or implies, that they did not, that they came from somewhere else, a subterranean world of spirits. How could a claim and its denial both be true? If I say that the earth is flat, and you say that it's round, how could we both be right?

Postmodernists like to respond to this sort of point by saying that both claims can be true because both are true relative to some perspective or other, and there can be no question of truth outside of perspectives. Thus, according to the Zuni perspective, the first humans in the Americas came from a subterranean world; and according to the Western scientific perspective, the first humans came from Asia. Since both are true according to some perspective or other, both are true.

But to say that some claim is true according to some perspective sounds simply like a fancy way of saying that someone, or some group, believes it. The crucial question concerns what we are to say when what I believe— what's true according to my perspective—conflicts with what you believe— with what's true according to your perspective. The one thing not to say, it seems to me, on pain of utter unintelligibility, is that both claims are true.

This should be obvious, but can also be seen by applying the view to itself. For consider: if a claim and its opposite can be equally true provided that there is some perspective relative to which each is true, then, since there is a perspective—realism—relative to which it's true that a claim and its opposite cannot both be true, postmodernism would have to admit that it itself is just as true as its opposite, realism. But postmodernism cannot afford to admit that; presumably, its whole point is that realism is false. Thus, we see that the very statement of postmodernism, construed as a view about truth, undermines itself; facts about truth independent of particular perspectives are presupposed by the view itself.

How does it fare when considered as a claim about evidence or justification? So construed, the suggestion comes to the claim that the Zuni story and the archaeological theory are equally justified, given the available evidence. Now, in contrast with the case of truth, it is not incoherent for a claim and its negation to be equally justified, for instance, in cases where there is very little evidence for either side. But, prima facie, anyway, this isn't the sort of case that's at issue, for, according to the available evidence, the archaeological theory is far better confirmed than the Zuni myth.

To get the desired relativistic result, a postmodernist would have to claim that the two views are equally justified, *given their respective rules of evidence*, and add that there is no objective fact of the matter which set of rules is to be preferred. Given this relativization of justification to the rules of evidence characteristic of a given perspective, the archaeological theory would be justified relative to the rules of evidence of Western science, and the Zuni story would be justified relative to the rules of evidence employed by the relevant tradition of myth-making. Furthermore, since there are no perspective-independent rules of evidence that could adjudicate between these two sets of rules, both claims would be equally justified and there could be no choosing between them.

Once again, however, there is a problem not merely with plausibility, but with self-refutation. For suppose we grant that every rule of evidence is as good as any other. Then any claim could be made to count as justified simply by formulating an appropriate rule of evidence relative to which it is justified. Indeed, it would follow that we could justify the claim that not every rule of evidence is as good as any other, thereby forcing the postmodernist to concede that his views about truth and justification are just as justified as his opponent's. Presumably, however, the postmodernist needs to hold that his views are better than his opponent's; otherwise what's to recommend them? On the other hand, if some rules of evidence can be said to be better than others, then there must be perspective-independent facts about what makes them better, and the thorough-going relativism about justification is false.

It is sometimes suggested that the intended sense in which the Zuni myth is "just as valid" has nothing to do with truth or justification, but rather with the different purposes that the myth subserves, in contrast with those of science. According to this line of thought, science aims to give a descriptively accurate account of reality, whereas the Zuni myth belongs to the realm of religious practice and the constitution of cultural identity. It is to be regarded as having symbolic, emotional and ritual purposes other than the mere description of reality. And as such, it may serve those purposes very well—better, perhaps, than the archaeologist's account.

The trouble with this as a reading of "just as valid" is not so much that it's false, but that it's irrelevant to the issue at hand; even if it were granted, it couldn't help advance the cause of postmodernism. For if the Zuni myth isn't taken to compete with the archaeological theory, as a descriptively accurate account of prehistory, its existence has no prospect of casting any doubt on the objectivity of the account delivered by science. If I say that the earth is flat, and you make no assertion at all, but instead tell me an interesting story, then that has no potential for raising deep issues about the objectivity of what either of us said or did.

Is there, perhaps, a weaker thesis that, while being more defensible than these simple-minded relativisms, would nevertheless yield an anti-objectivist result? It's hard to see what such a thesis would be. Stanley Fish, for example, in seeking to discredit Sokal's characterization of postmodernism, offers the following (Opinion piece, the *New York Times*):

> What sociologists of science say is that of course the world is real and independent of our observations but that accounts of the world are produced by observers and are therefore relative to their capacities, education and training, etc. It is not the world or its properties but the vocabularies in whose terms we know them that are socially constructed . . . [pt. 3, "Professor Sokal's Bad Joke"].

The rest of Fish's discussion leaves it thoroughly unclear exactly what he thinks this observation shows; but claims similar to his are often presented by others as constituting yet another basis for arguing against the objectivity of science. The resultant arguments are unconvincing.

It goes without saying that the *vocabulaires* with which we seek to know the world are socially constructed and that they therefore reflect various contingent aspects of our capacities, limitations and interests. But it doesn't follow that those vocabularies are therefore incapable of meeting the standards of adequacy relevant to the expression and discovery of objective truths.

We may illustrate why by using Fish's own example. There is no doubt that the game of baseball as we have it, with its particular conceptions of what counts as a "strike" and what counts as a "ball," reflects various contingent facts about us as physical and social creatures. "Strike" and "ball" are socially constructed concepts, if anything is. However, once these concepts have been defined—once the strike zone has been specified—there are then perfectly objective facts about what counts as a strike and what counts as a ball. (The fact that the umpire is the court of last appeal doesn't mean that he can't make mistakes.)

Similarly, our choice of one conceptual scheme rather than another, for the purposes of doing science, probably reflects various contingent facts about our capacities and limitations, so that a thinker with different capacities and limitations, a Martian for example, might find it natural to employ a different scheme. This does nothing to show that our conceptual scheme is incapable of expressing objective truths. Realism is not committed to there being only one vocabulary in which objective truths might be expressed; all it's committed to is the weaker claim that, once a vocabulary is specified, it will then be an objective matter whether or not assertions couched in that vocabulary are true or false.

We are left with two puzzles. Given what the basic tenets of postmodernism are, how did they ever come to be identified with a progressive political outlook? And given how transparently refutable they are, how did they ever come to gain such widespread acceptance?

In the United States, postmodernism is closely linked to the movement known as multiculturalism, broadly conceived as the project of giving proper credit to the contributions of cultures and communities whose achievements have been historically neglected or undervalued. In this connection, it has come to appeal to certain progressive sensibilities because it supplies the philosophical resources with which to prevent anyone from accusing oppressed cultures of holding false or unjustified views.

Even on purely political grounds, however, it is difficult to understand how this could have come to seem a good way to conceive of multiculturalism. For if the powerful can't criticize the oppressed, because the central epistemological categories are inexorably tied to particular perspectives, it also follows that the oppressed can't criticize the powerful. The only remedy, so far as I can see, for what threatens to be a strongly conservative upshot, is to accept an overt double standard: allow a questionable idea to be criticized if it is held by those in a position of power—Christian creationism, for example—but not if it is held by those whom the powerful oppress—Zuni creationism, for example. Familiar as this stratagem has recently become, how can it possibly appeal to anyone with the slightest degree of intellectual integrity; and how can it fail to seem anything other than deeply offensive to the progressive sensibilities whose cause it is supposed to further?

As for the second question, regarding widespread acceptance, the short answer is that questions about truth, meaning and objectivity are among the most difficult and thorny questions that philosophy confronts and so are very easily mishandled. A longer answer would involve explaining why analytic philosophy, the dominant tradition of philosophy in the English-speaking world, wasn't able to exert a more effective corrective influence. After all, analytic philosophy is primarily known for its detailed and subtle discussion of concepts in the philosophy of language and the theory of knowledge, the very concepts that postmodernism so badly misunderstands. Isn't it reasonable to expect it to have had a greater impact on the philosophical explorations of its intellectual neighbors? And if it hasn't, can that be because its reputation for insularity is at least partly deserved? Because philosophy concerns the most general categories of knowledge, categories that apply to any compartment of inquiry, it is inevitable that other disciplines will reflect on philosophical problems and develop philosophical positions. Analytic philosophy has a special responsibility to ensure that its insights on matters of broad intellectual interest are available widely, to more than a narrow class of insiders.

Whatever the correct explanation for the current malaise, Alan Sokal's hoax has served as a flashpoint for what has been a gathering storm of protest against the collapse in standards of scholarship and intellectual responsibility with which vast sectors of the humanities and social sciences are currently afflicted. Significantly, some of the most biting commentary has come from distinguished voices on the Left, showing that when it comes to transgressions as basic as these, political alliances afford no protection. Anyone still inclined to doubt the seriousness of the problem has only to read Sokal's parody.

Selected responses

20 December 1997

Sir,

Although I have never considered myself much of a postmodernist, the more attacks I read on the decision of the journal *Social Text*'s editors to publish Alan Sokal's bogus article, the more I sympathize with them. Paul Boghossian (December 13) provides a perfect example of the source of my irritation. If we should beware of cultural-studies scholars passing themselves off as experts on cultural implications of contemporary science, we should be even more wary of philosophers who try to reduce cross-disciplinary scholarship to lessons in elementary logic.

Postmodernists may talk a lot about blurring "genres," but I do not recall any of their number ever saying they wanted to blur the difference between true and false. Their claim, rather, is that the difference between true and false—however clearly one wishes to draw it—does not explain either the initial acceptance or the subsequent persistence of beliefs. The reason is that the embrace of truth and the avoidance of falsehood are things that everyone claims for themselves and can usually demonstrate to their own satisfaction. The deeper question is how does a particular way of drawing the true/false distinction come to predominate over other possible ways. An adequate answer transcends the resources of logic, and requires some understanding of the history and sociology of knowledge-production. From this perspective, Professor Boghossian's brief on behalf of "realism" and "objectivity" is, as philosophers like to say, "true but trivial."

Not surprisingly, then, when Boghossian tries to find reasons why postmodernists appear to deny the true/false distinction, he is forced into a far-fetched speculation about their need to believe whatever satisfies their political prejudices. He tries to make this speculation stick in the case of the *Social Text* editors by presuming that to accept an article for publication is to agree with its conclusions. Unfortunately, had Boghossian read the introduction to the offending *Social Text* issue, he would have noticed that the editors failed to mention Sokal's piece altogether in their attempt to lace together the political interests that unify the issue's contributors. Considering Sokal's strained efforts to play to the gallery by evoking a "liberatory science" led by cultural-studies scholars, this fact is rather striking. It would seem, then, that the editors are guilty of no more than being able to tell the difference between what they agree with and what they are willing to publish.

Although I, unlike Boghossian, do not presume to be privy to the psychological make-up of *Social Text*'s editors, their actions seem to imply that they believed Sokal's piece to be sufficiently well crafted to merit academic discussion, which presumably includes discussion of whether or not its inferences from scientific to cultural matters are unwarranted, but I would stand behind the editors in arguing that it is better to have this point revealed in open debate than to have the article censored in the editorial boardroom. To my mind, Alan Sokal does the most damage to postmodernism when his own designation of it as a "hoax" is taken as the authoritative reading of the piece.

Steve Fuller
Department of Sociology and Social Policy,
University of Durham, Elvet Riverside, Durham.

10 January 1997

Sir,

Steve Fuller (Letters, December 20) acts perhaps out of excessive modesty in failing to mention the fact that, as a contributor to the special "Science Wars" issue of *Social Text* in which Alan Sokal's parody appeared, he is better placed than most to explain and defend that journal's editorial decisions. Unfortunately, his letter is an example of the sort of careless argument that my article (December 13) deplored.

Dr. Fuller claims never to have met a postmodernist who denies that there is a distinction between what is true and what is false. His formulation omits the crucial word "objective"; and he neglects to mention that I also consider post-modernism as a thesis about justification rather than truth. According to Fuller, postmodernists believe only the far more innocuous thesis that a belief's being true doesn't explain its acceptance or persistence. It's certainly encouraging to hear that no one asserts the extreme and, as I argued, incoherent thesis about truth. Alas, Fuller's claim here would appear to be an instance of what Raymond Tallis calls, in his eloquent and impassioned letter (January 3), one of those "U-turns conducted with such guile that no one feels the centrifugal force."

Fuller doesn't tell us whether he thinks that the truth of a belief doesn't *necessarily* explain its acceptance or persistence, or that it *never* explains it.

The former thesis is so obvious that no one has ever denied it; if the truth of a belief necessarily explained its acceptance, no one would ever believe anything false. So Fuller had better mean the second thesis. But how are we to understand the claim that the truth of a belief *never* explains its acceptance or persistence? If I believe that there is a cup on my table, and there is a cup on my table, can't that fact sometimes enter into the *causal explanation* of why I believe what I believe? If, on the other hand, the claim is supposed to be that I can never *justify* my belief that the cup is on my table by appealing to that very fact, whose view is that supposed to contradict? To appeal to a fact, in order to justify one's belief in that very fact, would be obviously circular and self-serving. What one appeals to is not the fact itself, but the evidence at one's disposal. So I have no idea what interesting thesis Fuller wishes to attribute to postmodernism, nor how he proposes to explain postmodernist denials of the distinction between science and myth, fact and superstition, explicit examples of which are cited in my article.

Steve Fuller also seeks to defend *Social Text*'s decision to publish Sokal's essay by suggesting that it stemmed from their justified view that it was "sufficiently well crafted to merit academic discussion." Has he not read Sokal's essay, or even my brief summary of it? The essay contains literally dozens of claims that anyone with the least familiarity with their content would see right through, including, inter alia: that the geometrical constant pi is a variable; that complex-number theory, which dates from the nineteenth century and is taught to schoolchildren, is a new and speculative area of mathematical physics; that the axiom of choice in set theory is intimately related to the issue about freedom of choice in the abortion debate. Does Fuller really wish to claim that an essay that is basically a tissue of such transparent nonsense is "sufficiently well crafted to merit academic discussion"?

What is much more plausible is that the editors of *Social Text* were simply not qualified to judge whether Sokal's essay merited discussion and that this fact didn't hinder them in the least. This peculiar behavior seems to me to call for special explanation, and I can think of nothing more compelling than to appeal to the independently confirmable fact that they have bought into a set of misguided philosophical views that allow them to pooh-pooh the importance of reasonable argument, plausible evidence and factual correctness. There are, surely, less charitable explanations also available.

As for David Weissman's contention (Letters, December 27) that *Social Text*'s relativism is akin to the views of Carnap, Wittgenstein, Quine and Putnam, one can at least be thankful that he does not try to beat the sort of hasty tactical retreat that Steve Fuller attempts. However, it would take more than a letter to sort out the various confusions that lead Weissman blithely to rope these important but disparate thinkers together, and to equate their views with the sort of simple-minded relativisms at issue.

Finally, Tallis wonders whether he is alone in agreeing with the general tenor of my remarks and arguments. I can assure Dr Tallis, on the basis of the very large correspondence I've received, that he is not.

Paul Boghossian

31 January 1997

Sir,

In his comments about Alan Sokal's hoax (December 13), Paul Boghossian grossly misrepresented postmodernist critiques of objectivism. He was less than honest, since he said nothing about the failures of the analytic philosophy he championed against postmodernism, failures which have provided over the years much force for the postmodernist argument. Having said this, Steve Fuller has been equally dishonest in his response (Letters, December 20), by failing to acknowledge that there is something profoundly disturbing about the failure of the editors of *Social Text* to recognize Sokal's essay for what it was, a hoax which has left no one untarnished.

Anyone familiar with the literature on postmodernism will know that defining this term is a notoriously difficult problem even among self-styled postmodernists themselves. The crisis of analytical philosophy and the diversity of traditions in continental philosophy open too many disparate ways of criticizing objectivism to be as coherently assimilated and labeled as Professor Boghossian does. The editors of *Social Text* certainly failed to live up to good standards of academic conduct, such as calling for evaluation by competent referees, when their own competencies to evaluate a manuscript on the problems of physics were clearly inadequate. This procedural failure, however, cannot be used to deny the intellectual integrity of all those who argue against objectivism. I want to be more specific than Boghossian, reflecting on just the work of the sociologists of scientific knowledge to whom he refers via Stanley Fish.

These sociologists, and Fuller is one of them, would agree with Boghossian that their actors often evaluate this or that affirmation on the grounds that they seem reasonable and they are patently supported by empirical observations. Nor do they have any problem with the view that claims to knowledge are bound by systems of rules and conventions, within which it is clearly possible to adjudicate between truth and falsity. The problem between the sociologists and Boghossian actually lies instead in how we, the observers, should understand who is allowed to establish the conventions allowing the actors in our various philosophical and sociological accounts of human action to move from evidence to choice in certain ways rather than others. At this point, the sociologists argue, the actors' claims to knowledge, to truth, must be viewed as problems about social and political order. Boghossian disagrees, and wants to invoke instead the putative facts of nature as ultimate arbiter between various competing systems of conventions, for example between those underpinning theological and naturalistic explanations.

Boghossian points out, quite rightly, the inconsistency of postmodernist scholarship when it takes on the objectivist, Archimedean standpoint in its criticism of objectivism itself. Like David Weissman (Letters, December 27), I suspect that the editors of *Social Text* fell into this trap when they thought they had found a physicist who would tell the world (or better, the largely already convinced readers of their journal) about the objective validity of their particular outlook. Incidentally, I fear that such insularity greatly contributes to the fracturing of the academic community into needlessly and perniciously opposed camps. Not only does it mean that it is increasingly impossible to call on trustworthy and competent expertise to comment on the merits of seemingly promising, interdisciplinary exchanges such as Sokal's infamous essay, but it also weakens the academic community's position against far more powerful, external enemies of meaningful intellectual exchange. Many postmodernists take the view that the most effective strategy to defeat any objectionable system of beliefs, such as objectivism, is not to fall for the alluring Archimedean perspective, but to show instead the faultiness of arguments for said system according to its own conventions. In the case of objectivism, this has already been done, as Weissman has correctly indicated and Boghossian continues to ignore in his reply to his critics (Letters, January 10). Once this leveling work is accomplished, choosing between one conventional system and another becomes a matter of local and specific, ethical and political commitments.

I take it that Paul Boghossian would claim that the Bible provides only a mythical account of the world, but for many who don't believe in its account of creation or the miracles, it has been and still is nonetheless a source of great strength to act justly and morally in the world. I would like to know for whom, and for what ends, Boghossian wants to resurrect a now outdated notion of analytical philosophy which refuses to reflect on the ethical and political implications of its appeal to the objective facts of nature.

Paolo Palladina
Department of History, Furness College,
Lancaster University, Lancaster.

KURT GOTTFRIED

Was Sokal's Hoax Justified?

Physics Today, January 1997

Physicists rarely make the front page of the *New York Times*, but Alan Sokal of New York University did last 18 May. The *Times* reported the hoax he published in *Social Text*,[1] and immediately revealed,[2] in which he lampooned certain sociologists and humanists engaged in science studies. The story reverberated in the popular press, and was then taken to a loftier level by the *New York Review of Books*.[3]

Some believe that such a prank in an academic journal is unacceptable, but I claim that Sokal was justified.

As this debate has an irreducible ideological dimension, I must first state where I come from. Because science has an enormous impact on society, decisions about the exploitation and support of science must be made by society as a whole. This imposes serious obligations on us as scientists— obligations rarely discharged with commensurate urgency and devotion. The natural sciences also provoke questions few scientists are qualified to tackle—such as the influence of the cultural and political context on the creation of scientific knowledge. Here, there are serious obligations on scholars in science studies, and in my view they too are often not met. Finally, I know that "an oral tradition [employing] intuitive modes of thought, inference by analogy and other stratagems plays an essential role in the creation of physics."[4] Nevertheless, I believe that physics ultimately produces knowledge that is not contingent on culture or personalities, in contrast to more difficult pursuits in which reproducible phenomena under carefully controllable conditions either do not exist or are of little interest.

When Sokal's hoax surfaced, I heard arguments that the editors of *Social Text* should be excused for not catching on—that respected physics journals sometimes publish articles that editors and referees know they do not understand and suspect to be wrong. I found these arguments rather compelling. Afterward, however, evidence from the ultimate source, *Social Text* itself, changed my mind.

The editors of *Social Text*, Bruce Robbins and Andrew Ross, with commendable candor, stated publicly that their journal has a political agenda, which is overlooked by those who charge Sokal with defiling academic ethical standards. This perspective is evident in Robbins and Ross's letters to the *New York Times* on 23 May 1996, and to *In These Times* on 8 July, the latter stating that "*Social Text* was hoaxed not because we liked Sokal's jargon-filled references to postmodern authorities . . . but because we thought he was a progressive scientist, a physicist who was willing to be publicly critical of scientific orthodoxies. . . . Anyone who thinks this stuff is characteristic of *Social Text* is invited to read the rest of the 'Science Wars' issue from which Sokal's prank has unfortunately diverted attention."

I then read an article from which Sokal diverted attention: "The Politics of the Science Wars" by Stanley Aronowitz.[5] To put it succinctly, had I been shown both Sokal's and Aronowitz's articles, and asked which might be a hoax, I would have said that both are either hoaxes or nonsense! Why? Because Aronowitz, like Sokal, (1) makes statements about physics that are factually wrong, (2) displays deep misconceptions about physics and (3) seems ignorant about what physicists did in the past and try to do now. And to boot, Aronowitz, like Sokal, speaks with a self-confidence that would assure lay readers that they are in the hands of an erudite expert.

What's wrong with the Aronowitz piece?

Exhibit 1: "Most theoretical physicists, for example, sincerely believe that however partial our collective knowledge may be . . . of physical reality, one day scientists shall find the necessary correlation between wave and particle; the unified field theory of matter and energy will transcend Heisenberg's uncertainty principle."

Readers of *Physics Today* don't need me to explain how absurd that is.

Exhibit 2: "At the end of the day, the many questions of science and its influence cannot be settled by means of a fail-safe method of inquiry . . . passionate partisans of wave and matrix mechanics explanations for the behavior of electrons were unable to reach agreement for decades."

The facts: Heisenberg discovered matrix mechanics in July 1925, and his theory was developed that fall by him, Born and Jordan, and independently by Dirac. Schrödinger announced his discovery of wave mechanics in January 1926. Everyone was puzzled that two such different formulations gave identical results. Six weeks later, Schrödinger submitted the paper that proved that the two theories were mathematically equivalent. End of passionate debate.

Now you may say this is a quibble. It is not. For it goes beyond not knowing the simplest facts about an important development in the science one is supposedly analyzing. This incorrect statement is used to argue that scientists cannot settle their disputes with better experiments or theories, a claim also made by some other sociologists, though not on the basis of such a flagrant error.

Exhibit 3 is far more complicated. Aronowitz's article rests, in part, on a study by Paul Forman,[6] which, according to Aronowitz, "shows" that the "shift from the Old Quantum Theory, which retainted large elements of classical physics, to [quantum mechanics]" was linked to the "pessimism that afflicted the rest of the academic elite" in Weimar Germany.

This claim that the Weimar *Zeitgeist* led to the triumph of indeterministic quantum mechanics floored me. I have, for some 45 years, indulged myself in an amateurish infatuation with the original literature of modern physics, and was unaware of this thesis. That atomic physics was in crisis was known before Weimar was a gleam in France's eye. In 1912, Einstein in Prague, looking out on a mental hospital below, told a visitor that the people pacing the yard were the lunatics who did not have to worry about the quantum theory. Long before 1925, practitioners of the old quantum theory knew it was not a theory, but a hodgepodge of ingenious and often contradictory recipes grafted onto classical physics.

The intellectual leader of the whole quantum enterprise in the Weimar period was a Dane, Niels Bohr. In 1924, Bohr published the most radical pre-Heisenberg proposal for a new theory with a Dutchman, Kramers, and an American, Slater. They were not humiliated Teutons obsessed by Nietzsche and Spengler, pining for a Wagnerian crisis.

I looked up Forman. His is an erudite paper with 246 footnotes, many very long. Forman makes a convincing case that Hermann Weyl[7] and other important German-speaking mathematicians and physicists (in contrast to Anglo-Saxon ones) did ponder the philosophical implications raised by their attempts to solve the atomic enigma. But Forman's paper has no explicit discussion of the famous puzzles that the old quantum theory could not solve, such as the helium spectrum, or of the phenomena it could not even address, such as collisions. Nor does it relate that once the matrix mechanics and wave mechanics papers appeared, those Germans stopped philosophizing and used the new theory like pragmatic Anglo-Saxons because it obviously worked, even if its interpretation was then a mystery.

Other publications by Forman show that he knows all this and much more. Furthermore, he could assume that his readers, professional historians of science, do too, and could make an informed judgment about the plausibility of his astonishing thesis, as some did with sharp critiques[8] that go beyond my curbside remarks. But most readers (and authors) of *Social Text* do not have such knowledge, and would be unable to assess the extent to which cultural factors influenced the development of quantum mechanics.

So, in this setting, Aronowitz's presentation becomes the unadorned contention that the triumph of one scientific theory over another is due to factors exterior to science and not to what we physicists claim produces the final decision—experimentally established facts and mathematical coherence.

Indeed, Aronowitz implies that Forman showed that the shift from the old theory was due to the *Zeitgeist*, whereas Forman's thesis is more subtle: "And while it is undoubtedly true that the internal developments in atomic physics were important in precipitating this widespread sense of crisis among German-speaking Central European physicists, . . . [t]he *possibility* of the crisis of the old quantum theory was, I think, dependent upon the physicists' own craving for crisis, arising from participation in, and adaptation to, the Weimar intellectual milieu."[9] Here, developments within physics are considered, though with far less weight than I find plausible.

Now a few words about Sokal's paper. I claim that any well-informed layman should have recognized it as a hoax, because Sokal was reckless. Consider, for example, his hilarious note 3, citing the literary scholar David Poroush who, according to Sokal, claims that computer scientists subverted "the most revolutionary implications of quantum physics." Sokal then admonishes Poroush for not taking his case further—for not pointing out that "Claude Shannon worked for the then telephone monopoly AT&T," and not analyzing carefully whether "the victory of cybernetics over quantum physics in the 1940s and 1950s can be explained in large part by the centrality of cybernetics to the ongoing capitalist drive for automation of industrial production, compared to the marginal industrial relevance of quantum mechanics." Where did the editors of *Social Text* hear of the victory of cybernetics over quantum physics? And are they, while putting out an issue on science and society, unaware that the transistor, the Rosetta stone of modern electronics, was invented at AT&T at that very time, and depends on quantum processes in solids?

To summarize, I hope that Sokal's hoax will play a beneficial role—not just in the debate at this interface between the natural sciences and other fields, but for the academic enterprise as a whole. People who allow others to call them university professors do not have academic freedom and—if they're lucky—tenure only to protect that freedom. They also have responsibilities. Surely they must—not should—have a modicum of knowledge about the topics they pass judgments on. That does not mean that they must follow a narrow path, or refrain from voicing outrageous opinions—but not opinions based on junk thought and junk knowledge.

Physicists should not, however, jump to the conclusion that *Social Text* is representative of science studies. Sociologists with knowledge of physics voice opinions that I find outrageous and perplexing. Consider, in particular, Andrew Pickering's *Creating Quarks: A Sociological History of Particle Physics*.[10] It gives a superb account of the birth of the Standard Model of particle physics, and is better suited for most of the readers Weisskopf and I had in mind when we wrote our 1984 book. Nevertheless, here is the lesson Pickering draws from his well-told tale: "The [Standard Model] should be seen as a culturally specific product . . . a communally congenial representation of reality. . . . [O]nly singular incompetence could have prevented [the] high energy physics community [from] producing an understandable version of reality at any point in [its] history. . . . [T]he preponderance of mathematics . . . is no more difficult to understand than the fondness of ethnic groups for their native language. . . . [T]here is no obligation upon anyone framing a view of the world to take account of what twentieth century science has to say."[11] Pickering's later work offers a more nuanced and complex viewpoint, though he appears to adhere to the same bottom line.[12] Some other sociologists who study physics also assert that scientific knowledge is a cultural artifact (as discussed in David Mermin's column, "The Golemization of Relativity," *Physics Today*, April 1996, page 11), and this view is taking hold in audiences in no position to evaluate the assertion. Scientists must respond in a thoughtful and persuasive manner, and learn how to reach those audiences effectively. Mere polemics will not do.

Notes

I thank Gerald Holton, David Mermin and Sam Schweber for criticism and advice.

1 A. D. Sokal, *Social Text* (Spring/Summer 1996), p. 217.

2 A. D. Sokal, *Lingua Franca*, (May/June 1996), p. 62.

3 S. Weinberg, *New York Review of Books*, 8 August 1996, p. 11; see also letter to editor, 3 October 1996, p. 54.

4 K. Gottfried, V.F. Weisskopf, *Concepts of Particle Physics*, vol. 1, Oxford U.P., New York (1984), p. vii.

5 S. Aronowitz, *Social Text* (Spring/Summer 1996), p. 177.

6 P. Forman, His. Stud. Phys. Sci., 3, 1 (1971).

7 H. Weyl, *Philosophy of Mathematics and Natural Science*, Princeton U.P., Princeton, N.J. (1947); largely translated from the original *Handbuch der Philosophie* (1926).

8 J. Hendry, His. Sci. 18, 155 (1980); P. Kraft, P. Kroes, Centaurus 27, 76 (1984).

9 Ref 6, p. 62, emphasis in original.

10 A. Pickering, *Creating Quarks: A Sociological History of Particle Physics*, U. of Chicago P., Chicago (1984).

11 Ref. 10, p. 413.

12 A. Pickering, Soc. Stud. Sci. 20, 682 (1990); *The Mangle of Practice*, U. of Chicago P., Chicago (1995).

DAVID DICKSON

The "Sokal Affair" Takes Transatlantic Turn

Nature, 30 January 1997

A dispute that has been simmering since last summer in the United States over the validity of "postmodernist" ideas about the nature of scientific knowledge has finally reached the point where many such ideas originated— the banks of the river Seine in Paris.

Over the past month, the newspaper *Le Monde* has been running a series of articles triggered by an account of the widely publicized hoax perpetrated last year by Alan Sokal, a theoretical physicist at New York University, on the journal *Social Text*.

The hoax took the form of an article submitted to and accepted by the journal. It purported to demonstrate the social and political origins of ideas in quantum mechanics—but in fact was fabricated out of miscellaneous (but accurate) quotations from prominent postmodern writers and dubious statements of scientific "fact."

Sokal's article has added fuel to a conflict that has been growing in recent years between scientists who argue that science is based on empirical fact, and sociologists of science who argue that much of scientific knowledge is "constructed" out of debates between researchers (see, for example, *Nature* 375,#39; 1995).

In the United States, the hoax article and its implications—namely that sociologists of science have little regard for empirical truth and are more interested in intellectual fashions—has set off a wide debate on university campuses. "The reaction has been a factor of ten bigger than I expected," says Sokal. "And it is not letting up."

Until now, the response in Europe has been relatively muted, even though many of the writers quoted tend to be European, usually either British or French. The main reaction has been a defense of European academics whose work and U.S. colleagues have come under attack.

Positions, Postmodernism, and Politics

Last October, for example, many of those attending a joint meeting of the US-based Society for Social Studies in Science and the European Association for Studies of Science and Technology, held in Bielefeld in Germany, signed a petition protesting that some of the recent US criticism of work by sociologists of science could, in Europe, be regarded as potentially defamatory.

But the recent series of articles in *Le Monde*, widely regarded as the main public forum for both intellectual and political debate in France, as well as coverage in French publications *Libération* and *Le Nouvel Observateur*, indicate that the issue is now hotting up in Europe too.

Further evidence comes from the fact that an article by Paul Boghossian, a philosopher also at New York University, attacking postmodernist views of science, which appeared in the *Times Literary Supplement* in December, has already been published in *Die Zeit*, one of Germany's leading newspapers.

One of Sokal's strongest supporters is Jean Bricmont, a theoretical physicist at the University of Louvain in Belgium. He is writing a book with Sokal on what both argue is the frequent misuse of scientific concepts by prominent—and mainly French—intellectual figures ranging from the psychoanalyst Lacan to Bruno Latour, an influential sociologist of science.

When is a fact is not fact? Bricmont wrote in his contribution to the debate in *Le Monde* that such allusions tended to be "at best totally arbitrary and at worse erroneous." He says he is keen to see a reinstatement of ideas about science based on empiricism and the analytical philosophy of individuals such as the mathematician Bertrand Russell, rather than those of German idealists such as the philosopher Martin Heidegger.

He says he is concerned at a growing tendency to see ideas in socially relative terms, criticizing, for example, official guidelines on epistemology used by high school teachers in Belgium for stating that a fact is not an empirical truth, but "something that everyone agrees upon."

Like Sokal, Bricmont says that he has been surprised by the level of interest he has stirred up. "I seem to have put my finger on something bigger than I realized," he says.

But some of those under attack, having initially held back from the fray on the grounds that the debate was primarily based on issues internal to the United States, are now fighting back, arguing that it is their critics who have an idealistic—and increasingly outdated—vision of science and its role in contemporary culture.

Last week, for example, Latour, who teaches the sociology of innovation at the Ecole Supérieure des Mines in Paris, one of France's so-called *grandes écoles*, complained in *Le Monde* that he and fellow sociologists were being treated as "drug peddlers" who were corrupting the minds of American youth.

In fact, says Latour, one of his main concerns has been to demonstrate how modern society—as reflected in the public response to concerns about bovine spongiform encephalopathy ("mad cow disease")—is transforming itself from a culture "based on Science, with a capital S," to one based on research more broadly, including the social sciences.

He writes: "In place of an autonomous and detached science, whose absolute knowledge allows us to extinguish the fires of political passions and subjectivity, we are entering a new era in which scientific controversy becomes part of political controversy."

The latest salvo in the French debate comes from Sokal himself. In a response due to be published this week, Sokal repeats his claim that every scientist is aware that, although scientific knowledge is always partial and subject to revision, "that does not prevent it from being objective."

Sokal eschews charges of chauvinism, saying that his target is not—as some have suggested—French intellectuals as such, but "certain intellectuals who happen to live in France." He also dismisses the criticism that his concern about the growing influence of "constructivist" ideas about science reflects worries about a decline in both funding for physics and its social status with the end of the Cold War.

Differences in Culture and Education

But Latour, too, who makes both claims, has his supporters—and not just in France. Simon Shaffer, a lecturer in history and philosophy of science at the University of Cambridge, points to the irony that Latour and others are trying to develop the public understanding of science that, in other contexts, Sokal and others argue is essential if they are to retain respect.

Shaffer also points to the different cultural environments, partly a product of different educational traditions, in which French and American scientists operate. "In France, everyone believes that the sciences are self-validating, and that the social sciences refer to a world that exists outside themselves," he says.

In contrast, he argues, the empiricism that tends to dominate the Anglo-American approach to science means that "no one in the scientific community sees themselves as an epistemologist or a constructivist."

With Europe facing important issues concerning the relationship between science and politics—ranging from the likely science policy of the British Labour party if it wins the imminent general election, to the squeeze by Germany on international spending on particle physics—the public debate set alight by Sokal appears unlikely to die down rapidly.

PETER OSBORNE

Friendly Fire: The Hoaxing of Social Text

Radical Philosophy, January–February 1997

When the editorial committee of the U.S. journal *Social Text* chose "Science Wars" as the title for last year's special double issue (nos. 46–47, Spring/ Summer 1996), they could hardly have guessed how apt it would prove to be—not as a description of its contents, but of the furor it would provoke. For with this issue of *Social Text*, a new front was opened up in the "culture wars" which rage in the USA over the disputed terrain where academic discourse meets mainstream politics in the distorting mirror of the media: a complex and treacherous battleground of "science," where political allies can be swiftly transformed into ideological foes in a hail of friendly fire.

The spark was the revelation that *Social Text* had been subjected to a carefully managed hoax. Several months previously, Alan Sokal, a professor of physics at New York University, had submitted an article, "Transgressing the Boundaries: Toward a Transformative Hermeneutics of Quantum Gravity," claiming to offer support from recent physics for various "postmodern" epistemological positions. After some hesitation, *Social Text* decided to carry it in their special issue on science. However, the day after it appeared, another article by Sokal was published in the bimonthly *Lingua Franca*, in which he exposed his own *Social Text* piece as a "parody" of cultural studies of science, intended to unmask its "shoddy scholarship."

His method, Sokal revealed, was to structure the article around "the silliest quotes about mathematics and physics" from "the most prominent academics," "inventing an argument praising them and linking them together." All of which, he claimed, was "very easy," since he "wasn't obliged to respect any standards of evidence and logic"—although it will have taken considerable industry, since the text is liberally referenced, being accompanied by over twenty-one pages of notes and bibliography. Furthermore, Sokal argued, he had perpetrated his hoax on behalf of the Left: specifically, that section of the Left increasingly fed up with the "trendy" obscurantism and wrong-headedness of a postmodern cultural studies which, it believes, is undermining the prospect for "progressive social critique" by insisting upon the "social construction" of reality. Nowhere are its idiocies more apparent, so the argument runs, than in the "cultural" treatment of physical theory.

We were thus presented with a set-piece confrontation between a new, culturally based academic Left and its scientifically oriented predecessor, in which the latter, apparently, worsts the former by publicly revealing the illusory character of its clothing (intellectual standards), and gains a rare opportunity to show off its own sense of humor into the bargain.

The media had a field-day. The story made the cover of the *New York Times* (18/5/96); it was picked up in Britain by the *Observer* (19/5/96); it became a subject of debate on National Public Radio; and follow-up articles and exchanges appeared in everything from *Newsweek* (3/6/96), the *THES* (7 & 21/6/96) and *The Village Voice* (21/6/96) to a host of smaller US Left periodicals such as *Tikkun* and *In These Times*. Letters columns were clogged with competing voices, with Sokal comically complaining about the number of Stanley Fish's column-inches in the *NYT* (38) and refusing to continue playing there when his own 12-incher was cut down to "7.3" by the letters' editor (7.3!). Sokal chose instead to post his reply on the Internet with commentary on his threatened inches, although how many inches it can be said to have occupied there is anyone's guess. Sokal was not alone in making use of the Internet, though, and its communities of interest have played a significant role in framing and sustaining the affair. But what, exactly, is the affair about? And what does it actually show?

Misplaced Solidarity

For Sokal and his supporters, there is little doubt (they have few doubts): it demonstrates the bogus intellectual credentials of "postmodern" cultural studies and reaffirms the need for the Left to turn away from the "wishful thinking, superstition and demagoguery," to reclaim its Enlightenment roots in the "scientific worldview" (Sokal, talk at the NYU forum, 30/10/96). For the editors of *Social Text*, matters are predictably more complex. Clearly, they regret the publication of Sokal's essay and acknowledge it to have been an error of editorial judgement. But, they argue, it was a mistake generated by a misplaced sense of cultural-political solidarity, rather than any particular intellectual affinity with the offending piece—as its comparison with any of the sixteen other articles in the "Science Wars" issue (by the likes of Steve Fuller, Sandra Harding, Ruth Hubbard, Joel Kovel, Emily Martin, Les Levidow and Hilary Rose) shows.

Both stylistically and in tone, Sokal's essay stands out as an anomaly, but in Andrew Ross's words: "the editors considered that it might be of interest to readers as a 'document' of that time-honored tradition in which modern physicists have discovered harmonic resonances with their own reasoning in the field of philosophy and metaphysics." And in its own perverse way, it undoubtedly is. According to Robbins (the other main editor of the journal, besides Ross): "*Social Text* was hoaxed not because it liked Sokal's jargon-filled references to postmodern authorities—in fact we asked him to cut them out—but because we thought he was a progressive scientist, a physicist who was willing to be publicly critical of scientific orthodoxies."

The mistake was thus to allow the lure of an ally within the scientific establishment to dictate judgment about the piece; to allow political convenience to suspend intellectual judgment. In this respect, for some, it was a *representative* error, whatever one's conception of physics, and however much one may disagree with Sokal's views about science: representative of an overly *strategic* approach to intellectual matters, characteristic of that section of the cultural Left to which *Social Text*, broadly speaking, belongs. (Although it should be noted that it also represents a certain cultural Marxism, which is one reason it fell for the hoax in the first place. It takes science seriously; seriously enough to be skeptical of its conventional self-understanding.) But what of the politics of the hoax itself?

Media Wars

One of the most salient aspects of the affair has been Sokal's recourse to the mainstream media to conduct an ideological campaign against another section of the Left. Sokal has used the media skillfully, both to register his hoax and to generalize its point into a full-scale attack on "cultural studies of science" and "postmodern cultural studies" (which he tends to treat as equivalents).

And for many on the Left, his hoax was a welcome *public* counter to the attention-grabbing "relativism" of much recent cultural theory. Yet Sokal has also provided the press with an ideal occasion to prosecute two of its favorite pastimes—disparaging intellectualism, of any kind, and travestying the Left—while bolstering the sagging image of the "scientist" as a figure of authority and a man of reason and good sense. (Relishing the "impenetrable hodge-podge of jargon [and] buzzwords" in Sokal's hoax essay, the *New York Times* (18/5/96) selected "hegemony" and "epistemological" for especial derision . . . postmodern nonsense indeed!)

This was Sokal's major media card: his status as an "expert" in modern physics legitimated his views about the philosophy of science, and thereby about the cultural study of science, from whence it was but one small step to cultural studies as a whole.

That these views are simplistic, at best, and never short of commonsensical was an added bonus. Stanley Fish (Professor of English and Law at Duke University and executive editor of its Press, which publishes *Social Text*) was wheeled in by the *Times* to provide an alternative account of "social construction," but nobody in the press thought to ask the likes of Hilary Putnam what he thought about Sokal's bracingly down-to-earth conception of "reality," or the casual confidence with which he distinguishes "truth" from "claims of truth," and "knowledge" from "pretensions to knowledge." Nor was anybody interested in the decidedly non-commonsensical character of Sokal's own scientific work, as spelled out in such papers as "New Lower Bounds on the Self-Avoiding-Walk Connective Constant."

Philosophy has been notable by its absence, which is just as well for Sokal, since, as Linda Martín Alcoff has pointed out, his robust views would be rejected by nearly all contemporary philosophers of science—irrespective of their politics. Yet, weirdly, philosophy is precisely what Sokal now claims his hoax was all about. "*Social Text* is not my enemy, nor is it my main intellectual target," he insisted at the recent Forum at NYU. In fact, "this affair is in my view *not* primarily about science . . . What I believe this debate *is* principally about . . . is the nature of truth, reason and objectivity." But this is not what it has been about for the media. Nor is it what it was originally about for Sokal, when he started it all off by feeding the press yet another version of one of its most relentlessly promulgated narratives: the story of a decline in "standards." It was about knocking the cultural Left, and if that meant reinforcing conservative dogmas about "declining standards," the "emptiness" of fashion and the "obscurantism" of cultural minorities, so be it.

There has always been a section of the radical left which is more comfortable in the company of Burkeans than sexual libertarians. And it is here, perhaps, rather than in the philosophical disputes about science (which have been going on since the 1960s), that the heart of the matter lies: in a heightening of intellectual antagonisms between generations of the Left. It is an aspect of the affair that has been most prominent in the parade of opinions on the Internet.

Fantasies of "Pomos"

One of the functions of the Internet has been to expose to immediate public scrutiny exchanges that would previously have taken place in private, over a longer period of time. One of the dangers of this exposure is that intemperate and hastily conceived thoughts can readily take on the character of "positions" in highly charged debates. One of the advantages, however, is that the motivations underlying different views are more legible than usual.

So it is that the *ad hominem* attacks on Stanley Aronowitz and Andrew Ross—against which Sokal himself has recently protested—have much to tell us about the anxieties, fantasies and displacements sustaining what is an increasingly harmful divide between an older "scientifically" oriented and a younger "culturally" oriented Left.

It is tempting (and no doubt, to some, reassuring) to conceive of the divide as structured by differing attitudes to Marxism. But this is too simple. Not just because the intellectual culture of Marxism is pervasive, if uneven, on both sides, but because antipathy to the cultural Left tends to be focused on a particular composite image: "pomos" (postmodernists), who have allegedly taken over the academy, dismissing material interests and laying waste to intellectual standards in their dogged pursuit of identity politics, fashionable clothing and academic careers. In the exchanges provoked by Sokal's hoax, "pomos" are the ideal imaginary others of the "true Marxists" (and vice versa), and they are modeled on the media's fantasy projection of Andrew Ross. (Clothing plays a key metaphorical role in these invectives.)

One might, I think, be forgiven for finding this spectacle both intellectually irritating and politically depressing: irritating, because of the lowering of the level of debate that it involves; depressing, because it is so clearly the product of a political defeat, from which it distracts attention. At a time when the Left needs all the solidarity it can muster just to survive, there has to be a better way for it to conduct its debates than this.

STANLEY ARONOWITZ
Alan Sokal's "Transgression"
Dissent, Winter 1997

Explaining his now famous parody in *Social Text*'s "Science Wars" issue, Alan Sokal writes in *Dissent* ("Afterword," Fall 1996):

> But why did I do it? I confess I'm an unabashed Old Leftist who never quite understood how deconstruction was supposed to help the working class. And I'm a stodgy old scientist who believes, naively, that there exists an external world, that there exist objective truths about that world, and my job is to discover some of them.

There is much to note in this "confession." Why choose a hoax on *Social Text* to make these points? Did Sokal believe its editors were unabashed deconstructionists who doubted the existence of an external world or that they were anti-science? If so, he has either misread the burden of its seventeen-year history or was capricious in his choice or has perpetuated the saddest hoax of all: on himself. For the fact is that *Social Text*, of which I am a founder and in whose editorial collective I served until 1996, has never been in the deconstructionist camp; nor do its editors or the preponderance of its contributors doubt the existence of a material world. What is at issue is whether our knowledge of it can possibly be free of social and cultural presuppositions.

Social Text was founded, and remains within, the Marxist project, which is profoundly materialist. When Fredric Jameson, John Brenkman, and I started the journal we gave it the subtitle "Theory, Culture, Ideology." Our objective was to interrogate Marxists' habitual separation of political economy and culture and to make a contribution to their articulation, even reunification. We were appalled by the orthodox Marxist claim that culture had nothing to do with burning issues of economic justice and were equally opposed to a "culturalist" deconstruction of reality in which all that mattered was language. The use of the term "ideology" in our subtitle revealed our critical intent. For us, ideology was not "false consciousness" but a form of "lived experience." This marked us decidedly as not "old leftist" because we questioned the naive old materialism that holds that knowledge simply reflects reality. We followed the contemporary Marxist view that all processes of knowledge, including science, are mediated by their practices; for us "practice" was not a mental, but a material category.

So the issue is not whether reality exists, but whether knowledge of it is "transparent." Herein lies Sokal's confusion. He believes that reason, logic, and truth are entirely unproblematic. He has an abiding faith that through the rigorous application of scientific method nature will yield its unmediated truth. According to this doctrine there are "objective truths," because the earth revolves around the sun, gravity exists, and various other laws of nature are settled matters. So Sokal never interrogates the nature of evidence or facts, and simply accepts them if they have been adduced within certain algorithms that bear the stamp of "science."

Sokal cites Andrew Ross and Sandra Harding as representative deconstructionists. Neither fits this characterization. Harding, in her essay on "Why 'Physics' Is a Bad Model for Physics," argues that (a) facts do not speak for themselves but are subject to interpretations marked by the values and beliefs of scientists as well as the political imperatives of ruling groups who fund scientific work. Physics, *like any other human activity*, is subject to these influences; (b) there is no such thing as "pure description." She cites racial theories using scientific conventions, which have recurred through the modern era; (c) "we need critical social theory" to account adequately for causality and other scientific ideas.

At a recent forum on the so-called Sokal/ *Social Text* Affair, Sokal readily agreed that facts must be interpreted, but maintained that proper scientific method filters out social and cultural influences in the process of discovery. This, it seems to me, is an article of faith akin to a religious belief. In the history of science it was invoked by scientists as a defense against the attacks of the Church and the state to which it was allied in the sixteenth and seventeenth centuries, and became relevant again during the era of Nazi science and of Lysenkoism in the Soviet Union.

But it is one thing to insist on the autonomy of science from the state—the sort of battle leading scientific institutions have not really engaged since some atomic scientists sought to prevent further production of the bomb in the late 1940s—and another thing to make the flatfooted statement that the "objective truth" of science's postwar discoveries has nothing to do with its alliances with the military. The trajectory that Sokal presents—quantum mechanics gave rise to solid state physics which, in turn, is the basis of quantum electronics—is indisputable. What it leaves out is what influence military sponsorship has had on the selection of appropriate scientific objects and on the results of scientific work.

What did science *not* study because of its funding sources? What determines what it actually studies? Has not science increasingly directed its energies in biology as well as physics to technical applications? Is the emergence of bio-engineering, for instance, not subject to political, even economic interrogation? Harding acknowledges, as I do, *both* the liberatory as well as the questionable sides of the history of science. Bioengineering is a case in point. On the one hand, its applications fight disease with salutary effects. On the other hand, it may be linked to a revival of eugenics; indeed, some molecular biologists have declared its relevance to "perfecting" our species.

So: are the uses made of such knowledge part of science? If interpretation and the consequences of discovery are integral to the meaning of scientific knowledge, it takes more than the conventional procedure of repeatable experiments or calculations to "prove" that molecular biology is not a technoscience when most of its practitioners have eagerly sought alliances with drug companies and other commercial interests.

Beyond immediate issues concerning the relation between science and politics lie important metatheoretical questions. How do cultural influences—worldviews, for instance—bear on science? It was not deconstruction but the Frankfurt School that pointed to a dialectic of the Enlightenment, arguing that the modern cultural ideology of the scientific-technical domination of nature has direct political parallels. It was not deconstructionists but many historians of science who demonstrated that Newton's *Principia* is rooted in the mechanical worldview that was widely shared by scientists and laypersons in his time. Newton made true discoveries but, needless to say, they were overturned by "better" truths—relativity and quantum mechanics.

If one acknowledges that the domination of nature is intimately linked to the domination of humans, we can better grapple with racial "science" than by simply arguing that theories of racial and gender inferiority—like those of Shockley, Herrnstein, and Murray, or the nineteenth-century mainstream scientists who held women to be incapable of reason because of their biology—are false. Of course they are false, not only because one can adduce counterfactuals to refute them but because they violate the criterion of humanistic universalism according to which together humans have evolved into a unified species. I would conjecture that this underlying belief informs the widely-held judgment that what Murray and Herrnstein have asserted is bad science *as much* as the counterfactuals that may be offered in evidence.

Racial science reappears when society experiences a sense of economic and social crisis and needs scapegoats to explain its panic. But we cannot abstract the steady drumbeat of these pseudosciences from the degree to which the ideal of *domination* informs all scientific inquiry. To ignore the universal of domination is to fail to understand why, in the face of "definitive" refutations such as Stephen J. Gould's *The Mismeasure of Man*, they come back to us like a stopped-up toilet and in each generation win new adherents, even among some reputable scientists. Nor can we fully grasp the ubiquity of artificial intelligence apart from its uses in the computerized workplace or the devolution of molecular biology into a commercially configured technoscience.

However, I hold that an account of science that ascribes to it what Harding calls a "political agenda" is necessary but not sufficient to understand its tendencies. Among other questions a materialist science of sciences asks are what is the role of laboratory life where, after all, much of science is still done, in the configuration of scientific knowledge?; what is the influence of the power relations within the scientific community on what counts as legitimate knowledge?; and what are the ideological frames within which science is done? These have been standard questions in the sociology of science since its emergence as a line of inquiry in the 1930s. The questions bear on how we understand how science is done, not whether what it does is a "distortion" of truth.

A few examples: Shapin and Schaeffer examined the debate between Thomas Hobbes and Robert Boyle about the nature of knowledge. They put into question one of the underlying precepts of modern science: seeing is believing. Their point is not to deny the importance of observation but to show that its role in knowing is not free of presuppositions, that to show the social origins of observation as a foundation for scientific knowledge is at the very least worthy of inquiry. Latour and Woolgar and Sharon Traweek are among those who have investigated everyday life in the laboratory to figure out how science is produced. In their *Laboratory Life*, a study of the Salk laboratory in La Jolla, Latour and Woolgar discerned the relevance of conversation, inscriptions, and machine technologies for producing knowledge. In these and other cases ethnographic and historical studies proceed from Vico's idea that "making is knowing."

The point is not to debunk science or to "deconstruct" it in order to show it is merely a fiction. This may be the postmodern project, but it is not the project of science studies. The point is to show science as a social process, to bring it down to earth, to remove the halo from its head. Scientific truth cannot be absolute; otherwise we might agree with those who have proclaimed the "end" of science. If all knowledge, including natural science, is mediated by the social and cultural context within which it has developed, then its truths are inevitably relational to the means at hand for knowing. In fact, in much of microphysics what is called observation is often the effects of machine technologies, a reading of effects. But the reading is theory-laden. Which means pure description based on observation is not possible. Scientists require other tools such as machines and mathematics, and infer what they see from what they believe.

To say that the increasing dependence of science on socially and economically permeated technology, the culture milieux within which science is done or the political agendas of the funders invalidates results would be foolish. What it means is that scientific knowledge is not immune from broad cultural or narrow political influences and its methods cannot function as a filter. Cultural change, as much as internal debate among scientists, contributes to science—social and natural—as an evolving activity; what the scientific communities believe to be the case today may be revised, even refuted tomorrow. And, reasonably, logically, this must include the most accepted propositions. If this is so, and science reflects on social and cultural influences, on its visions, revisions, and its practices, and perhaps more to the point, on its *commitments*, then there is hope for a liberatory science.

MEERA NANDA

The Science Wars in India

Dissent, Winter 1997

What do left intellectuals do when they know that they are too marginalized to change the world? They get busy interpreting the world, of course. And interpreting how we interpret the world, and how the non-Western "Others" interpret it, and how we interpret others' interpretations . . . and ad infinitum. The interpretive turn allows the left to create in discourse what it is unable to realize in the rough and tumble of real politics: a world where all ideologies have been deconstructed, revealed, and readied for overthrow; a world where all can live by their own lights. The inverse relationship between an explosion of high theory and a decline in political efficacy appears to be as true today as it was when Perry Anderson first observed it nearly two decades ago in his *Considerations of Western Marxism*.

What follows here is an appeal by an "Other," in whose name many contemporary left theorists justify their interpretive turn, to think about how their epistemological egalitarianism affects the urgent task of transforming oppressive social structures and cultural values in non-Western societies. I will argue that the recent rise in political and cultural visibility of the religious right (the Bharatiya Janata party, or BJP, and its affiliates) in my native India[1] should give pause to all those academics in the West and in the third world who describe the rationality of "Western" science itself as a source of imperialism and racism.

Hindu nationalists have heeded the call for "decolonizing" science, and responded with aggressive propaganda for "Hindu ways of knowing," which they present as the locally embedded alternative to the alien and colonizing Western science. The two examples of the right's "Hinduization" of science and politics that I will discuss—the introduction of Vedic mathematics in public schools and the spread of "Vastu shastra" (ancient Indian material science)—do indeed meet the criteria of decolonized science advocated by left theorists: both are opposed to "Eurocentric Northern" ways of knowing; both are "situated knowledges" of non-Western people. The question I want to pose in the light of the BJP's victory is whether such knowledge is a step forward for women, minorities, and the desperately poor in non-Western societies. Does the project of de-Westernizing science deserve the support of my fellow progressive intellectuals?

As a one-time biologist, science writer, and a partisan of science-for-the-people movements in India and in the United States, I have watched with increasing unease the transnational alliance that has emerged around the idea that the rationality of modern science encodes Western and imperialistic social-cultural values, and is therefore inimical to the interests of non-Western peoples. The alliance brings together some of the most avant-garde scholars in U.S. universities with the neopopulist, cultural-nationalist, "postcolonial" intellectuals from the third world, most notably India.

Indeed, the cluster of ideas that postmodernist intellectuals deploy to deconstruct the supposedly Eurocentric assumptions of modern science appears with high frequency in the discourse of Hindu fundamentalist parties. The Hindu right has proclaimed the twenty-first century a "Hindu century" on the theoretical grounds made respectable by left critics of science. These reverse Orientalists who glorify whatever the Western powers devalued are walking through the door that the critics of Orientalism opened for them. The tools that deconstruct also construct.

Constructivist theories of science have cleared a discursive and political space that the nationalistic right is only too eager to move into. Indeed, the right could not have wished for a more fashionable neighborhood to pitch its own tent in. Making the content and rationality of science an epiphenomenon of the wider cultural and social structures is no doubt useful for exposing the play of power in supposedly objective accounts of the world. But when science is joined to culture at the hip in the constructivist fashion, it also opens the door to the so-called "ethno-sciences"—"Hindu science," "Islamic science," "third world women's science"—wherein scientific rationality is subordinated to the "forms of life" of different communities. When the existing social values are allowed to decide the validity of knowledge, knowledge loses whatever power it has to critique these often oppressive values. It is this deference to the existing "forms of life" that makes the project of constructing different ethno-sciences for different peoples so hospitable to all kinds of conservative social forces.

Thus, when the secular and mostly left-inclined critics claim—in the language and tone that Alan Sokal managed to feign so convincingly in his *Social Text* hoax of last year—that scientific facts cannot be judged as objectively true or false, but only from within the "regime of truth" established by social power, the religious right reads in it a justification for its demand that the validity of Hindu science be judged only on its "own terms." When the academic critics argue that scientific rationality must be subordinated to cultural instrumentalities, the religious right finds in it an affirmation of its own cultural chauvinism. One cannot avoid a shock of recognition when one reads, for instance, the BJP's recent *Humanistic Approach to Economic Development*, which insists that the cultural ethos of the Hindu *Rashtra* (nation) must become "a light onto itself," and have the final authority over what aspects of "foreign" science and technology are admitted into schools and other institutions. Hasn't one encountered similar appeals for integration of values and politics in knowledge-seeking activities in more academic, self-described "progressive" critiques of science? If the critics see science as a dystopian, arrogant and "God's-eye view of the world," supposedly transcending the material lives and beliefs of people, the BJP is only too happy to offer a supposedly humbler and more situated "Mother India's view of the world." If, as the critics charge, the very logic of modern science is a cultural expression of a Western "will to power," then the Hindu nationalists justifiably consider it their patriotic duty to resist modern science, and to replace it with ways of knowing informed by the imagined Hindu values of holism, communitarianism, and androgyny. Interestingly, the ruthlessness with which the critics interrogate "Western" science is matched in intensity only by their charity and solicitousness toward non-Western, pre-scientific ways of knowing.[2]

I do not for a moment believe, and neither should I be read as claiming, that the cultural critics of science knowingly speak for the Hindu right. In fact, both from personal association and from their written works, I know these critics to be motivated by deeply egalitarian, radically democratic, and staunchly antiracist sentiments. I know that they have no sympathy whatsoever for the anti-Muslim and anti-Christian platform of the Hindu right. But their personal politics and good intentions are not the issue here. What is an issue is the unintended impact of their theories on the lives of distant strangers. It is time the left critics of science ask: why is it that the religious right in India (and to a far more dangerous extent in Islamic countries) has been able to appropriate the theoretical language and conclusions of their intellectual labors? Isn't this appropriation reason enough to rethink some of their basic assumptions regarding science as social "all the way down"?

What fuels the antipathy of science critics toward those who wish to defend the traditional virtues of scientific realism, including the idea that, although not free from cultural biases, scientific reasoning does incrementally lead to knowledge that corresponds to the actual state of affairs in the world? There was a time, not so long ago, when popularizing science was considered a progressive cause, and science was seen as a weapon against ancestral authority. (The flowering of a vigorous people's science movement in India through the seventies and the eighties, which openly advocated

"Western" science for social revolution, motivated me to give up a career in biotechnology and become a science popularizer instead.) How has the left become so alienated from the institutional practices of natural science that it can find no use for them, in their present form, for progressive politics?

Limiting myself only to the recent battles in the "science wars," I believe I have a rough diagnosis of the left's disenchantment with science. The key word of my diagnosis is "empathy." As even a cursory reading of their work will show, the left academics who defend some variant of cultural relativism as "liberatory" believe that claims of universality of modern science prevent Westerners from fully empathizing with the moral and cognitive logics of others. Andrew Ross, for instance, seems to believe that supporting popular beliefs, say, in alternative medicine (his example) is a sign of "democratization from below," while those who demand that the popular beliefs be scientifically tested are elitist. According to Ross, only when we attenuate the claims of empirical rationality—and recognize "different ways of doing science, ways that downgrade methodology, experiment, and manufacturing in favor of local environments, cultural values, and principles of social justice"—can we begin to move toward true diversity of knowledge systems.[3]

Sandra Harding extends the empathy argument to non-Western "Others" when she claims that modern science is an "ethnoscience" of the West, with no more global purchase than any other culturally specific, local knowledge system. Because the West's ethnoscience has been molded on the twin templates of capitalist greed and imperialist expansion, she believes that it is "incapable of producing the kinds of knowledge needed for sustainable human life under democratic conditions," especially in societies with different natural and social orders. The need to empathize with other cultures in a multicultural world, Harding insists, requires that we give up the dream of a "one true science," and begin to live with a "borderland epistemology"— an epistemology that "values the distinctive understandings of nature that different cultures have resources to generate." Knowers in different cultures can pick and choose sciences and combine them in a "knowledge collage" that serves whatever particular goal might be of interest to them at any given time. Thus, in Harding's "borderlands," the appropriation of modern science by other cultures can be defended only for pragmatic or political reasons, not on epistemological grounds.[4]

For Harding, as for many other advocates of multicultural science, the impulse to empathize with non-Western "Others" requires that knowledge systems not be rank-ordered in terms of better or worse accounts of reality. They are "different" accounts that different social orders produce in order to cope with their culture- and language-bound perceptions of reality. And yet, cultural critics of science continue to deny that they have erased the line between science and nonscience. Such denials are surprising, for it has been shown many times over that *any* account of knowledge that makes the standards of validity (for example, logic, experiment, and evidence) internal to a culturally conditioned consensus cannot escape epistemological and judgmental relativism. But constructionists simply refuse to play ball with philosophers—one more symptom, I presume, of the skepticism toward all abstractions that has come to define the post-all academy.

No doubt this empathy with the long-oppressed Others is liberatory for Western outsiders. But I contend that those insiders whose interest in a fuller, freer life has long been frustrated by the oppressive elements of local, "situated" knowledge—women, the "lower castes," and working people—need a richer kind of empathy that includes respect, but also critique; love, but also anger. The oppressed Others do not need patronizing affirmations of their ways of knowing, as much as they need ways to *challenge* these ways of knowing. They do not need to be told that modern science is no less of a cultural narrative than their local knowledges, for they need the findings of modern science, *understood as transcultural truths*, in order to expose and challenge local knowledges.

I submit that the moment the Indian left began to talk the language of cultural constructionism, it lost the battle to the Hindu nationalists. Those of us associated with the people's science movements of the 1970s and the 1980s could use modern scientific knowledge to contest the dominant, largely Hindu world views on caste and women, precisely because we could claim that the content of science was not Western in any substantive way, and that it gave us a picture of the natural world that was as true for us in India as it was for anyone living anywhere on this planet. But when a small but highly influential group of Indian intellectuals, borrowing heavily from Western critics of the Enlightenment, began to argue that scientific rationality itself is a colonial construct, the people's science movements were left with no principled defense against accusations that popularization of modern science means internal colonization. Gradually, almost imperceptibly, the old, bold slogans of "science for social revolution" gave way to a parochial, almost obsessive compulsion to search and destroy any contaminating traces of the Western/colonial "episteme." Correspondingly, the cosmopolitan vision of socialism and secularism gave way to communitarian fantasies of Gandhian village republics—which sound much more egalitarian than they have ever been in reality.

In this context, is it any surprise at all that the Hindu nationalists have been able to position themselves as the true defenders of non-Western ways of knowing? Themselves leading the charge for "decolonizing knowledge," what principled argument could the alliance of left-leaning and neo-Gandhian critics of modern science have offered when the Hindu fundamentalist parties began to replace modern mathematics with so-called "Vedic mathematics" in public schools? One of BJP's first acts after coming to power in the state of Uttar Pradesh in 1992 was to make the study of Vedic mathematics compulsory for high school students. Explicitly stating an interest in "awakening national pride" among students, the government-approved textbooks replaced standard algebra and calculus with sixteen Sanskrit verses proclaimed by their author, Jagadguru Swami Shri Bharati Krishna Tirathji Maharaj, the high priest of Puri, to be of Vedic origin. Prominent Indian mathematicians and historians who have examined these verses believe that there is nothing Vedic about them, and that the Jagadguru has tried to pass off a set of clever formulas for quick computation as a piece of ancient wisdom. But that has not stopped BJP and other revivalist cultural movements in India from equating Jagadguru with Ramanujan in their hagiographies of Indian knowledge systems.

The problem with introducing supposedly indigenous and ancient knowledge is not that it is indigenous and ancient: there can, of course, be instances of ancient lore that can help us see a contemporary problem in a new light. The real issue is that the supposed Vedic mathematics, as many progressive Indian mathematicians and critics have argued, offers students mere tools for computation in place of the allegedly "Western" algebraic equations of which they are instances. In the name of national pride, students are being deprived of conceptual tools that are crucial in solving the real-world mathematical problems they will encounter as scientists and engineers.

Hinduization is not limited to mathematics alone. History curricula have always been favorite targets of religious nationalists. Under the growing influence of religious nationalists in the state and central governments, the earlier emphasis on secularism is being reversed. New history textbooks celebrate all things Hindu (including even the caste system), propagate the myth of India as the original home of the "Aryan race," and deplore all "foreigners," including the Muslims. The history of Indian science and technology is not exempt. It is described as an unfolding of the Hindu genius, although material accomplishments (ancient technologies, for example) are emphasized over the penchant for critical inquiry that exists in some Indian traditions.

I have not come across any critique of Vedic mathematics from any of the intellectuals who have been so vocal in their criticism of "Western" science. The only opposition to the communalization of education has come from scientists, mathematicians, and other intellectuals associated with the people's science movements. It is quite likely that when confronted with the blatant nationalism driving such attempts, those who criticize modern science as a "Western" implant often try to distance themselves from the BJP's zeal for institutionalizing Vedic knowledge. But the fact remains that the BJP is not doing anything that those who see modern science as "inherently Western" have not themselves clamored for in the past. A good example is the well-known "Penang Declaration on Science and Technology" signed by prominent proponents of ethno-sciences in 1988. Among many other demands, the declaration calls for a system of education that "appreciates the value of indigenous scientific and technological culture. . . . The teaching of science should never be divorced from the value-system of the indigenous civilization. The students should also develop a critical faculty so that they may judge the cultural and ideological bias of western science and technology."[5] (The declaration is silent on the biases of indigenous civilizations.)

The BJP may be on the wrong side of the egalitarian ideals espoused by science critics, but it is by no means on the wrong side of their constructivist logic. The irony is that the largely academic critics who offer sophisticated theoretical justifications for indigenous sciences have the material resources and the opportunities to escape being grounded in them. Vedic mathematics and other projects for Hinduization of education do not personally affect most of the academic critics of science, for their own children hardly ever attend the state-run schools that cater to the poor or the BJP-run schools that cater to small businesses. Those who are most ardent about locally situated knowledges are the least embedded locally: most of them have one foot in the transnational academic world to which they regularly escape.

Another illustration of the co-option of the left's advocacy for indigenous knowledges by the powers-that-be is the recent craze for *Vastu Shastra*, the Sanskrit name for the ancient Vedic rules that govern the construction of sacred buildings on the basis of the "auspiciousness" of space. If the practice of this Hindu science were limited to the *nouveau riche* in Delhi and Bombay, who build their houses to maximize the "positive energy" that comes with spatial correctness, one could ignore it. But last June we witnessed how cultural ideas can play a role in politics. N.T. Rama Rao, the late chief minister of the southern state of Andhra Pradesh, sought the help of a traditional *Vastu Shastri* to help him out of some political rough weather, and was told that his troubles would vanish if he entered his office from an east-facing gate. But on the east side of his office there was a slum through which his car could not pass. The chief minister ordered the slum to be demolished.

If the Indian left were as active in the people's science movement as it used to be, it would have led an agitation not only against the demolition of people's homes, but also against the superstition that was used to justify it. In a case like this, modern science and social justice were clearly pulling in the same direction, and the left could easily have made the pure irrationality of *Vastu Shastra* an opportunity for consciousness raising. A left movement that was not so busy establishing "respect" for non-Western knowledge would never have allowed the power-wielders to hide behind indigenous "experts."

I tried out this case on my social constructionist friends here in the United States. Although they see the injustice of the situation, they do not see why I am so exercised about the irrationality that led to it. We have our superstitions in the West, they tell me. Did not Nancy Reagan consult astrologers? As for my suggestion that if we want justice, we must challenge the irrationality of ideas that lead to injustice, I am told that there is no need for proving that *Vastu Shastra* is wrong and modern science correct. I am told that seeing the two culturally bound descriptions of space at par with each other is progressive in itself, for then *neither* can claim to know the absolute truth, and thus tradition will lose its hold on people's mind. I am told that this desire to prove that traditional knowledge is an incorrect representation of nature is a sign of a scientific mind-set, a hangover from my training in biology that I must overcome if I do not want to re-engineer the society of my birth on technocratic lines. Finally, I am told that I am an incorrigible modernist if I believe that Western science has any democracy-enhancing potential in my part of the world.

After all this, I should hardly be surprised when I hear my position labeled as that of the "antidemocratic right," as it often is within the radical circles of science critics. I plead guilty to believing that modern science is not something to be deconstructed and overcome. It must have an active role in progressive politics. The alternative is staring us all in the face. It is called religious fundamentalism, and it is not pretty.

Notes

1   The Hindu-nationalist BJP won 194 (about 36 percent) of the 543 seats in the lower house of India's Parliament in the general elections held in May 1996, with the secular Congress party trailing with only 139 seats (25 percent). As the short-lived BJP government failed to come up with the two-thirds majority needed, it had to hand the reins of power to a coalition of center-left parties. However, most observers don't expect the current coalition government to last for long, and anticipate that BJP will emerge even stronger in the next elections.

　　The BJP's rise to national prominence is truly impressive—and frightening. Until the last decade or so, the BJP was considered a communal party, a pariah with barely 2 percent of seats in the parliament. Its increased popularity represents a defeat of the ideals of secularism and modernity that India set for itself after its independence from the British.

2   For representative postcolonial science critiques, see Ashis Nandy (ed.), *Science, Hegemony and Violence: A Requiem for Modernity* (Oxford University Press, 1988). For a representa-

tive science critique from a Western multicultural perspective, see Sandra Harding, "Is Science Multicultural?" *Configuration* (2:301–330, 1994). The Hindu right's views on science and technology mentioned in this paper are gleaned from press reports from India.

3   See Andrew Ross, "Introduction," *Social Text* (46–47 Spring/Summer, 1996), p. 4.

4   See Sandra Harding, "Science is 'Good to Think With,'" *Social Text* (46–47, Spring/Summer, 1996).

5   Reproduced in Ziauddin Sardar (see note 2).

BARBARA EPSTEIN

Postmodernism and the Left

New Politics, Winter 1997

Alan Sokal's Hoax, "Transgressing the Boundaries: Toward a Transformative Hermeneutics of Quantum Gravity,"[1] which was published in the "Science Wars" issue of *Social Text*, and the debate that has followed it, raise important issues for the left. Sokal's article is a parody of postmodernism, or, more precisely, the amalgam of postmodernism, poststructuralist theory, deconstruction, and political moralism which has come to hold sway in large areas of academia, especially those associated with cultural studies. These intellectual strands are not always entirely consistent with each other. For instance, the strong influence of identity politics in this arena seems inconsistent with the poststructuralist insistence on the instability of all identities. Nevertheless, no one who has participated in this arena can deny that it is dominated by a specific, highly distinctive subculture. One knows when one finds oneself in a conference, seminar, or discussion governed by this subculture, by the vocabulary that is used, the ideas that are expressed or taken for granted, and by the fears that circulate, the things that remain unsaid. There are many critiques of the literature that informs this arena, which can for convenience be called postmodernism (though the term "poststructuralist" points more specifically to the dominant theoretical perspective).[2] But there is little if any discussion of postmodernism as a subculture.

The subculture of postmodernism is difficult to locate precisely. It is more pervasive in the humanities than elsewhere, but it has also entered the social sciences. It cannot be entirely identified with any particular discipline, but in some sense constitutes a world of its own, operating outside of or above disciplinary categories. Within the world of postmodernism, intellectual trends take hold and fade into oblivion with extraordinary rapidity. Many of the people who play major roles in shaping it refuse such labels as "postmodernist" (or even "poststructuralist"), on the ground that such categories are confining.[3] The difficulty of defining postmodernism discourages discussion of it as a particular intellectual arena. Nevertheless it does constitute a subculture. It has increasing reach and power within the university; it has become increasingly insistent that it is the intellectual left.

Many people, inside and outside the world of postmodernism (and for that matter inside and outside the left), have come to equate postmodernism with the left. There are many academic departments and programs that associate themselves with progressive politics in which the subculture of postmodernism holds sway. This is especially the case in interdisciplinary programs, especially those in the humanities; postmodernism is most likely to be the dominant perspective if the institution is relatively prestigious and if the faculty has been hired since the '60s. These programs tend to draw bright students who regard themselves as left, progressive, feminist, concerned with racism and homophobia. The result is that many students with this sort of orientation have come to associate progressive concerns with a postmodernist perspective. Many professors and other intellectuals, of all political shades, also accept this equation. Left intellectuals who object to postmodernism tend to complain in private but remain largely silent in public, largely because they have not learned to speak the postmodernist vocabulary. The equation of postmodernism with the left poses problems both for the intellectual work conducted under the aegis of postmodernism and for efforts to rebuild the left in the U.S. Alan Sokal's hoax, and the debate that has followed it, provide an opportunity to address these issues.

Some of us who were delighted by Sokal's hoax, at one time had a more positive view of postmodernism. The constellation of trends that I am calling postmodernism has its origins in the writings of a group of French intellectuals of the '60s, most preeminently Michel Foucault, Jacques Derrida, Jacques Lacan, and Jean-François Lyotard. Those who developed postmodernism tended to be associated with the radicalism of the '60s, and to see May '68 as a formative moment in their intellectual and political development. French postmodernism expressed many aspects of the ethos of May '68: its anti-authoritarianism, its rejection of Marxism and view of it as implicated in unacceptable structures of authority, its celebration of the imagination and resistance to all constraints.[4]

In addition to being shaped by the politics of May '68 (including the French Communist Party's betrayal of the student movement and support for the authorities), French postmodernism developed out of the debates that were taking place in French intellectual circles at that time. It included a rejection of humanism, in particular of Sartre's view of the self as the center of political resistance and his quest for an integrated, authentic selfhood. Postmodernism rejected aspects of the structuralist legacy, particularly its emphasis on the stability of social structures, but retained its focus on language, the view that language provides the categories that shape self, and society. This could be extended to the view that all reality is shaped by language; it could suggest that language is real, everything else, constructed or derived from it. Such an approach could suggest a critique of social analysis or radical politics emphasizing the economic level, or overt structures of political power. It could suggest the need for a critique of culture and a call for cultural transformation.

Postmodernism entered the U.S. in the late '70s and early '80s, by a number of routes simultaneously. There were academics, especially philosophers and literary critics, who were drawn to poststructuralist philosophy. Many feminists and gay and lesbian activists became interested in the work of Michel Foucault, whose attention to the social construction of sexuality, view of power as dispersed through society, and insistence on the connection between power and knowledge intersected with their own concerns. Foucault's work seemed to provide a theoretical ground for shifting the focus of radical analysis away from macrostructures such as the economy and the state, and toward daily life, ideology, social relations and culture. Foucault's view of state power as always repressive and his identification of resistance with the marginalized and suppressed made sense at a time when radical struggles were being led by groups peripheral to mainstream culture and power relations, such as disaffected youth and women, blacks and other racial minorities, gays and lesbians.

The attractiveness of postmodernism, in the late '70s and early '80s, had something to do with the cultural and political currents with which it was associated. It was loosely affiliated with avant-garde trends in architecture and art, and also with the impulse of many intellectuals to set aside the old distinction between high and low culture and begin taking popular culture seriously. Poststructuralist theory emphasized flux, instability, fragmentation, and questioned the validity of claims to authenticity and truth. These concerns overlapped with emerging themes in popular culture: distraction, absence of rootedness in the past, a sense of meaninglessness. More important, these poststructuralist, or postmodernist, concerns spoke to levels of reality that seemed increasingly salient and that more conventional theories, including left theories, did not address. Postmodernism seemed to refer to a set of cultural changes that were taking place around us (and within us) as much as it referred to a literature or set of theories about those changes. The increasing use of the term "poststructuralism" to refer to a set of theories in part grew out of the need to distinguish between theory and the cultural realities to which it responded.

In the latter part of the '70s, many young people whose center of attention was shifting from the movements of the '60s to intellectual work, often in the academy, were avidly reading Foucault. Many were also reading other French intellectuals, including French feminists such as Luce Irigaray, Monique Wittig, the eclectic theorists of society and psychology Gilles Deleuze and Felix Guattari, the Marxist structuralist, Louis Althusser, the psychoanalytic structuralist, Jacques Lacan. Through the works of these writers and the debates in which their work was embedded, the poststructuralist ideas that had come to dominate French radical intellectual circles in the late '60s and '70s filtered into parallel intellectual circles in the U.S. By the early '80s an intellectual subculture was emerging in the U.S. which tended to use the term "postmodernism" to describe its outlook. Though it was located primarily in the university, it had links to avant-garde developments in art and architecture and a strong interest in experimental trends in popular culture. Postmodernists tended to feel strong sympathies for feminism and for gay and lesbian movements, and were especially drawn to a politics that was tinged with anarchism and oriented toward spectacle—a politics that happened to be quite salient in a cluster of movements that emerged in the U.S. around the late '70s and early '80s.

The excitement of postmodernism, certainly in the early '80s and to some degree through the decade, had to do with its links to vital cultural and political movements, and to the fact that it was pointing to rapid changes in culture and examining these through the poststructuralist categories of language, text, discourse. Through the '80s, original and provocative books and articles appeared, loosely associated with a postmodernist perspective or at least addressing questions raised by postmodernism. Though everyone would have a different list, most would no doubt include James Clifford's *The Predicament of Culture: Twentieth-Century Ethnography, Literature, and Art,* Donna Haraway's *Primate Visions: Gender, Race and Nature in the World of Modern Science,* Ernesto Laclau and Chantal Mouffe's *Hegemony and Socialist Strategy: Towards a Radical Democratic Politics,* Jean Beaudrillard's *For a Critique of the Political Economy of the Sign,* Jean François Lyotard's *The Postmodern Condition.*

Others examined postmodernism as a cultural phenomenon and criticized it from a broadly Marxist perspective. Works in this vein would include David Harvey, *The Condition of Postmodernity,* and Frederic Jameson, *The Political Unconscious: Narrative as a Socially Symbolic Act* (and his influential article, "Postmodernism, or the Logic of Late Capitalism.")[5] In the '80s and '90s a great deal of European postmodernist (or poststructuralist) literature was being published in English, and was widely read in the U.S. In fact, postmodernist books by European authors may have been read more widely in the U.S. than in their authors' home countries, since by this time interest in postmodernism had faded considerably in France and elsewhere in Europe.

Despite the attractions of postmodernism, some of us were uneasy about it from the start. Postmodernism not only pointed to processes of flux, fragmentation, the disenchantment or draining of meaning from social life, but tended to be fascinated with them. It often seemed that postmodernists could see nothing but instability, and that a new set of values was being established without ever being acknowledged, according to which the shifting and unstable was always preferable to the unified or integrated. Despite the brilliance of much of the literature, there seemed at times to be a kind of flatness of vision, a tendency to insist on one set of qualities while refusing to recognize their necessary counterparts, as if one could have up without down, hot without cold. There seemed to be a celebration of the fragmentation of self and society that ignored the need for balance, for a new level of coherence. Not that all writers who addressed the questions posed by postmodernism fell into this trap. But on the whole those who escaped it were those who addressed questions raised by postmodernism rather than adopting it as their own perspective.

By the late '80s and early '90s, postmodernism seemed to have been taken over by the pursuit of the new or avant-garde. Radicalism became identified with criticism for the sake of criticism, and equated with intellectual or cultural sophistication. The aestheticization of postmodernism corresponded to the attenuation of its ties with any actual social movements, as the movements with which postmodernism had felt the greatest rapport shriveled. Postmodernism had always been pulled between the agendas of the academy and the social movements; the agenda of the academy now took over. Politics became increasingly a matter of gestures or proclamations. By the '90s, the quest for success in an increasingly harsh and competitive academic world became the driving force. Claims to radicalism, oddly, seemed to serve this purpose.

One way of understanding postmodernism is to say that there are strong and weak, or more ambitious and more restrained versions of it. According to the strong version, there is no such thing as truth. Because all perception of reality is mediated, because what we regard as reality is perceived through discourse, there is no truth, there are only truth claims. Since there is nothing against which these claims can be measured, they all have the same standing. Another way of putting this would be that there is nothing prior to interpretation or theory, nothing that stands outside of interpretation and can be taken as a basis for judging its validity. In the postmodernist or poststructuralist lexicon, the terms "essentialism" and "foundationalism" are used to denote a host of presumably bad attitudes, including the view that interpretation or theory can and should be judged in relation to some reality external to itself, the view that some social groups have characteristics or interests that are given rather than continually constructed and reconstructed—and reductionism, stereotyping, as in the view that all women are nurturent, or that African Americans have innate musical abilities. The fact that the term essentialism refers simultaneously to an epistemological approach and also to racist, sexist or at least naive politics tends to link these two and makes it difficult to have a calm discussion of whether there is such a thing as truth, and whether theory should be judged by reality external to itself. In many discussions the use of the term "essentialist" is enough to identify the philosophical stance as politically retrograde and therefore unacceptable.

Those of us who disagree with the strong postmodernist position do not object to the premise that our perception of reality is mediated. What we object to is the leap of logic between this premise and the conclusion that there is no truth, that all claims have equal status. We would argue that although we do not possess ultimate truth and never will, it is nevertheless possible to expand our understanding, and it is worth the effort to gain more knowledge—even if that knowledge is always subject to revision. This version of the strong postmodernist position is—in my experience—rarely explicitly argued in the literature; it is in discussion (in conferences, seminars, and private conversations) that one encounters it. It is often posed against a straw-person argument that would claim that the truth is readily accessible, completely transparent, unaffected by culture. This straw-person argument is used as a foil, to excuse the implausibility and logical weakness of the strong postmodernist view. On the whole, postmodernist literature, instead of arguing this position explicitly, assumes an attitude of radical skepticism toward truth, or toward claims that there is an objective reality that is to some extent knowable, without ever clearly defining the grounds for this skepticism.

The strong position, as it appears in postmodernist or poststructuralist writing, tends to take the form of an extreme social constructionism, a view that identities, relations, political positions are constructed entirely through interpretation, that there is no identifiable social reality against which interpretations can be judged, no ground in material or social reality that places any constraints on the formation of identities or perspectives. Joan Scott, for instance, in her influential article "Experience," argues that any account of experience takes for granted categories and assumptions that ought to be questioned, that to accept the category of experience, or to use the word without distancing oneself from it by surrounding it with quotation marks, is dangerous, and opens the way to essentialism and foundationalism. Scott admits that the concept of experience is too deeply embedded in culture to be done away with easily. In the end she suggests that we retain it but treat it with suspicion.[6]

Ernesto Laclau and Chantal Mouffe, in their book *Hegemony and Socialist Strategy*, apply the same approach to the formation of political positions. They argue that all political identities or perspectives are constructed, that there is no particular relation between class position, for instance, and political stance. In support of this, they argue that workers are not automatically socialist or even progressive: often they support right-wing politics. Laclau and Mouffe are of course correct that there is no automatic connection between class and politics, or between the working class and socialism, but this does not mean that there is no connection between the two, that all interpretations or constructions of class interest are equally possible and equally valid. For instance, it is hard to imagine a situation in which a socialist program, proposed by the capitalist class, was defeated by working-class opposition. Laclau and Mouffe make their argument by setting up a straw argument (that workers are automatically socialist—a view held by no one that I know of), knocking it down, and substituting a position that is equally extreme, namely that there is no connection at all between class position and political perspective. Without this straw economism as a foil, the problems of the extreme social constructionist argument become more apparent.[7]

An even more extreme example of strong postmodernism is Judith Butler's argument, in her book *Gender Trouble*, that sexual difference is socially constructed. Butler accepts Foucault's now widely accepted view that gender is socially constructed; she goes beyond this and criticizes Foucault for his unwillingness to extend an anti-essentialist perspective to sexuality itself. She argues that not only gender but sex itself, that is, sexual difference, should be seen as an effect of power relations and cultural practices, as constructed "performatively"—that is, by acts whose meaning is determined by their cultural context. Butler argues that the conventional view of sex as consisting of two given, biologically determined categories, male and female, is ideological, and defines radical politics as consisting of parodic performances that might undermine what she calls "naturalized categories of identity." Her assertion that sexual difference is socially constructed strains belief. It is true that there are some people whose biological sex is ambiguous, but this is not the case for the vast majority of people. Biological difference has vast implications, social and psychological; the fact that we do not yet fully understand these does not mean that they do not exist. Butler's understanding of radicalism shows how the meaning of the word has changed in the postmodernist arena. It no longer has to do with efforts to achieve a more egalitarian society. It refers to the creation of an arena in which the imagination can run free. It ignores the fact that only a privileged few can play at taking up and putting aside identities.

There is a weak, or restrained, version of postmodernism which is much more plausible than the strong version described above. This version argues that language and culture play a major and often unrecognized role in shaping society, that things are often regarded as natural which are actually socially constructed. This is a valid and important perspective. Those of us on the left who criticize postmodernism reject the strong version, not this more restrained approach. The difference between the two lies in the excessive ambition, and the consequent reductionism, of the strong approach, and the greater modesty or caution of the weak or restrained approach. Strong postmodernism is cultural reductionism: it represents the ambition to make culture the first or only level of explanation. It is no better to argue that everything can be understood in terms of culture or language than to argue that everything is driven by economic forces, or by the quest for political power. The project that frames postmodernism is the critique of Enlightenment rationality; there are aspects of that tradition that deserve to be criticized, such as the tendency to take the white male as the model of rational subjectivity, and the equation of truth with the discoveries of Western science, excluding other contributions. But the postmodernist critique of the Enlightenment is one-sided. It forgets that a universalist view of humanity was a major (and only partially accomplished) step away from narrow nationalisms, and that the concept of truth is a weapon in the hands of progressive social movements, that they rely on opposing the truth of oppression to hollow official claims that society is just.

The problems of postmodernism that I have named, and more, have been displayed in the public response to the Sokal article. The first response was from Stanley Fish, Professor of English at Duke University and a leading figure in the field of cultural studies. In an op-ed piece in the *New York Times*, "Professor Sokal's Bad Joke,"[8] Fish tried to shift the terrain of the debate from postmodernism to the social sciences, suggesting that the field of science studies consists of scholars whose modest aim is to investigate the ideas that drive scientific research. The work of these scholars, he implied, hardly goes beyond the bounds of conventional sociology. In this article, Fish appeared not to have noticed the more extreme positions that have been taken in the name of postmodernism or cultural studies, inside or outside the field of science studies. It is hard not to see Fish's piece as a strategic move, a slide to the weak or restrained position when the strong position has begun to look foolish.

The next piece to appear was a statement in *Lingua Franca,* by Andrew Ross and Bruce Robbins, editors of *Social Text.*[9] Robbins and Ross wrote that they had regarded Sokal's article as "a little hokey" and "not their cup of tea" but that they published it to encourage a natural scientist who appeared to be interested in Cultural Studies. Next, *Tikkun* published an article by Bruce Robbins,[10] who wrote that the editors of *Social Text* had published the article because of the merit they saw in its argument. Robbins asked what conclusions should be drawn and what should not be drawn from the fact that *Social Text* had published Sokal's piece. One conclusion not to draw, he wrote, is that postmodernists can't recognize an unintelligible argument when they see one.

> When Sokal said his essay was nonsense, most reporters instantly followed his lead. After all, he should know, right? But we thought Sokal had a real argument, and we still do. Allow me to quote John Horgan, senior writer at *Scientific American,* summarizing in the July 16 *New York Times*: Sokal, Horgan says, "proposed that superstring theory might help liberate science from 'dependence upon the concept of objective truth.'" Prof. Sokal later announced that the article had been a hoax, intended to expose the hollowness of postmodernism. In fact, however, superstring theory is exactly the kind of science that subverts conventional notions of truth. (p.58)

Robbins went on to argue that the concept of truth is questionable on political grounds:

> Does subverting conventional notions of truth really have anything to do with being politically progressive? . . . Is it in the interests of women, African-Americans, and other super-exploited people to insist that truth and identity are social constructions? Yes and no. No, you can't talk about exploitation without respect for empirical evidence and a universal standard of justice. But yes, truth can be another source of oppression. It was not so long ago that scientists gave their full authority to explanations of why women and African-Americans (not to speak of gays and lesbians) were inherently inferior or pathological or both. Explanations like these continue to appear in newer and subtler forms. Hence there is a need for a social constructionist critique of knowledge. (p.59)

Here we have an argument that has become hopelessly tangled, perhaps through the effort to see everything through a postmodernist lens while refusing to acknowledge that postmodernism is a lens, that it is anything other than pure Truth. Robbins is of course right that some people say things about African Americans, women, etc., that are not true. This does not mean that we should reject the concept of truth. It means that we should reject false assertions.

Robbins goes on to deride critics of postmodernism as "know-nothings of the left [who] delude themselves: Capitalism is screwing people! What goes up must come down! What else do we need to know?" Robbins continues, "It seems likely that what is really expressed by the angry tirades against cultural politics that have accompanied the Sokal affair is a longing for the days when women were back in the kitchen and it was respectable to joke about faggots and other natural objects of humor. These are not the family values I want my children to learn" (p.59). Presumably Robbins is referring to people who have expressed support for Sokal, such as Ruth Rosen (a feminist historian), Katha Pollitt (a feminist journalist), Jim Weinstein (editor of *In These Times*), Michael Albert (editor of *Z Magazine*), myself. Robbins' remark is self-righteous posturing, and unfortunately it is not an isolated example. In the arena of postmodernism, left politics is often expressed through striking poses, often conveying moral superiority, greater sophistication, or both. There often seems to be a sneer built into postmodernist discourse, a cooler-than-thou stance. This enrages the critics of postmodernism, and it is one reason why it has been so difficult for supporters and critics of Sokal to discuss their differences calmly.

There are serious problems within the postmodernist subculture. There is an intense ingroupyness, a concern with who is in and who is out, and an obscurantist vocabulary whose main function often seems to be to mark those on the inside and allow them to feel that they are part of an intellectual elite. This is not to object to the use of a technical vocabulary where it is needed to express ideas precisely. The world of postmodernism has unfortunately come to be flooded with writing in which pretentiousness reigns and intellectual precision appears to have ceased to be a consideration. There is the fetishization of the new: the rapid rise and fall of trends, the collective deference to them while they last. For a while it seemed that every debate in this arena entailed accusations of essentialism. The exact definition of essentialism was never clear, but it nevertheless seemed that essentialism was the source of all error, and the use of the term as invective was enough to halt discussion. There is the inflation of language and the habit of self-congratulation: it has become common practice in this arena to advertise one's own work as radical, subversive, transgressive. All this really means is that one hopes one is saying something new. There is the worship of celebrities. This is a culture that encourages and rewards self-aggrandizement and grandiosity. There is intellectual bullying, the use of humiliation, ridicule, implicit threats of ostracism, to silence dissent. All of this stands in direct contrast to the endless talk of difference that takes place in this arena.

Efforts to raise criticisms from within this arena have not had much effect; those who have made such efforts have been treated with hostility or at best ignored. Those of us who supported Sokal's hoax felt that a public act of mockery was required to open up discussion. Now that postmodernism has lost its aura of invincibility people have begun to laugh, and it does not seem likely that the laughter will stop anytime soon. For instance, in a review of a book entitled *Male Matters: Masculinity, Anxiety, and the Male Body on the Line,* by Calvin Thomas (University of Illinois Press), reviewer Daniel Harris writes,

> In the fast-paced intellectual environment of postmodern cultural studies, the line between ostensibly serious scholarship and outright parody is not just thin but, in many instances, nonexistent, as became embarrassingly evident last month to the editors of one of the house organs of contemporary theoretical discourse, *Social Text.* . . . One can only hope that Sokal's brilliant act of intellectual terrorism . . . will be the first of many similar practical jokes. If even a handful of the numerous critics of cultural theory did their part, postmodern journals and academic presses would be swamped with fraudulent manuscripts that would shatter the self-confidence of the entire field. This vast industry would collapse into a state of total disarray were its tightly-knit ranks to become infiltrated by jargon-spewing moles posing as the real McCoy, double agents cloaked in the uniform of the American university's elitist new brand of paper radicals.

Harris goes on to speculate that the book under review must be another hoax. How else, he asks, can one explain the bewildering statements that appear in this book, such as:

> The excrementalization of alterity as the site/sight of homelessness, of utter outsideness and unsubiatable dispossession figure(s) in . . . Hegel's metanarrational conception of Enlightenment modernity as the teleological process of totalization leading to absolute knowing.

> The anal penis . . . function(s) within a devalued metonymic continuity, whereas the notion of the phallomorphic turd functions within the realm of metaphorical substitution. If the bodily in masculinity is encountered in all its rectal gravity, the specular mode by which others become shit is disrupted.

Harris suggests that if Thomas wants to become an academic success, he should follow Sokal's example and proclaim his book to be a prank. Only slightly less tongue in cheek, he speculates that what he describes as the central metaphor of this book, the comparison of writing to "productions" of the body, especially shit, may be apt in a field in which jargon is used as an offensive weapon, to score points against competitors in the battle for tenure and prestige.[11]

Postmodernism did not invent intellectual bullying. This is not the first instance of dogmatism on the left. In the '30s people on the left (at least those in or close to the Communist Party) felt considerable pressure not to admit, or even consider the possibility, that the Soviets were anything less than angels. In the late '60s a kind of Maoist politics swept the left, in particular the radical core of the anti-war movement. Under the aegis of "Marxism-Leninism," a politics was put forward that revolved around the assumption that revolution was possible in the U.S. if only people on the left would follow the example set by revolutionaries in the Third World. Strategies were proposed that were utterly inappropriate to the U.S.; questioning these strategies, or for that matter suggesting that a revolution was not very likely in the U.S., was tantamount to labeling oneself a defector from the cause. Similar things took place in the radical wing of the women's movement: extreme conceptions of feminism, such as the belief that having anything to do with men amounted to fraternizing with the enemy, took hold in many circles, and questioning these ideas was likely to earn one a reputation as a friend of the patriarchy. The left in the U.S. seems prone to being seized by ideas which, when recollected a few years later, look somewhat mad. But it is worth asking why particular ideologies take over at particular moments. After all, in the case of postmodernism, it is not clear why culturalism, a social constructionism set in competition with other levels of social analysis, should be equated with radicalism.

Terry Eagleton, in his article "Where Do Postmodernists Come From?" argues that left intellectuals in the U.S. have adopted postmodernism out of a sense of having been badly defeated, a belief that the left as a political tendency has little future. Culturalism, he argues, involves an extreme subjectivism, a view of the intellect as all-powerful, a mindset that might be described as taking the May '68 slogan "all power to the imagination" literally, combined with a deep pessimism, a sense that it isn't worth the effort to learn about the world, to analyze social systems, for instance, because they can't be changed anyway.

I would add two points to Eagleton's analysis. First, postmodernism takes many of its ideas from the '60s. To some extent it represents a rigidification of ideas that were widespread in movements of that time, especially the voluntarism or hubris of a generational cohort that tended to think that it could accomplish anything. The widespread view among leftists of the '60s that revolution was waiting in the wings, and the fact that so few people openly challenged this, reflected a grandiosity, a loosening of the collective grip on reality. In the heated atmosphere of the late '60s it was possible for radicals to take fairly crazy positions without utterly losing their audience or becoming irrelevant to politics. In the '90s there is considerably less room for extreme voluntarism, or grandiosity, cast as a political position.

There was also a widespread tendency in the movements of the '60s to equate personal and cultural change with broader social change. One of the most important contributions of the movements of the '60s (especially feminism and the countercultural left) was the critique of a culture that promoted consumerism, that equated happiness with individual striving for power and wealth. But in rejecting a politics that left this element out, it was easy to fall into the opposite problem of believing that creating communities in which people tried to live according to different values would inevitably move society as a whole in the same direction. This made change seem easier than it was. The prosperity of the late '60s and early '70s allowed alternative communities to flourish, and it seemed plausible that the more egalitarian relationships and humane values developed in them might serve as models. But as it turned out the egalitarian impulse that found expression in these communities was overshadowed by the shift to the right that has taken place in American society as a whole since the mid-to late '70s. Alternative communities themselves were weakened and destroyed by social changes over which they had no control, especially the depression of the '70s and the withdrawal of support from the public sector in the '80s and '90s. In the '90s it would be very hard to make a convincing case that cultural change equals social change. The equation of the personal or the cultural with the political was a mixed blessing for the movements of the '60s. In the '90s it tends to mean retreating into one's own community and allowing politics to drift further and further to the right.

Postmodernism suffers not only from its reliance on a conception of radicalism that made more sense in the '60s than it does now, but also from the fact that it is located in academia and reflects its pressures. The logic of the market is not a new presence in the American academy, but it now seems to be sweeping all other values and considerations aside. There has been a dramatic increase in the pressures toward intellectual specialization and a frantic pace of publication. There is intense competition between and within fields. In the years following World War II there was a widespread belief, in government and business circles, that the U.S. economy would benefit if a broad liberal higher education were widely available. In the wake of Sputnik there was a sudden rush of support for science education; this resulted in more government support for universities without diminishing its commitment to the humanities. Through the '60s it was mostly the children of the white middle class who attended universities, public or private. Since the '60s the economy has changed, the values governing public spending have changed, and the composition of university student bodies has changed. In a society increasingly stratified between haves and have-nots, an economy in which technical expertise seems more important than familiarity with history and literature, support for liberal education is hardly reliable.

In the '50s and '60s academics could believe that their profession was held in high esteem. They were well paid, and at least some found their opinions sought by the White House or by large corporations. Over the last few decades it has become harder to believe that public esteem of the academy is unqualified. The loss of prestige (and of resources) is felt most sharply in the humanities. In the '50s the social sciences tried to show that they could be as rigorous, quantitative, and ostensibly value-free as the natural sciences. This encouraged huge quantities of unimaginative, narrowly-conceived, jargon-ridden papers. Now it seems to be the turn of the humanities to try to raise their stock within academia, though this time the strategy is not to imitate science but to assert the supremacy of a vocabulary and theoretical perspective nurtured in the humanities over all fields of knowledge. But postmodernism only highlights its own weaknesses when it overreaches its scope. I have heard many postmodernists denounce Sokal on grounds that his hoax could lead to funds being withdrawn from cultural studies or the humanities generally. It seems more useful to look at postmodernism's internal problems. Sokal's hoax and the laughter it generated shows that the field had become ripe for parody.[12]

What are the implications of this for the left? As restraints on capitalism have loosened and the logic of the market has crept into virtually every area of life, the more human values of the left have come to seem archaic and irrelevant. We certainly need a critique of this culture. But postmodernism is not that critique. There are too many respects in which postmodernism accepts or revels in the values of the marketplace for it to serve as a critique. On a deeper level, the problem is that postmodernism is a stance of pure criticism, that it avoids making any claims, asserting any values (or acknowledging its own implicit system of values, in particular its orientation toward sophistication and aesthetics). Left politics requires a conception of a better society and an assertion of a better set of values than those that now prevail. This does not mean that any particular vision of society or any particular definition of those values is the last word; a left perspective requires ongoing discussion and debate. But it is not possible for a purely critical stance to serve as the basis for left politics.

No doubt, one reason that postmodernism has taken hold so widely is that it is much easier to be critical than to present a positive vision. Being on the left means having a conception of the future and confidence that there is a connection between the present and the future, that collective action in the present can lead to a better society. It is difficult these days to articulate any clear vision of the future, even more difficult to figure out how we might get from where we are to a more humane, egalitarian, and ecologically balanced society. A friend of mine recently told me that her image is that we are on a log that is slowly drifting down the Niagara River, and we can begin to hear the roar of the Falls. But because we do not know what to do, we are not roused from our lethargy. It seems to me that postmodernism has become an obstacle to addressing urgent issues, including impending environmental and social disasters, and how to build a movement that might begin to address them. Clearing away the fog won't automatically provide us with any answers, but might make it easier to hold a productive discussion.

Notes

1 Alan Sokal, "Transgressing the Boundaries: Toward a Transformative Hermeneutics of Quantum Gravity," *Social Text* 46–47, Spring/Summer 1996: 217–252.

2 For critiques of postmodernism, or poststructuralist theory, see Brian Palmer, *Descent into Discourse: The Reification of Language and the Writing of Social History* (Philadelphia: Temple University Press, 1990); Peter Dews, *Logics of Disintegration: Post- Structuralist Thought and the Claims of Critical Theory* (London: Verso, 1987); Alex Callinocos, *Against Post-Modernism* (London: Methuen, 1982); Christopher Norris, *Deconstruction: Theory and Practice* (London: Methuen, 1982), and *Deconstruction and the Interests of Theory* (London: Pinter, 1988); Terry Eagleton, *The Illusions of Postmodernism* (Oxford: Blackwell, 1996); Perry Anderson, *In the Tracks of Historical Materialism* (London: Verso, 1984); and Somer Broberibb, *Nothing Mat(t)ers: A Feminist Critique of Postmodernism* (North Melbourne: Spiniflex Press, 1992).

3 See, for instance, Judith Butler, "Contingent Foundations: Feminism and the Question of 'Postmodernism,'" 3–21, in *Feminists Theorize the Political,* ed. Judith Butler and Joan W. Scott (New York: Routledge, 1992).

4 See Luc Ferry and Alain Renault, *French Philosophy of the 60s: An Essay on Antihumanism* (Amherst: University of Massachusetts Press, 1985) on the ways in which poststructuralism and the spirit of May '68 coincided, and differed. Ferry and Renault point out that while a politics of authenticity, of the self as agent of social change, was central to May '68, poststructuralism emphasizes fragmentation and incoherence to the point of denying the existence of the self and the possibility of authenticity.

5 David Harvey, *The Condition of Postmodernity: an Enquiry into the Origins Of Cultural Change* (Oxford: Basil Blackwell, 1989); Frederic Jameson, *The Political Unconscious: Nar-*

rative as a Socially Symbolic Act (Ithaca: Cornell University Press, 1981), and "Postmodernism, or the Logic of Late Capitalism," first published in *New Left Review* 146 (July–August 1984): 53–92, later included in Jameson's book of the same title (Durham, N.C.: Duke University Press, 1991).

6   Joan W Scott, "Experience," in *Feminists Theorize the Political*, (New York: Routledge, 1992), ed. Judith Butler and Joan W. Scott: 22–40.

7   Ernesto Laclau and Chantal Mouffe, *Hegemony and Socialist Strategy* (London: Verso, 1985), pp. 82–85.

8   Stanley Fish. "Professor Sokal's Bad Joke," *New York Times,* Op Ed, May 21, 1996.

9   "Mystery Science Theater," Bruce Robbins and Andrew Ross, Co-Editors of *Social Text*, *Lingua Franca*, July/August 1996: 54–57.

10 Bruce Robbins. "Anatomy of a Hoax," *Tikkun* Vol. 11, No. 5, September–October 1996, pp. 58–59.

11 Daniel Harris, "Jargon Basement," review of *Male Matters: Masculinity, Anxiety, and the Male Body on the Line*, by Calvin Thomas (University of Illinois Press). *Bay Area Reporter*, June 13, 1996, p. 40.

12 For a discussion of the public view of academics and how postmodernism has made a bad situation worse, see Loic J.D. Wacquant, "The Self-Inflicted Irrelevance of American Academics." *Academe,* July–August 1996, 18–23.

KEN HIRSCHKOP

Cultural Studies and Its Discontents:
A Comment on the Sokal Affair

Social Text, Spring 1997

Alan Sokal's hoax was a childish gesture, but his motivations cannot be dismissed as trivial. His parody was unmistakably aimed not at science studies in general but at those who would install cultural studies as the new queen of the sciences. Over the past few years the very idea of "culture" has served as a Trojan horse for cultural studies, providing it with an access to other intellectual territories that it has consistently abused. The admission that the subject matter of one's discipline is part of human culture has been interpreted by cultural studies' devotees as an invitation to call the shots, and they have not been shy or reticent about calling them. In this situation a justified, if messy, rebellion was always in the cards.

Sokal may not have been aware of these incursions into neighboring disciplines, but he clearly had a sense of what would follow once it was agreed, as George Levine has put it, that "science *is* culture" (114).[1] For however much cultural studies has urged us to pursue a provisional, positional, or local form of knowledge, it has always displayed a disturbing confidence when it comes to knowledge of the working of culture itself. Those who do cultural studies write as if it were self-evidently the case that cultural institutions and forms confine and constrain the discourse flowing within them, and as if there could be no doubt that the inner structure of every cultural form is bound to a discrete, nonuniversalizable historical project. I always wonder how people who are apparently skeptical of everything under the sun can be so sure that they know how discourse, language, or culture works, so sure that they can guarantee, without need for empirical demonstration, that every attempt to create something with universal significance (in politics, science, art, or whatever) is doomed. How do we know that the very structure of discourse and culture militates against the universal and renders every claim to knowledge relative? Well, we don't know, and anyone who thinks he or she does know wants the theory of culture to assume the throne vacated by philosophy.

Social Text and others working in cultural studies claim that Sokal has nothing to fear, because they are not the card-carrying relativists of his fevered imagination. In a way that is certainly true, but in another way it is disingenuous. Practitioners of cultural studies of science (and I am speaking of them in particular, and not of science studies as a whole) are not relativist for the simple reason that no one can be a relativist consistently, and certainly not writers with social criticism in mind. In his introduction to the "Science Wars" issue, Andrew Ross reminds us that relativism leaves everything just as it is, and he accordingly opts for something he calls *diversity* instead. But one can be inconsistently relativist—relativist in theory but not in practice, or relativist about some matters and not others—and this is the tack we find here. Although many contributors to the "Science Wars" issue acknowledge the epistemological claims of natural science, others assure us that there is no knowledge except that produced by (self-contained?) "knowledge systems" (22); that belief in the explanatory power of science or in its intellectual logic is old hat (except to those blind to the latest in scholarship!) (130–31); and that we cannot maintain the universalist claims of "empirical rationality" (4). In these and other cases, the fact that "science is culture" renders the achievements of natural science relative to its immediate context, to the interests of a professional elite, to the political project of the European and American nation-states, or to whatever else is deemed a relevant limiting factor. Thus conveniently packaged, modern natural science becomes just one of many options we might select, given the right occasion. For in the night of culture, every knowledge is local and black.

These theoretical commitments do not hamstring their writers only because they know how and when to abandon them. Strikingly, the most telling criticisms of science in the issue—that science should not have its agenda set by the profit-making interests of U.S. industry or the Department of Defense; that scientists should be aware and self-critical about sources of bias, be they gender, race or something else, in their work; that science should engage in dialogue with the wider public—amount to the charge that current scientific research compromises the universalistic aspirations that legitimate it. For all the theoretical huffing and puffing, the main complaint of most of the contributors is that science could do more—granted, a lot more—to be scientific. There are moments, however, when some contributors realize this is a pretty modest payoff for their theoretical exertions, and decide to have a go at the very epistemology of natural science itself. But having dismissed out of hand the possibility of a critique based on the principle that some knowledges are better than others, they have to make their stand on far more dangerous ground—the principle that some knowledge makes better politics than others. When Ross asks us to do science in a way that favors "local environments, cultural values, and principles of social justice" (4), he is certainly being critical rather than relativistic, but he is being critical only by abandoning the claims of knowledge altogether. As is common enough in the cultural studies game, he displays an uncanny faith that whereas no one can agree on what should constitute natural science, everyone will know what the principles of social justice are. Relativism in epistemology finds its counterweight in dogmatism in politics; the best knowledge will be that which advances the politics we just know is right.

Shouldn't that much-vaunted sense of the historical set off some alarm bells here? Putting politics in the driving seat of science makes both for bad science (the historical record speaks for itself) and for bad politics. Democracy-advancing social movements (to use Sandra Harding's phrase [15]) don't need sciences shaped by their needs, because that kind of science will only tell them what they want to hear. Social movements need knowledge that is independent of their immediate political horizon. They need knowledge that can justify itself in scientific terms (in the broadest sense), not knowledge that justifies itself by being in tune with this or that political or cultural value.

Or to put it another way: cultural studies should recognize that it, too, is science, and should drop the frequently encountered pretense that it is the natural ally, or (worse still) the theoretical reflection, of the new social movements. The critique of universalism is a matter of science, not politics: cultures may be context-bound in the way cultural studies believes, or they may not be, but politics will never provide the answer. In her contribution to the issue, Hilary Rose points out that some feminists believe in science and some critique it, the point being that the political movement itself has no particular epistemological stance. So it is with the other social movements with which cultural studies likes to identify itself: they are held together by political passions and interests, not by epistemological ones, and while there are elements in these movements that share the Herderesque concept of culture with cultural studies, there are elements that do not. Sokal says he is a leftist and I have no reason not to believe him; certainly he is not more or less of one because of his epistemological beliefs. He is right to protest at the comfortable equation cultural studies makes between its style of intellectual work and its political commitments. For if it continues to ask the politics of its time to provide ballast for its positions, it will find itself either left out in the cold when political winds change, or leading the Left back toward a grim Stalinist history from which it surely should have learned something. There would be little point in jumping from the frying pan of a linear history into the fire of a cyclical one.

Notes

1 All page references are to *Social Text*, nos. 46–47 (spring–summer 1996).

BRUCE ROBBINS

Just Doing Your Job: Some Lessons of the Sokal Affair

Yale Journal of Criticism, Fall 1997

The December 3, 1996, issue of the French left-wing newspaper *Libération* contains a full-page article, plus photograph and interview, devoted to Alan Sokal's hoax in *Social Text* and the media coverage that has followed. The article begins like this: " 'Does reality exist?' It's difficult to believe, but for the past six months, the American intellectual left has been gorging itself on the question."

This is not an even approximately accurate account of the Sokal affair—no one in this argument has in fact taken the position that reality does not exist—but it is a representative sample of how scrupulously journalists have reported it, in the U.S. as well as abroad, on the left as well as elsewhere on the political spectrum. That's a load of inaccuracy to crawl out from under. And these are the people who complain that others don't respect standards of evidence! As the journalists will sometimes tell you off the record, they are "just doing their Job." Perhaps it's in the nature of their Job that they need not worry whether anyone remembers the provenance of this excuse. But it would be too easy simply to blame either them or their profession. After all, the professional deformation is not all on their side.

Asked how it feels to know he has provoked this avalanche of malicious half-truths and outright misrepresentations, Alan Sokal could of course respond that it's not his field, not the point he wanted to make about science studies, not his responsibility. As a physicist, should he have been required to consider what the media would do with his stunt? What are a physicist's responsibilities in—or to—the public sphere? (This is of course one of the questions that science studies was attempting to bring to the public's attention when the hoax came along and diverted that attention elsewhere.) But in addition to being a physicist, Sokal has also declared himself a leftist. As a leftist, he could surely be expected to weigh the likely consequences— consequences not just for the quantity of his email correspondence and lecture invitations, but for untenured, highly vulnerable students of culture around the country, some of whom are already seeing their projects endangered and their reappointments blocked in a gathering backlash. Still, to appeal to politics is not to end the discussion. For *Social Text*, too—and it's also our mistake that has brought discredit on the work of so many other practitioners of cultural politics—a certain obscurity lingers over the question of how responsibilities to politics and to everyday academic business are supposed to be balanced or reconciled.

Toward the beginning of Sokal's essay, there is a little sentence which goes as follows: "physical 'reality,' no less than social 'reality' is at bottom a social and linguistic construct." To the best of my knowledge, no one on the *Social Text* collective believes this. After more than a decade of editorial meetings, I can't think of anyone who is entirely comfortable within the constructivist paradigm, anyone who doesn't bump up against its limits with every intellectual move they make. Andrew Ross's largely unread introduction to the largely unread "Science Wars" issue does what it can to move the focus away from epistemology to matters like the politics of funding and agenda-setting, and I think that's both right and more characteristic of the journal. For years I've been using Diana Fuss's *Essentially Speaking* (1989) to tell incoming graduate students they cannot assume they are doing anything intellectually or politically significant by sole virtue of showing that something is a social construct since saying that X is a social or cultural construct only displaces the "reality" question from the X and onto the "society" or the "culture" that's supposedly doing the constructing. The papers I want from my students, and the submissions we have tended to welcome for *Social Text*, have the tact or savvy to acknowledge the potential interpretive regress (what constructs "society" and "culture"? and so on) without getting carried away by it, without losing their worldly focus on what for the moment at least is undeniably there.

Still, the line about physical reality as construct passed. It might have provided grounds for such large disagreement as to disqualify the article; many other disagreements would have. It wasn't our line, but it wasn't definitively unacceptable either. And the fact that it could pass says something troubling about the compromise that underlies the term "cultural politics," a compromise between the left and the study of culture which has changed and enriched both sides, but in which there is also an element—perhaps an unavoidable element—of professional deformation. Extending the empire of culture, even to the very limit, is not guaranteed to incur the displeasure of cultural professionals.

This might also be phrased as the problem—other editors must also face it—of how to run a journal of cultural politics in a time when, in the humanities at least, the concept of politics seems to be everywhere and therefore nowhere, when it is the common currency into which all interpretations of culture must obligatorily be converted, a synonym for interpretive value itself. To many, then, the phrase "cultural politics" would be a redundancy. Culture is nothing *but* politics, and politics—at least as the profession sometimes understands it—is nothing but culture.

One lesson to be drawn from the Sokal affair (though many of us had already been making the point for years) is that this equation will not do. A genuine dialogue of the sort that this episode might well have created, but hasn't so far, would perhaps have begun by restricting and nuancing both terms. It could have acknowledged, for example, that what the cultural left means by politics is often perceived by disgruntled outsiders as blatant favoritism to the humanist's priorities and workday routine—a routine of writing and pedagogy—as against the schedules and possibilities of nonhumanists. Over the last few months a certain number of progressive people outside the humanities and/or outside the academy have expressed resentment against us cultural types for an oddly oblique reason: because we cultural types seemed to be claiming that we were doing progressive and significant political work simply by doing our jobs. This was rarely if ever an option, they implied, for natural scientists and engineers like themselves. And they were probably right to see it as an insidious display by the humanities of a sort of holier-than-thou status—our implicit exemption from the bothersome necessity of spending all those extra hours leafleting or on committees or whatever. Since we have the good luck to deal with culture, the logic goes, and since culture is always already political, we are doing politics simply by doing what we would be doing anyway, doing what we're paid to do.

This is too good to be true, no? Yes, it is. And there is no way of rationalizing the exclusiveness that's built into it. And yet I cannot help but wonder—assuming such unfair temporal advantages are real and not simply distortions of both culture and politics—whether anyone can afford to give them up. Harried as we all are, our workplaces increasingly separated from our residences, our time increasingly spent in transit, our responsibilities multiplied and diversified, who has time enough even for minimal citizenship, let alone for more strenuous commitments? Editors of journals of cultural politics feel this constraint in their own specialized and especially acute way. Surely we would all like our exchanges with aspiring contributors to sound more like sustained and mutually instructive community-building and less like a mere thumbs-up or thumbs-down on a one-shot effort. But where is the time supposed to come from, say, to write back to authors of promising yet rejected manuscripts? And if the time is *not* found, then what is to prevent a journal like *Social Text* from assuming in the eyes of many readers and potential authors the uncongenial, even forbidding countenance of an academic gatekeeper or expert authority, coolly inspecting and appraising goods in an academic marketplace?

The fact that for better or worse "politics" has become an intellectual *lingua franca* means that, like *Social Text*, many other journals are now located at the murky, disorganized juncture of the political and the professional. Thus we are all potential targets or scapegoats for certain slow-burning frustrations, the experiential result of insistent structural contradictions between the two. Many would-be writers see themselves, and assume naturally enough that they will be treated, as comrades in arms. It is a sense of common political project that brings them to a given journal, and they have some natural expectation that the shared purposes will be recognized. Yet they receive what appears to be hasty and summary judgment, as if they were not comrades but inconveniently overabundant aspirants to that scarce professional privilege, respectable publication. This is not just a matter of numbers; it also shows up in an uncertainty about the criteria of acceptance. A writer may want to take something already known and repeat it, perhaps giving it extra emphasis so as to adapt it to a particular moment—an acceptable and sometimes desirable procedure in a political movement, but less so by more strictly academic standards. For all of us whose writing is simultaneously, naturally enough, trying to satisfy the ever-rising requirements of a job and a career, the experience of contradiction seems unavoidable. What better revenge, then, than to see the judges judged and their imperfections so dramatically exposed? I would be surprised if much of the emotional energy that has given the Sokal story such legs did not come out of a logic like this, a logic that interpolates ideological allies at least as intensely as outright enemies.

Let me take another example. In the debate about the Sokal affair at New York University in November 1996, someone from the audience, clearly speaking in good faith, asked a question that went something like this: "I understand that the choices of which scientific research is being done and how much it's funded are political, but tell me, how is the lab work I do every day political?" Perhaps no good answers could be expected to a question so general. Much work in science studies, like Bruno Latour's, has offered specific answers about the politics of specific labs. But if this point has not been brought home to people outside science studies, it's in part because we who do cultural politics have a bigger professional investment in the principle that *everything* is political than we do in a practical discrimination of the modes and degrees to which *any given thing* is political. It *takes* work to see how a given sort of work is political. For things are not just political in some easy universal sense, nor are they political to the same extent. To say that science isn't neutral is not to say it's always political in the same way, or even in a significant way. Every judgment that something is political should assume the possibility of its being political only in an *in*significant sense.

Another thing that politics ought to mean is making oneself part of a conversation that is larger than one's usual professional conversations. This is not a problem of language, as the media have gleefully and predictably repeated. On the whole *Social Text* has a pretty good record at avoiding unnecessary jargon and flights of verbal virtuosity that go nowhere. But politics in this scale-of-conversation sense is indeed in conflict with some of the often unconscious criteria for academic publication. Some readers will perhaps have seen Alan Sokal's "Afterword" to the hoax in *Dissent* (Fall 1996, 93–97). The piece was turned down by *Social Text*, as *Dissent*'s editors note with a certain understandable pleasure. At the risk of exposing dirty laundry, I would like to say a couple of words about that refusal. There were approximately six hours of official debate over whether to accept Sokal's piece or not. I myself was in favor of publishing it. Not because of its inherent quality, however. I agreed with other members of the editorial board that it contained little that he had not already said in print and, more to the point, that it persisted in the same lazy, ignorant caricature of us, and our readers, as postmodernists whose suspicions of absolute truth left us unable to make any contact at all with social reality. I could certainly understand why, personal hostility aside, others felt that the article did not raise the level of the discussion enough to warrant giving it any space. I felt nevertheless that we had to publish Sokal, and then go on to show where and how he was wrong. Not because of the quality of his ideas, which on their own warranted rejection, but because of who he is—because, for better or worse, he had become the symbol of the hoax, and because *Social Text* desperately needed to demonstrate its openness to dialogue with the many people of intelligence and good will on the left who thought the hoax in some sense a useful or well-deserved exercise.

Though we did invite Sokal to submit his opinions in another form, not publishing the afterword left me with a sour feeling—the feeling that we had lost an opportunity to assert our responsible membership in a larger political world, preferring instead to reassert a commitment to avant-garde, cutting-edge scholarship within a niche of the cultural studies market, while also asserting the (to me) strangely misplaced meritocratic notion that submissions can be judged on their intrinsic intellectual value alone. It may not have been arrogant, but it looked arrogant, and even the appearance of arrogance does a lot of damage to the democratic ideal of constructive dialogue. Of course, who knows how possible such a dialogue actually was? Witness for example the reply by James Weinstein, publisher of *In These Times*, to a letter saying that his editorial denouncing *Social Text* and company as sordid careerists was groundlessly and gratuitously insulting to many of his own readers and hardly an invitation to dialogue. Weinstein wrote back, regretting the loss of a subscriber, but also agreeing with the former subscriber's account. No, his editorial was not intended, he said, "as an invitation to dialogue (I'm sure I wouldn't understand what the post-structuralists were saying)."

Even people like this can be tricked or shamed into dialogue. But if that's going to happen—and a good deal is riding on it—certain founding assumptions of our kind of periodical have got to be a lot better understood, by us and by others, than they are now. Please note, for example, that my argument for publishing Sokal's afterword is entirely consonant with what many people consider the prime motive and source of our failure: that is, publishing him because of who he was, a friendly physicist. What I was proposing was, once again, publishing someone not solely for the intrinsic value of what he or she says, but also because of who she or he is—what his or her reputation and credentials represent to others. And I continue to think that, if you take out the article's silly bowing to authorities (which we in fact asked Sokal to take out) as well as the deliberate mistakes (which we didn't catch), we would have been right to publish the piece assuming it had been what it professed to be, that is, an informed opinion *by a physicist* reporting to non-scientists that quantum physics, properly understood, makes one think again about certain conventional notions of truth in the sciences. This is not to say that we have no standards, but only that who the author of certain ideas is forms a legitimate part of our standards. We're right to want intelligent opinions on cultural studies from Richard Johnson and from Fredric Jameson, because of who they are, and we're right to want intelligent contributions from graduate students, from women, from people of color, even from physicists, because of who they are, because they belong to groups whose opinions on issues of cultural politics matter to a democratic project that is larger than the advancement of knowledge for its own sake.

One might say that to set up an opposition between truth and objectivity, on the one hand, and a nihilistic, relativistic constructionism or postmodernism, on the other, is to display a certain intellectual incompetence. It's not just that there are lots of serious positions between these two extremes. As philosopher Linda Martin Alcoff remarked last fall in Syracuse, *all* the serious positions fall between these extremes, including positions that have nothing postmodern about them. Sokal apparently thought he was attacking postmodernism, in other words, but in fact he was attacking philosophical thought as such. He did not do his homework, and not doing his homework—which the media were not going to notice, of course, but left academics *should* notice—has meant contributing to an enraged anti-intellectualism from which all intellectuals suffer. Or all of us who agree that changing the world also requires interpreting the world, and even interpreting *how* we interpret the world. Ellen Willis summed up the alternative pretty well in her *Village Voice* piece: "Capitalism is screwing people! What goes up must come down! What more do we need to know?" [pt. 5, "My Sokaled Life"]. In fact we need to know a lot.

But there are more generous interpretations of Sokal's simplification than dogmatic know-nothingism. The one that is perhaps most useful for Sokal's opponents to reflect on would connect it to what Kant called the conflict of the faculties. According to this interpretation, Sokal was not so much defending science against its left-wing critics (with whom he admits he largely agrees) as trying to assert the pertinence of physics and its particular protocols of validity to areas outside physics, specifically to social and political analysis. This is what he is doing, for example, when he offers physics' idea of absolute, de-contextualized truth for application to intelligence testing and Zuni creation myths. I think this is a truly terrible idea. As Aristotle said (by Sokal's standards, he would have to count as an early postmodernist), social and political phenomena do not lend themselves to the sorts of certainty that physicists and mathematicians demand. But I can understand where the impulse comes from. With the end of the Cold War and cuts in defense-related research, scientists have been feeling the pinch of serious defunding, as well as the threat to their "disinterested" image that comes of more visible dependence on profit-making corporations. As people in the humanities should know, making a public display of the relevance of your field to matters usually located outside it is one way of seeking public legitimation for it in periods when it is more than usually vulnerable.

In fact the comparison with the humanities extends further. This overreaching on the part of physics, flailing away in all directions with the big stick of Truth, is really only a mirror image of the overreaching of fields like literary criticism. For criticism too has claimed a sort of disciplinary inside track on territory already staked out by other disciplines, for example political phenomena to which it is not always or self-evidently better suited. Our side has often assumed that the right way to talk about politics is with the sensitivity to multiple interpretations and indeterminacies and so on that we in the humanities bring to culture. If piracy like this has its benefits, it also has its liabilities: for example, a conveniently purist weakness before the task of making policy proposals, and a reluctance to recognize that our positions on truth may entail very little about our positions on politics in some other, perhaps larger sense. No interdisciplinary ethics or law of the seas exists to assert jurisdiction over such intellectual wayfaring. But if the humanities cannot thus be assumed to be guilty, neither can the natural sciences.

I won't try to adjudicate any further between these two parallel claims to leadership of the disciplines, though the adjudication would be interesting. In fact, the adjudication is perhaps what we should have been talking about all along. At any rate, it cannot be avoided by the simple expedient of, say, leaving politics to political science. On the one hand, politics is not and cannot be monopolized by anyone's job. On the other hand, everyone's job, at least among the intellectual disciplines, requires the kind of extra-disciplinary legitimation that both the physicists and the cultural critics have lately been discussing with such enthusiasm. So much remains here for debate.

The debate could also use some frank talk about the versions of truth that the cultural left does respect and indeed relies on all the time in its everyday work routines, the sorts of logic and evidence that we do not simply leap to deconstruct, but accept at least provisionally as necessary in order to get down to business. In the talk he delivered at NYU, now published in *Tikkun* (11:6, November/December 1996, 58),[1] Sokal has included a swipe at something I said to this effect in an earlier article in *Tikkun*. In answer to the question of whether the critique of truth was really in the interests of oppressed people, I had said, yes and no. No, in the sense that of course we had to leave ourselves with the resources of logic and evidence, which indeed we had never given up. But yes, in the sense that the supposed singleness of "the" truth has been used and is still being used to claim the last, authoritative word on highly ideological issues. Sokal's response was that though *claims* to truth might be against the interests of oppressed people, the truth itself never could be. Let us not confuse truth, he said, with mere claims to truth.

For what it's worth, I'll make one more brief effort to explain what I take to be a reasonable position on truth for the left—a left which, I repeat, has no good reason to allow itself to be defined by any one epistemology. What I believe is 1) that, at least in situations of social and political controversy, there is no such thing as "Truth" with a capital T, an absolute that is good in all possible times and places, from all possible perspectives. Hence there are *only* claims to truth. And from this perspective, those who claim to be beyond mere claims, to lay their hands on the truth itself, will seem to be behaving with a familiar sort of fundamentalist arrogance. But I also believe 2) that there is all the difference in the world between *better* claims to truth and *worse* claims to truth. It would certainly help if we could get people to see how many of their fears of relativism that difference allays. And perhaps also to see that the real legacy of the Enlightenment lies in carefully specifying the limits and conditions of what we know: protecting the value of what we do know by being modest enough to admit what we don't.

Note

1   The talk delivered at NYU was published in *New Politics* and is reprinted here in part 6 ("A Plea for Reason, Evidence, and Logic"). The *Tikkun* article, entitled "Truth or Consequences: A Brief Response to Robbins," contains the same comment alluded to by Robbins as well as other material.

6

Colloquies

ANDREW ROSS

Reflections on the Sokal Affair

Forum at New York University, October 1996

In the six months that bookstores stocked the special Science Wars issue of *Social Text,* under eight hundred copies were sold, a modest number for a double issue on a topical subject, even for an obscure, small-circulation journal like *Social Text.* It's reasonable to conclude that relatively few people actually read the issue, and yet there seemed very few who did not have a strong opinion about the Sokal affair, as it came to be known, and not a few who used the occasion to cast judgment on entire fields of scholarship, such as science studies and cultural studies, without showing much evidence of having read one word of the scholarship.

For a brief time, the contents of this issue were a scandal of public record, bringing down ridicule upon *Social Text* and its editors for opinions that we do not hold, let alone represent. This is not a good situation to find yourself in, although it is quite typical of life in the Culture Wars. Nor did it come as much of a surprise to those who study the workings of public-opinion making. After all, *Lingua Franca*'s scoop of the Sokal hoax framed the story to fit the template of a particular kind of yellow media exposé, and virtually all the press reports ran a version of the Sokal/ *Lingua Franca* narrative without questioning any of its inflated claims. As a result, public discussion was limited to this frame in its treatment of concepts with a complex intellectual background. Social constructivism and other approaches in science studies were reduced to the status of disbelief in the physical world, a blatantly dishonest reduction introduced by Sokal himself. So, too, ideas associated with postmodernism/cultural studies/poststructuralism/critical theory— widely perceived, for much the same reasons, as interchangeable terms— were reduced to the status of gibberish, in the name of no-nonsense appeals to the moral fundamentalism of plain speech and plain thinking. None of this was surprising. Radical ideas, no less than radical politics, are fringe topics in the public media, sources of highly processed material for genre stories and op-eds about the silly excesses of radicals, whether in the academy or elsewhere. Denied a place on the spectrum of media opinion, the Left is used to berating itself for performing ineptly when thrust in the spotlight to play a prescripted role. Under circumstances framed as a scandal, the *Social Text* editors had very few choices that offered dignity. Our response, which ran in the summer issue of *Lingua Franca*, tried to summarize our regret for having erred, our offense at having been deceived by a fraudulent author, and our obligation to describe the editorial process that led to the publication of Sokal's article. Our response satisfied some, and inflamed others.

If the Sokal affair had been just one more incident worked up by the Right to fuel the media-oriented Culture Wars and Science Wars, its impact would have been limited. But the story also played well in the left-wing press and in liberal and neoliberal publications. The attacks begun by Gross and Levitt attracted sympathy from some unlikely quarters, and Sokal's call to "reclaim the Enlightenment roots of the Left" was accompanied by a minor bout of intolerance among those who had decided they belonged to the true Left, morally authorized to punish the backslidden.

How did this happen and what can be done about it? Two points might be emphasized: (1) the degree to which these attacks are different from the Culture Wars, and (2) the degree to which they are the same.

(1) While most progressives (including scientists) welcome criticism of science's serviceability to corporate, military, and state needs, many are less willing to question science's close affiliation with positivist rationality and value-free knowledge, for fear that compromising the path of positivism somehow amounts to a betrayal of those "Enlightenment roots," or that it represents the first step down a slippery slope to nihilism. Many others, however, believe that progress in social thought is not possible without a thorough critique of the Enlightenment, whether for its justification of the domination of nature, or its authoritative support for belief systems like scientific racism or sexism, or for the monocultural legacy of its assumptions about universality. Still others believe that the critique of technoscience is an extension of the radical skepticism generated, in large part, by the Enlightenment. And yet discussion of the Sokal hoax has invariably been presented in the form of a needlessly polarizing dispute about the Enlightenment—are you for or against? If these are the only choices, most progressives would choose the former. But does this choice then bind us to the view that scientific knowledge is not like all other forms of knowledge, and that it is somehow off-limits to critical inquiry of its social, cultural, and historical components—inquiry of the sort that the Science Warriors see as irrationalist or counter-Enlightenment? Of course not. Then why are we so easily seduced into arguing along these lines? In whose interests exactly is it to polarize opinion in this way?

(2) The Sokal hoax played into and reinforced many of the divisions that have been opened up in the Culture Wars' prolonged backlash against feminism, multiculturalism, and the queer renaissance. We hear more and more progressives, not unlike Sokal himself, appealing to Enlightenment ideals of universality and common value as a prescription for rescuing the Left from its patronage of the politics of social identity. Left-wing jeremiads inform us that in our preoccupation with race, gender, and sexuality, we are being led astray. Inevitably, such voices recall the reason why the label of political correctness was first devised—in order to temper the knowingness of those who dwelled on the errors of others. What made the Sokal affair an unusual, but germane, event in the Culture Wars was that it gave rise to an outbreak of old-style correctness, complete with impatient calls for purges of a faux Left. This is always a sad spectacle, especially when it features anti-intellectual sentiment masquerading as "sufficient" political consciousness. Ellen Willis satirized this disposition well in her *Village Voice* article [pt. 5, "My Sokaled Life"]: "Capitalism is screwing people! What goes up must come down! What more do we need to know?" To which, I would again add: in whose interests is it to believe that this is all we need to know?

What use then can knowledge be to public politics? This is surely one of the questions that arises out of incidents like the Sokal affair, and it certainly lies close to the heart of cultural studies, conceived as an intellectual movement that seeks not only to bridge traditional (though not ancient) divisions in the field of knowledge but also to transcend the rift between the academic specialist and the public generalist/cultural critic. Inevitably perceived as an overreacher, cultural studies often focuses on material that is "out of place" in academic life, just as it brings critical analysis considered too "complex" to the life of public discourse. Complaints about the lack of scholarly standards from one side compete in volume with protests against overcerebrality on the other. These grievances often find common cause in the objection to high-theoretical language, infamously, though not exclusively, associated with cultural studies. If nothing else, the Sokal affair generated widespread agreement on this particular charge, though it was a long-standing complaint, even within the cultural studies community. I am no dissenter in this matter. There is no excuse for obscurantism, just as there are no critical insights that cannot be phrased in a readily intelligible manner, without causing eyes to glaze over. If folks who subscribe to the loosely shared ideals of cultural studies do not make the effort to forge an inclusive language, then many of these ideals will become objects of antiquarian nostalgia and not daily customs of intellectual life. I happen to believe that the language problem is a serious one (there is a high-theory ghetto, and there is a way out), but I also suspect that the most significant resistance to cultural studies stems from its intellectual activism—its challenges to specialist turf and the disciplinary carve-up of the field of knowledge, its challenges to proprietary journalistic self-interest and to left-wing piety about pure politics.

While I do not think the Sokal affair proved anything (it was an anomaly in almost every respect), it did expose a landscape of resentments and suspicions that may have to be negotiated. More than ever, we will have to learn to forge alliances while respecting our disagreements. But this will involve choosing carefully: some struggles are simply not worth the energy, just as some caricatures are not worth rebutting. Self-criticism always helps: guilt-tripping and abjection do not. Encouragement improves all of us, intolerance does not. The deceptive basis of Sokal's hoax might have generated widespread distrust for scientific authority, while reinforcing the fierce insularity of many scientists. This is unfortunate, coming at a time when the call for the public accountability of science has never been more critical. But let us hope that the mutual embarrassment—for scientists and nonscientist commentators alike—will generate new and unforeseen kinds of dialogue. First, we will have to agree to put aside the false polarities—such as realism versus relativism—that have framed so much of the Science Wars, compelling people to take sides over spurious choices. And while we're at it, we might lay to rest another phantom in the Left's version of the Culture Wars by fully acknowledging that social identity and cultural politics are a component of, and not a diversion from, the fight against economic injustice.

As a postscript, something ought to be said about the role of a publication like *Social Text,* since some commentators averred that the Sokal affair demonstrated the academic impropriety of a nonrefereed journal. *Social Text* is not simply a nonrefereed journal, it is a journal of tendency, edited by a collective that meets to discuss manuscripts in a face-to-face manner. This is an anomaly among academic publications, although there are a number of collectively edited journals of leftist and feminist persuasion—such as *Socialist Review, Camera Obscura, Radical History Review, Feminist Review, Rethinking Marxism*—which share some of our history, and which tend to favor some version of that editorial procedure. Without heroicizing the work of these journals, they have managed to survive, usually with scant institutional support, and to carry on the practice of face-to-face collective work primarily in an academic environment geared to rewarding individual careerism. To most academics, this is a concept that belongs with the dinosaurs, or else one that is anathema to scholarly standards. But enough is surely known about the often stultifying outcomes of a blind-review process (and the corruptions of peer-reviewing in general) to believe that there is still an important role, however anomalous, for such journals to play.

ALAN SOKAL

A Plea for Reason, Evidence, and Logic

Forum at New York University, October 1996

This affair has brought up an incredible number of issues, and I can't dream of addressing them all in 10 minutes, so let me start by circumscribing my talk. I don't want to belabor *Social Text*'s failings either before or after the publication of my parody: *Social Text* is not my enemy, nor is it my main intellectual target. I won't go here into the ethical issues related to the propriety of hoaxing (although in the question period I'd be glad to defend my ethics). I won't address the obscurantist prose and the uncritical celebrity-worship that have infected certain trendy sectors of the American academic humanities (though these are important questions that I hope other panelists will address). I won't enter into technical issues of the philosophy of science (although again I'd be glad to do that in the question period). I won't discuss the social role of science and technology (though these are important issues). Indeed, I want to emphasize that this affair is in my view not primarily about science—though that was the excuse that I used in constructing my parody—nor is it a disciplinary conflict between scientists and humanists, who are in fact represented on all sides of the debate. What I believe this debate is principally about—and what I want to focus on tonight—is the nature of truth, reason, and objectivity: issues that I believe are crucial to the future of left politics.

I didn't write the parody for the reasons you might at first think. My aim wasn't to defend science from the barbarian hordes of lit crit or sociology. I know perfectly well that the main threats to science nowadays come from budget-cutting politicians and corporate executives, not from a handful of postmodernist academics. Rather, my goal is to defend what one might call a scientific worldview—defined broadly as a respect for evidence and logic, and for the incessant confrontation of theories with the real world; in short, for reasoned argument over wishful thinking, superstition and demagoguery. And my motives for trying to defend these old-fashioned ideas are basically political. I'm worried about trends in the American Left—particularly here in academia—that at a minimum divert us from the task of formulating a progressive social critique, by leading smart and committed people into trendy but ultimately empty intellectual fashions, and that can in fact undermine the prospects for such a critique, by promoting subjectivist and relativist philosophies that in my view are inconsistent with producing a realistic analysis of society that we and our fellow citizens will find compelling.

David Whiteis, in a recent article, said it well:

> Too many academics, secure in their ivory towers and insulated from the real-world consequences of the ideas they espouse, seem blind to the fact that non-rationality has historically been among the most powerful weapons in the ideological arsenals of oppressors. The hypersubjectivity that characterizes postmodernism is a perfect case in point: far from being a legacy of leftist iconoclasm, as some of its advocates so disingenuously claim, it in fact . . . plays perfectly into the anti-rationalist—really, anti-thinking—bias that currently infects "mainstream" U.S. culture.

Along similar lines, the philosopher of science Larry Laudan observed caustically that "the displacement of the idea that facts and evidence matter by the idea that everything boils down to subjective interests and perspectives is—second only to American political campaigns—the most prominent and pernicious manifestation of anti-intellectualism in our time." (And these days, being nearly as anti-intellectual as American political campaigns is really quite a feat.)

Now, of course, no one will admit to being against reason, evidence and logic—that's like being against Motherhood and Apple Pie. Rather, our postmodernist and poststructuralist friends will claim to be in favor of some new and deeper kind of reason, such as the celebration of "local knowledges" and "alternative ways of knowing" as an antidote to the so-called "Eurocentric scientific methodology" (you know, things like systematic experiment, controls, replication, and so forth). You find this magic phrase "local knowledges" in, for example, the articles of Andrew Ross and Sandra Harding in the "Science Wars" issue of *Social Text*. But are "local knowledges" all that great? And when local knowledges conflict, which local knowledges should we believe? In many parts of the Midwest, the "local knowledges" say that you should spray more herbicides to get bigger crops. It's old-fashioned objective science that can tell us which herbicides are poisonous to farm workers and to people downstream. Here in New York City, lots of "local knowledges" hold that there's a wave of teenage motherhood that's destroying our moral fiber. It's those boring data that show that the birth rate to teenage mothers has been essentially constant since 1975, and is about half of what it was in the good old 1950s. Another word for "local knowledges" is prejudice.

I'm sorry to say it, but under the influence of postmodernism some very smart people can fall into some incredibly sloppy thinking, and I want to give two examples. The first comes from a front-page article in last Tuesday's *New York Times* (10/22/96) about the conflict between archaeologists and some Native American creationists. I don't want to address here the ethical and legal aspects of this controversy—who should control the use of 10,000-year-old human remains—but only the epistemic issue. There are at least two competing views on where Native American populations come from. The scientific consensus, based on extensive archaeological evidence, is that humans first entered the Americas from Asia about 10–20,000 years ago, crossing the Bering Strait. Many Native American creation accounts hold, on the other hand, that native peoples have always lived in the Americas, ever since their ancestors emerged onto the surface of the earth from a subterranean world of spirits. And the *Times* article observed that many archaeologists, "pulled between their scientific temperaments and their appreciation for native culture, . . . have been driven close to a postmodern relativism in which science is just one more belief system." For example, Roger Anyon, a British archaeologist who has worked for the Zuni people, was quoted as saying that "Science is just one of many ways of knowing the world. . . . [The Zunis' world view is] just as valid as the archeological viewpoint of what prehistory is about."

Now, perhaps Dr. Anyon was misquoted, but we all have repeatedly heard assertions of this kind, and I'd like to ask what such assertions could possibly mean. We have here two mutually incompatible theories. They can't both be right; they can't both even be approximately right. They could, of course, both be wrong, but I don't imagine that that's what Dr. Anyon means by "just as valid." It seems to me that Anyon has quite simply allowed his political and cultural sympathies to cloud his reasoning. And there's no justification for that: We can perfectly well remember the victims of a horrible genocide, and support their descendants' valid political goals, without endorsing uncritically (or hypocritically) their societies' traditional creation myths. Moreover, the relativists' stance is extremely condescending: it treats a complex society as a monolith, obscures the conflicts within it, and takes its most obscurantist factions as spokespeople for the whole.

My second example of sloppy thinking comes from *Social Text* co-editor Bruce Robbins' article in the September/October 1996 *Tikkun* magazine, in which he tries to defend—albeit half-heartedly—the postmodernist/poststructuralist subversion of conventional notions of truth. "Is it in the interests of women, African Americans, and other super-exploited people," Robbins asks, "to insist that truth and identity are social constructions? Yes and no," he asserts. "No, you can't talk about exploitation without respect for empirical evidence"—exactly my point. "But yes," Robbins continues, "truth can be another source of oppression." Huh??? How can truth oppress anyone? Well, Robbins' very next sentence explains what he means: "It was not so long ago," he says, "that scientists gave their full authority to explanations of why women and African Americans . . . were inherently inferior." But is Robbins claiming that that is truth? I should hope not! Sure, lots of people say things about women and African-Americans that are not true; and yes, those falsehoods have sometimes been asserted in the name of "science," "reason" and all the rest. But claiming something doesn't make it true, and the fact that people—including scientists—sometimes make false claims doesn't mean that we should reject or revise the concept of truth. Quite the contrary: it means that we should examine with the utmost care the evidence underlying people's truth claims, and we should reject assertions that in our best rational judgment are false. [Robbins responds in an essay included in this collection, "Just Doing Your Job," pt. 5.]

This error is, unfortunately, repeated throughout Robbins' essay: he systematically confuses truth with claims of truth, fact with assertions of fact, and knowledge with pretensions to knowledge. These elisions underlie much of the sloppy thinking about "social construction" that is prevalent nowadays in the academy, and it's something that progressives ought to resist. Sure, let's show which economic, political, and ideological interests are served by our opponents' accounts of "reality"; but first let's demonstrate, by marshalling evidence and logic, why those accounts are objectively false (or in some cases true but incomplete).

A bit later in his article, Robbins admits candidly that "those of us who do cultural politics sometimes act as if . . . truth were always and everywhere a weapon of the right." Now, that's an astoundingly self-defeating attitude for an avowed leftist. If truth were on the side of the right, shouldn't we all—at least the honest ones among us—become right-wingers? For my own part, I'm a leftist and a feminist because of evidence and logic (combined with elementary ethics), not in spite of it.

This plea of mine for reason, evidence, and logic is hardly original; dozens of progressive humanists, social scientists, and natural scientists have been saying the same thing for years. But if my parody in *Social Text* has helped just a little bit to amplify their voices and to provoke a much-needed debate on the American Left, then it will have served its purpose.

Lingua Franca *Roundtable*

May 1997

The initial reactions to the Sokal hoax were highly charged and, quite frequently, strictly partisan. But the hoax's most valuable legacy may be the many informal conversations it sparked across the country. With that in mind, *Lingua Franca* invited three scholars to lunch to discuss the hoax.

Participants

David Z. Albert is professor of philosophy at Columbia University. He received his Ph.D. from Rockefeller University in theoretical physics. His recent works include *Quantum Mechanics and Experience* (Harvard University Press).

John Brenkman is professor of English at City University of New York. One of the founders of *Social Text*, his recent works include *Culture and Domination* (Cornell University Press) and *Straight, Male, Modern: A Cultural History of Psychoanalysis* (Routledge). He edits the literary magazine *Venue*.

Elisabeth (Lisa) Lloyd is professor of the history and philosophy of science at Indiana University at Bloomington. At the time of this roundtable, she was associate professor of philosophy at the University of California–Berkeley.

Lingua Franca was represented by two participants, including the journal's editor in chief, Jeffrey Kittay

Brenkman: The parody itself, it seems to me, was brilliant, but Sokal's explanation in *Lingua Franca* of what he'd done makes two massive claims, neither of which I think is true: On the one hand, that the whole of cultural studies is a morass of relativism and confused logic and lack of interest in empirical reality, and on the other hand, that we should espouse a very narrow realist position on the nature of scientific inquiry—which puts him out of tune with mainstream philosophy of science.

Albert: That's right. The character of the opposition (if there is one) between mainstream analytic philosophy of science and science studies or cultural studies attitudes towards science doesn't seem to me to be helpfully characterized in terms of a disagreement about philosophical propositions like realism or anything like that. You can find people indisputably within the standard mainstream analytic philosophy of science position, people like Nelson Goodman, whom no one in the poststructuralist camp is going to beat for anti-realism, or relativism, or social constructivism, or what you will. I think the way most people reacted to Sokal's piece was on another level. For them the article pointed to something alarming about standards of scholarship in certain quarters, and standards of argument, and highlighted how much could be gained by simply declaring allegiance to certain kinds of agendas. There was an enormous gap between what he presented himself as doing and what was actually interesting about what he was doing.

LF *representative:* When you say "most people," do you mean most philosophers of science, or most philosophers?

Albert: I surely think most philosophers read it like that. There were exceptions, however. There was for example an article in the *Times Literary Supplement* by Paul Boghossian [pt. 5, "What the Sokal Hoax Ought to Teach Us"], the NYU philosophy professor, which did take the form of an attack on certain kinds of anti-realism (although the kinds he chose didn't seem to me quite the strongest or most interesting ones). So *that* was a piece by a philosopher that did focus on the truth or falsity of certain philosophical propositions, but I think that's atypical from what I know of philosophers' reactions.

Lloyd: I don't think that Boghossian was alone in getting on the coattails of this to promote a philosophical agenda. It's sort of "I'm writing to all you intellectuals out there who I know are concerned about quality, and I'm a philosopher, I'm going to explain to you like I explain to my students how idiotic this mistake is, so you too will be able to refute these idiots in everyday life." Sort of take-home realist philosophy to use against your opponents in the academy. That's how I read the piece.

Albert: My personal style of doing philosophy of science, for reasons which are local to the specific problems I am interested in, is a very realist style. But certainly the most extreme social-constructivist, anti-realist positions have already been debated very seriously and with enormous respect— Nelson Goodman is again the perfect example—within standard analytic philosophy of science.

Brenkman: That's exactly right. This sort of very polarized debate between realist and anti-realist has a whole tradition within philosophy of science, without reference at all to the cultural studies debate itself.

Kittay: Do you think that Sokal is blameworthy because he behaves as if his opponents were idiots? Or, given that he is parodizing, is it rather the reader who is blameworthy for taking him literally?

Albert: Most of what we are saying here applies not to the parody itself but to what he wrote *about* the parody, in *Lingua Franca* and elsewhere. As a parodist, he's brilliant. As a theorist, he's very murky and unconvincing, although the thinking I've seen him do recently reflects a little more appreciation of the complexity of the situation. Initially, he did slightly misdescribe, or seriously misdescribe, what he did. My impression is that he is earnestly trying to figure out how it would be better to describe it.

Lloyd: As for his initial presentation in *Lingua Franca*, I have undergraduates who do better than he does in philosophy of science.

Brenkman: That *Social Text* accepted the original article is ironic, *not* because they didn't understand the physics and the mathematics, but because—no matter *what* the physics was—you cannot extrapolate from physics to feminism, or from mathematics to political and social equality. That is the most telling part of the editorial breakdown. But I guess the editors were seduced by the fact that this was a scientist writing. Contrary to the basic premise of critical science studies, which is to question the authority of scientific discourse, they fell for the authority of a scientist discoursing. What is ironic about that is that if a scientist writes a philosophical treatise, the appropriate response is to be extremely suspicious, because there is no reason to assume that a physicist is going to get the philosophy of science at all right, let alone getting right the politics and the social theory and all these other things.

Albert: That is a really important point, and one could make the irony even stronger: Within a lot of these discourses that present themselves as radical critiques of science, the degree to which individual scientists are valorized, the degree to which science carries authority, vastly outstrips the authority science carries within communities that are supposed to be much more sympathetic to it. It's the opposite of a project of demystification. There's such an aura that attaches to the ruminations of scientists in fields in which, as you say, there is no reason to expect that they have any expertise whatever.

Lloyd: Who does this?

Albert: First of all the editors of *Social Text*. It's also a technique you run into again and again in creationism—they find this or that scientist who doubts evolution . . .

LF *representative:* . . . Well, when an enemy comes over to your side, he is a very valuable ally.

Albert: But look, if you think about that, it is very puzzling that science should be so impressive to them. Scientists aren't the people, after all, whose opinions on philosophical or cultural or political issues ought to be considered the most important. And then, the credentialing of people who are entitled to produce critiques of science is something Ross and Robbins seem to be positioning themselves very strongly against. And indeed, over and over again the structure of the argument against science studies is: "Who the hell is this person anyway? She doesn't even have a Ph.D. in physics!"

Brenkman: Here we start to get at the heart of the missing interdisciplinary issue. There's a certain kind of anti-intellectualism on the part of scientists vis-à-vis work in the humanities and the "softer" social sciences, and clearly there is a very strong strand of anti-intellectualism as regards science on the part of a lot of people who do humanities and cultural studies. This whole controversy is an intensified version of this mutual antipathy, in which the attitudes on each side are, in a more general perspective, amazingly anti-intellectual: There is some underlying failure of education on both sides here on the rules of the game.

Albert: It is a complicated psychological situation. There is condescension and resentment on both sides—mixed with certain kinds of envy. It's a very complicated mix of things.

Brenkman: Speaking as a humanist, I thought that when the Gingrich Congress decided it was going to go after the National Endowment for the Humanities and the National Endowment for the Arts, it was even more alarming that they were going to go after basic science. This was a far more troubling symptom of conservative political and public opinion than the comparable attitudes about the arts and the humanities. It is very hard to have a functioning advanced modern society without the state supporting basic research in the sciences. But the natural alliances among the people who should all want to foster education and research are eclipsed in the Sokal debate.

Lloyd: You mentioned before that there was a failure of education—and certainly there is a pretty serious communications problem. But I actually see the context and birth of this debate as a lot more sinister. I think that *Higher Superstition,* the book by Gross and Levitt, did an unbelievable amount of damage. It goes beyond a failure of education. It was mis-education, the indoctrination of ignorance.

Brenkman: But it took hold within the community of science.

Lloyd: Yes, people who before Gross and Levitt didn't have any beliefs about what was being done in science studies or humanities, after reading the book had a bunch of beliefs that were false, based on hyperbole—to put it nicely—or complete misrepresentation of the positions of the feminist philosophers of science, but also of people like Bruno Latour. Before, there was ignorance; afterwards, there is ignorance with a self-righteous attitude, and misinformation, and disinformation, and that's what I think is sinister. But I do think that the situation arose because of cuts in science research funds and other institutional issues: the feud that that provoked in the scientific community required a scapegoat—a rhetoric of setting up an enemy. The scientific community needed an enemy at that point, and it couldn't quite be the people who were pulling the funding, could it?

Brenkman: You make it sound a little conspiratorial whereas it seems more like a misplaced reaction or something.

Lloyd: I don't mean to say it was a conspiracy. But it's more than a misplaced reaction. I think it *started* as a misplaced reaction, as a way to focus the concern that arose out of the undermining and challenges that were happening in the federal sphere. But after a certain point, the doors closed. Even if somebody said, "Look, that's not what we mean, that's not what I'm talking about, let me talk with you about that"—the doors had slammed.

Albert: In your article [Elisabeth A. Lloyd, "Science and Anti-Science: Objectivity and Its Real Enemies," in *Feminism, Science, and the Philosophy of Science,* ed. Lynn Hankinson Nelson and Jack Nelson (Kluwer 1996), 217–259], which I admire very much, and which I think was written before the Sokal incident . . .

Lloyd: . . . I finished it three weeks before . . .

Albert: . . . it was nicely argued that many science studies people are misunderstood as attempting to *delegitimize* science whereas what they're really doing is *demystifying* science. However, I wonder whether the Sokal business requires a different evaluation. I mean, unless one wants to argue that *Social Text*'s practice was wildly unrepresentative of what typically goes on in science studies, there is something alarming, and something of a radically anti-scientific agenda there. So I think you're letting people a little too much off the hook when you talk the way you were just now. It is no doubt true that if one isolates the best practitioners of science studies they are much, much more careful. But that a significant sector of science studies has a not particularly well-informed ideological hostility towards science—that position seems supported by what happened in the Sokal case, don't you think?

Lloyd: I hesitate to generalize from what happened with that editorial committee. What I did in the article was defend the targets that I knew, such as Helen Longino, Donna Haraway, Evelyn Fox Keller. These people—I knew what they said, and so I knew that what others said *about* what they said was *so* wrong that it raises a question for me about how they represent others.

Albert: Maybe it is worth distinguishing between two questions. One is:

"What are the positions of individual philosophers who do science studies?" To pursue it, one can go on a case-by-case basis, and see if Gross and Levitt are right or wrong about how they characterize this particular philosophical position. And the other is, in a more general way, "What kind of culture is it that now plays an important role in university life?" And it seems to me that the following two theses are consistent with one another. One is that all of the well-known and highly regarded practitioners of social constructivism aren't susceptible to the kinds of attacks that Gross and Levitt mount. At the same time, and not incompatible with that, it might be argued that there is an academic culture which is being conveyed to undergraduates, and maybe graduates too, which is quite different from a careful and intelligent reading of these philosophers of science.

Lloyd: I definitely would accept that.

Kittay: Let me switch our discussion to the institution called *Social Text*. I think you're saying that its role as a barometer of academic culture tends to be exaggerated. There are those who say, "I never read the thing anyway," or the guy in the audience at a session on the hoax at the Pacific Division of the American Philosophical Association, who asked: "What is this *Social Text*? Is it a respectable journal? Clue me in." So, how can we interpret the fact that it was *Social Text*, and not another journal, that was the center of the controversy? John, as you were a founder of *Social Text*, how was your understanding of *Social Text* either changed or confirmed by this affair?

Brenkman: My basic view is that anybody can be a victim of a hoax in the publishing world. Hoaxes come in all different types—from completely false journalism to authors who misrepresent their identity to promote their books, to something like this. So, that something like this can happen is not that meaningful. What made it meaningful was the particular context in which the article appeared. *Social Text* was trying to do a very difficult thing in the "Science Wars" issue: on the one hand, you are doing a critique of the epistemology of Western science, and on the other hand you are trying to talk about the political implications of the funding of scientific research, the application of science to industry and the military and to the inner workings of a capitalist economy, and so on. My view is that there is an unexamined tendency to believe that these two sets of problems are intimately related, if not identical. That is, that the problems in epistemology and the problems in the politics of science at some point meet, and are interwoven: Every argument about knowledge is an argument about power. It's the sort of Foucault paradigm run amok: at every moment knowledge is power, power is knowledge. Now this has become a very deep part of the common sense of cultural studies. That made the editorial board of *Social Text* susceptible to buying into an article whose basic argument resonates with the power/knowledge identification. Then you add all the fabulous details from physics and mathematics, and you're off and running. More disturbing to me is that, once the hoax was revealed, *Social Text* (and in particular Andrew Ross) defended their decision rather than simply admitting they made a terrible mistake and trying to examine some of the ramifications of that mistake.

Kittay: Are some of the personal characterizations that have been used appropriate? Both Ross and Sokal have been termed arrogant—and Sokal has certainly been deceptive. Is the vocabulary of arrogance, which is a kind of moralistic vocabulary, appropriate to this affair?

Brenkman: I think there has been an arrogance in the defense of *Social Text* that came particularly in the early phases, in the *New York Times*, and the stuff on the internet. That's because the journal had made the underlying stakes in this special issue on "Science Wars" the claim that there needs to be more public involvement in shaping of the direction of scientific research, and that in order for that to happen, the public discussion has to be ideologically broadened as regards the nature of intellectual disciplines, scientific authority, and so on. If you put yourself forward as leading the way in defining what that broad discussion might sound like, you cannot afford to make this kind of mistake. And then, when you do make a mistake like this, you can't afford not to admit having done so. And so to me, it throws retrospectively into question how well sorted out this project was from day one, and to what extent it was already overreaching and an overstatement of what is possible in this particular moment.

Lloyd: Was it you, John, who said that the project failed to take into consideration the low level of science education among the public and among the academics?

Brenkman: Yes, I felt that in the whole special issue of *Social Text* this was one major missing theme: we are by and large a scientifically uneducated populace. It is true in the schools, it is true among college students, it is true among professors, it's certainly true in the Congress, and I would worry more about raising the level of general science education than I would about how to constitute decision-making boards to direct scientific research that are going to involve the citizenry. There is something awry in the basic set-up of an argument which leaves out such a basic problem as whether or not the public, through the schools, is appropriately educated in science, and heads straight towards the notion that a certain very high level of epistemologically oriented critique of science begins already to outline a political intervention into the scientific process. This leaves out what—from the standpoint of basic democratic politics—is a sine qua non of more public involvement in scientific questions.

Lloyd: That remark really resonates with me, because at Berkeley I teach philosophy of science and philosophy of biology every year. Now, I get about half science majors and half philosophy majors, and I have to teach the philosophy majors the science and the science majors the philosophy, but I also have to teach a lot of scientific methodology to the science majors, and the one thing that is overwhelmingly clear is that the level of public education in science is one of the most serious self-perpetuating problems that there is. So I've got biology majors who are graduating in biology—they already work summer jobs, they are already doing research, they are already biologists—but they don't know evolutionary genetics or basic physiology. They don't know the parts of an organism. They don't know basic anatomy. They don't know basic physiology. This is weird to me.

Brenkman: Let's take up the converse. Do you think there is a tendency within the scientific community to try to hide from more general discussions? I mean, the corrosive influence of corporate and government and military imperatives in scientific research, such as what kind of labs universities set up, what kind of scientists you're going to hire, and so on. My guess is that a lot of that goes on behind closed doors, rather than being a part of an open discussion.

Albert: My own work is concerned mostly with the foundations of physics, and over the last 50 or 60 years there is an astounding tradition of hostility within the physics community to philosophically inclined investigations into the foundations of physics. Much of the history of physics in the twentieth century has been one of very urgent philosophical questions raised by developments in theoretical physics, and followed by an immediate reaction that took the form of a bizarre, ferocious hostility on the part of physics to investigations of those questions.

Lloyd: I have to say that we've been very lucky in biology to run across very little of that. It's something that has made doing the philosophy of biology ever so much easier.

Kittay: We've talked for an hour and a half and no one has mentioned the term "the Left."

Lloyd: It strikes me that so few journalists actually focus on what was officially Sokal's motivation, the issue of how all this contributes to an effective Left politics.

LF *representative:* I think I've read most of everything written on this, and there is not a single Left-Right exchange in the U.S.; whereas elsewhere, in Brazil, for instance, it's the core of the discussion.

Kittay: How appropriate is this political distinction? Sokal says, "I'm doing this for the Left . . . "

Lloyd: . . . well, there is a distinction between the old-fashioned Left and the Left as represented in parts of cultural studies. Or do you mean the distinction between the Left and the Right?

LF representative: Sokal considers himself of the Left for his *politics,* which is not the same as his academic work. Whereas *Social Text* considers the academic work they do to be political *and* to be of the Left, Sokal doesn't consider his *physics* to be of the Left, he considers his summer teaching in Nicaragua to be of the Left.

Albert: But he also considers the scientific tradition to be of the Left.

Kittay: When I visited Andrew Ross three days before the revelations, to alert him and show him Sokal's article, the first thing Ross said was something like: "Sokal's wrong: there is no relation between the traditional political Left and people who do cultural studies."

Albert: Wait a minute. Am I wrong in thinking that Ross advertises himself very explicitly as on the Left, and that he sees his work as having important political consequences?

Brenkman: You're absolutely right. But I've got to say that the positions that both Sokal and Ross have taken on this are absurd. Leftists will continue, as I think they have throughout the last two centuries, to disagree vehemently over almost every fundamental question that comes before them, including all kinds of theoretical questions that don't have very much to do with politics at all. Which may be the case in a good deal of this debate, as to what kind of epistemology you adhere to, or what kind of metatheory of science you're an advocate of. This has very little to do with the domain of politics per se. Similar problems in philosophy. In 1789, every revolutionary was a foundationalist. The most articulate counterrevolutionary voices in Europe were antifoundationalists, led by Burke. Two hundred years later, most academically trained Left-wing academics are antifoundationalists in their theoretical commitments, and most conservative culture critics claim to be foundationalists of one sort or another. Now, it is not that these things are totally arbitrary, but they are extremely contextualized, and though exactly how they match up is a really interesting problem, it is not the heart and soul of these issues.

Albert: But I mean, gosh, compared to a lot of other times in the 20th century, doesn't it seem like we're at a historical juncture now where there really is a more profound kind of uncertainty among people who think of themselves as progressives about what *is* the right way to proceed?

Brenkman: I agree. But what you think about *physics* is not going to clarify that issue . . .

Albert: . . . whereas both Sokal and Ross take the position (you're right, John) that what you think about physics *will* clarify that issue in an important way.

Brenkman: That's why I'm objecting.

Albert: Fair enough. But I think this is symptomatic of a crisis that does have a fair amount of historical singularity to it. I think I would resist assimilating this to the debates that have always been going on within the Left. We are at a moment now where on a political level the Left is unusually paralyzed and uncertain about what to do. And as there really is some kind of a crisis, it's not inexcusable to call for a reexamination of fundamental theoretical commitments.

Brenkman: True, but then those would have to be argued out over questions like the nature of social movements, political structure in the United States today, the international movement of capital, and so on, all of which are remarkably absent from this whole debate. Those things are all alluded to: everybody has something to say about feminism but it's a potshot, everybody says that ultimately the real problem is the economy, but it's a potshot, and so on. The whole controversy swirls and swirls. . . .

And now maybe I *will* make reference to the origins of *Social Text*. The first discussions to start the journal I think occurred in 1977. The first issue came out in 1980 (dated '79, it was already late, we had a tradition to maintain!). I think we were aware of the fact that our interest in theory, in trying to reconceptualize the field of culture, was coming in the wake of the decline of a significant period of political mobilization. There was a reflexive feel to it: basically we were asking ourselves, "How do we consolidate at an intellectual level the tremendous ferment that has gone on in politics and society?"

Albert: It is a kind of behavior that is appropriate under the circumstances.

Brenkman: Arguably it is. We may have made mistakes in that regard but, in the wake of the '60s, a preoccupying question was, "What does culture mean?" and also, "What is the role of culture in shaping political movements?" And so the project had a vitality and an urgency that before too long was lost. This was one little point of origin for culture studies—what *Social Text* did in its first few years.

LF representative: Why then—given that culture is extremely important for Right-wing movements too—why is there no such thing as Right-wing cultural studies?

Brenkman: My view is that in the last 30 years conservatives have contributed nothing to methodology in the humanities, they've contributed no new conceptual paradigms, they've opened up no new fields of research, they've brought no new texts into the archive for discussion. There is an extremely vital Right-wing presence in legal theory: original ideas, challenging things that have to be contended with. There is no such thing in literature and the humanities. The sheer lack of vitality of conservative thought within the humanities is a very striking thing.

LF *representative:* Maybe literature and art have come to be seen as extras, and conservatives work on the basics, the things that are "really important."

Lloyd: They've been focusing their energy on doing other things, on reducing market constraints and other 'important things.' But I also want to defend what I see as Sokal's and Barbara Epstein's [pt. 5, "Postmodernism and the Left"] good point: unfortunately there has seemed to be a drifting off of analytical and theoretical energies from anything that has to do with developing responsible political participation of *any* stripe. That's the criticism—activism and political participation of an effective kind is not a natural consequence, or even in some cases very compatible with the type of theory that has been developed. I see that very clearly in Epstein's complaints about all the posturing in the academy.

Brenkman: I am not sure that the most revealing connection here is the one between theory and activism. On this, my views have changed since the founding of *Social Text.* At that moment, the theoretical project had to do exactly with the notion that political activism would require a theoretically coherent framework. My favorite sentence in all of Marx in those years was something from the early Marx in which he says that critical philosophy was the self-clarification of the wishes and struggles of the age. That seemed to give theory a mission—What are the pertinent utopian aspirations? What are the social movements that need clarification (the role of theory being to provide that clarification)?

Now, I'd put it a little differently. In the most simplistic terms, our task is to try to illuminate what is going on. The way in which actual political mobilizations take up that kind of knowledge is a little bit unpredictable and tends to be an amalgamation of various intellectual endeavors and projects. So, one of the things that I find missing in cultural studies is a narrower conception of politics. The problem is that the conception of politics becomes so broad that things that are really ideology are seen as politics. Debates *within* particular fields of inquiry are seen as politics. Localized institutional politics are seen as politics writ large, and so on. And there's a deep tendency for that to happen within this sort of discussion. *That* is related to the posturing.

Lloyd: I don't disagree with your *conclusions* and your *instincts* about what needs to be done, so I'm trying to figure out what I disagree with in your *analysis.* And I think it is this idea of a theory that will intermesh in some way with political participation in an old-fashioned sense (not in the posturing sense, of course). On the one hand, this is a view I definitely still hold. I don't think you can develop effective action unless you have a good realistic view of what the situation is. That's what analysis is for, but, well, I see theory as the result of analysis, perhaps. But while I really hesitate to use the word theory, I *do* want to talk about analysis. Let me defend Epstein again, as well as Pollitt [pt.3, "Pomolotov Cocktail"], and say, whatever it is that is being produced in this abstract theoretical analysis doesn't seem to be doing a very good job. Why not? Because of this separation, this complete ungroundedness. There's a lack of information going back and forth, between what people in Congress think and what people in *Social Text* are thinking, or what people who are trying to keep the abortion centers open do, and what people are doing in *Social Text*, or what people who are running the homeless shelters think and what people are thinking in *Social Text*. I took it that that was the fundamental complaint of Epstein and others.

Albert: Let me put it this way. What the hoax should be construed as having pointed up is a failure of science studies, to the extent that science studies is represented by *Social Text*, to have done its job right. And the most elementary aspect of that job is that there has to be a capacity to distinguish between gibberish and intelligible discourse. And they failed that! OK? So something is radically wrong there. What the hoax points up is not an opposition of science to science studies but an opposition of science to bad science studies.

LF *representative:* John, you described *Social Text* in your piece [pt. 2, "Selected Letters"] as being different from journals like *PMLA* or *Critical Inquiry* which use "peer review to create a very different kind of journal, one which publishes a representative sampling of work in the field with a range of methodological, intellectual and political orientations, whereas *Social Text* represents by contrast a shared political and intellectual project intent on foregrounding *particular* methods, topics and debates." Does this play a role in the whole affair?

Brenkman: Social Text is a tendency journal, it always has been, and I think it's really important that there are tendency journals. I also think it is extremely important that there are peer-reviewed journals. Some of the stuff I've read about that in the controversy is very misguided. Toby Miller in a recent *Social Text* talks about peer review in a really disturbing rhetoric, he essentially attacks peer review as disciplinary policing—the exact wrong way to go. These different types of journals should coexist in our intellectual environment. If you had only tendency journals, there would be so many problems, for the coherence of academic life, and fairness, and the ability of people to negotiate the tenure process and so on. It would not be a healthy thing. By the same token, if the tendency journals disappeared, it would be terrible. The people who are involved in them, their reasons for being involved, the way they foster new kinds of work, all have a very different pattern from the inner workings of professional journals.

In this instance, I *don't* think *Social Text* should have given Sokal's article to a physicist or a mathematician, it should have given it to a philosopher of science because the article is a crossover between philosophy of science and politicized science studies, and clearly the editorial board didn't have anybody that could make that crossover and see what was going on: Otherwise somebody would have picked up that the science was screwy. They needed some outside review. But that's different from peer review. They had a decision to make, and if you're involved in a tendency journal, decisions happen a lot: you get a piece that exceeds the expertise of anybody you have on board so you find a sympathetic colleague whose judgment you trust and you have them give you an opinion. However, the Sokal incident is a *localized* flaw in *Social Text*'s editorial process. To me it is not the signal that this sort of editorial process is illegitimate.

The record speaks for itself: they've published fifty issues, and if you went through them, the quality of what has been in the bulk of those issues is extremely high by any standard (and that's why most of the nastiest attacks begin by saying "the most prestigious journal," "the most important journal of cultural studies" and so on). Now in physics I presume you could not have a tendency journal. . . .

Lloyd: But there *are* a number of what are called hypothesis journals, and it's the hypothesis journals that serve as the cutting edge for ideas, which is also done very well by the tendency journals you are talking about. I mean, there are new ideas out there that might eventually turn out to be useful and good ones . . .

Kittay: . . . and are too precarious for the moment to run the gauntlet of review by peers with entrenched notions.

Lloyd: Exactly. That's why hypothesis journals exist in all the sciences, and in medicine—a lot of them in medicine, actually. So I don't see them as totally alien to how science does its work.

Brenkman: Well, I think cultural studies is suffering from a kind of crisis of overconfidence, and it shows. A discourse develops which has so much underlying common sense among its practitioners and is so wide-ranging in the things that it can ostensibly talk about that you risk arriving at the point where—because something sounds right—it *must* be right. That's what happened here. Something sounded right, and they thought it must be right. And at a moment like that I think that huge doses of skepticism about your own project are totally in order. There is something awry when the coherence theory of truth so dominates your own work that if it all seems to make sense it must be right—whereas the point is that you're supposed to become *skeptical* if it all seems to make sense.

AMONG OUR ACADEMIC CONTRIBUTORS

David Albert is a professor of philosophy at Columbia University.

Stanley Aronowitz is a professor of sociology and director of the Center for Cultural Studies and Graduate Center at the City University of New York.

Michael Bérubé is a professor of English and director of the Illinois Program for Research in the Humanities at the University of Illinois at Urbana-Champaign.

Paul Boghossian is chairman of the Department of Philosophy at New York University.

John Brenkman is a professor of English at the Graduate Center of the City University of New York.

David Dickson is associate professor of actuarial studies at the University of Melbourne.

Barbara Epstein is a professor of history of consciousness at the University of California at Santa Cruz.

Stanley Fish is Dean of the College of Liberal Arts and Sciences at the University of Illinois at Chicago. At the time of the Sokal Hoax, he was director of Duke University Press, publisher of *Social Text.*

Kurt Gottfried is emeritus professor of physics at Cornell University.

Ken Hirschkop is a lecturer in English literature at the University of Manchester.

Bruno Latour is a professor at the Centre de Sociologie at the Ecole Nationale Superieure des Mines, Paris.

Elizabeth Lloyd is a professor of the history and philosophy of science at Indiana University.

Peter Osborne is a professor of philosophy at Middlesex University.

Bruce Robbins is a professor of English at Rutgers University.

Ruth Rosen is a professor of history at the University of California at Davis.

Andrew Ross is a professor of comparative literature and director of the American Studies Program at New York University.

Alan Sokal is a professor of physics at New York University.

Steven Weinberg is a professor of physics at the University of Texas at Austin.

Ellen Willis is a professor of journalism and director of the Cultural Reporting and Criticism program at New York University.

Thanks to Adriana Abdenur, Isis Costa, Kim Mrazek Hastings, Chauncy Gardner, Mark Edward Kehren, and Teri Reynolds for their contributions to the translations in this book.

SOURCE ACKNOWLEDGMENTS

Alan Sokal, "Transgressing the Boundaries: Toward a Transformative Hermeneutics of Quantum Gravity," *Social Text* 46/47 (spring–summer 1996): 217–52. Reprinted by permission of Duke University Press.

Alan Sokal, "A Physicist Experiments with Cultural Studies," *Lingua Franca,* May–June 1996, pp. 62–64. Reprinted by permission of *Lingua Franca, The Review of Academic Life,* published in New York.

Bruce Robbins and Andrew Ross, "Mystery Science Theater" [editorial response], *Lingua Franca,* July–August 1996, pp. 54–57. Reprinted by permission of *Lingua Franca, The Review of Academic Life,* published in New York.

The selected letters to the editor originally appeared in *Lingua Franca,* July–August 1996, pp. 54–64. Reprinted by permission of *Lingua Franca, The Review of Academic Life,* published in New York.

Linda Seebach, "Scientist Takes Academia for a Ride with Parody," *Contra Costa (Calif.) Times,* 12 May 1996. Reprinted by permission of Contra Costa Newspapers.

Mitchell Landsberg, "Is It Gibberish or Merely Obscure? Scientist Hoaxes Academic Journal," Associated Press wire, 16 May 1996. Reprinted by permission of the Associated Press.

Janny Scott, "Postmodern Gravity Deconstructed, Slyly," *New York Times,* 18 May 18 1996. Copyright © 2000 by the New York Times Co. Reprinted by permission.

John Yemma, "Hoakum for High-Brows," *Boston Globe,* 18 May 1996. Reprinted courtesy of the *Boston Globe.*

Stanley Fish, "Professor Sokal's Bad Joke," *New York Times,* 21 May 1996, op-ed sec. Copyright © 2000 by the New York Times Co. Reprinted by permission.

Scott McConnell, "When Pretension Reigns Supreme," *New York Post,* 22 May 1996, p. 21.

Ruth Rosen, "A Physics Prof Drops a Bomb on the Faux Left," *Los Angeles Times,* 23 May 1996, p. A11. Reprinted by permission of the author.

George F. Will, "Smitten with Gibberish," *Washington Post,* 30 May 1996, p. A31. Reprinted with the permission of the author and Scribner, a Division of Simon & Schuster, from *A Woven Figure* by George F. Will. Copyright © 1997 by George F. Will.

John Omicinski, "Hoax Article Yanks Academics' Legs," Gannett News Service, 3 June 1996. Reprinted by permission of the author and Gannett News Service.

Katha Pollitt, "Pomolotov Cocktail," reprinted with permission from the 10 June 1996 issue of

Bruce Robbins, "Just Doing Your Job: Some Lessons of the Sokal Affair," *Yale Journal of Criticism* 10, no. 2 (fall 1997): pp. 467–74. © 1997, The Johns Hopkins University Press.

The comments of Andrew Ross at the New York University forum have been published as "Reflections on the Sokal Affair," *Social Text* 50, vol. 15, no. 1 (spring 1997). Copyright 1997, Duke University Press. All rights reserved. Reprinted with permission of Duke University Press and the author. Alan Sokal's comments have been published as "A Plea for Reason, Evidence and Logic," *New Politics* 5, no. 2, whole #22 (winter 1997), and are reprinted with permission of *New Politics* and the author.

Permission to publish the transcription of the *Lingua Franca* roundtable has been granted by each of the participants.